REPUBLICANS FACE THE SOUTHERN QUESTION—
THE NEW DEPARTURE YEARS, 1877–1897

REPUBLICANS FACE THE SOUTHERN QUESTION –

The New Departure Years, 1877-1897

By

VINCENT P. DE SANTIS

GREENWOOD PRESS, PUBLISHERS
NEW YORK

Copyright © 1959, Johns Hopkins Press

Reprinted by permission
of the Johns Hopkins Press

First Greenwood Reprinting, 1969

Library of Congress Catalogue Card Number 69-13880

SBN 8371-1059-9

PRINTED IN UNITED STATES OF AMERICA

To the Memory of

MY MOTHER AND FATHER

PREFACE

A political heritage of Reconstruction has been the " Solid South," and its continued existence has frustrated the hopes and ambitions of Republican leaders for nearly a century for a vigorous life for their party in this section of the country. For the states [1] that make up the " Solid South " have been overwhelmingly Democratic, and the necessity of maintaining this party supremacy, through fear of Negro domination, has made the Republican party still the sectional party that it was at the time of its formation. " To many citizens of the South, a Republican is a rarity," a student of southern politics has written. " They may have heard about the Negro undertaker who goes to Republican conventions, or the eccentric railroad official who came from Ohio, but a genuine breathing Republican is a rarity in most counties of the South. . . . [And] when all the obstacles to southern Republicans are viewed together. . . . One wonders how the party can become a serious force in any southern state." Another observer of southern political life has pointed out that " One never knows who is and who is not a Republican [in the South]. The party places no imperative obligation of constancy upon its communicants. It scarcely deserves the name of party. It wavers somewhat between an esoteric cult on the order of a lodge and a conspiracy for plunder in accord with the accepted customs of our politics." [2] Such observations along with the election returns in the South since the end of Reconstruction heavily underscore the difficulties that the Republicans have in this part of the country.

The persistency of the " Solid South " has been a disturbing factor in our politics, for it has made for abnormal political life there by restricting the play of free opinion and by con-

[1] For the purpose of this study the South is defined as that area embracing those eleven states that formed the Southern Confederacy—Alabama, Arkansas, Florida, Georgia, Louisiana, Mississippi, North Carolina, South Carolina, Tennessee, Texas, and Virginia.

[2] Alexander Heard, *A Two-Party South* (Chapel Hill, 1952), pp 37, 133; V. O. Key, *Southern Politics* (New York, 1949), p. 277.

9

fining shifts and changes in policy to the Democratic party. That the " Solid South " is a major political problem has been a long-recognized fact. As early as 1877 a writer predicted that "A disruption of the white Democratic voters of the South would be everywhere regarded as the greatest political event in this country since the organization of the Republican party," and in our own day a student of the one party system has concluded that " the Solid South is the Nation's Number One Political Problem." [3] The attempt on the part of the Republican party to disrupt the Democratic supremacy in the South produced the Southern Question in American politics.

During Reconstruction the Southern Question, which included all the controversies relating to the Negro, the Civil War, and the military occupation of the South, was the most important issue in American politics.[4] Accompanying this was the Republican strategy of waving the bloody shirt which exploited the themes that southern whites were still disloyal and had learned nothing from the war, that northern Democrats were untrustworthy since they still had the same character and spirit as when they had sympathized with treason in the war, and that the nation required the rule of the party of patriotism which happened to be the Republican party. In some quarters the belief has prevailed that with the Compromise of 1877, which saw the removal of the troops from the South and the restoration of " home rule " to this section, the Southern Question was eliminated as the chief issue in national politics and the use of the bloody shirt as Republican campaign ammunition began to decline.[5] Actually both remained for some time after the end of Reconstruction as important features of American politics. By the turn of the twentieth century the bloody shirt

[3] New York *Times*, January 11, 1877; Marian D. Irish, " The Southern One-Party System and National Politics," *Journal of Politics*, IV (February, 1942), 94.

[4] For example see *Harper's Weekly*, XXI (February 17, 1877), 122. " As slavery was the commanding question of our politics for a generation before the war, so the ' Southern Question' which grows out of Reconstruction will long be the most important of all our political problems."

[5] Rayford W. Logan, *The Negro in American Life and Thought, the Nadir, 1877-1901* (New York, 1954), p. 37; Gunnar Myrdal, *An American Dilemma* (New York, 1944), p. 431; William B. Hesseltine, *The South in American History* (New York, 1943), p. 568; Paul Buck, *Road to Reunion* (Boston, 1937), pp. 107-112 shows quite clearly that the Republicans used the bloody shirt after 1877.

had just about disappeared, but the Southern Question has lasted to our own day.

The Southern Question may have become subordinated to other issues like the tariff, trusts, the money question, and civil service in the eighties and nineties, but it continued to be a principal political problem for the Republican party, and it began to take on a different character from that which it had during Reconstruction. In the years following the Compromise of 1877, the Southern Question, as far as the Republicans were concerned, meant a " Solid South " and the efforts to destroy the Democratic supremacy that had developed there as a result of military Reconstruction. This meant a shift in Republican appeals from Negroes to southern whites, and if it is a truism of Reconstruction that the Republicans enfranchised the freedman to build a party in the South, it is a truism that after Reconstruction they practically abandoned him to do the same thing. For the Republicans the "new" Southern Question took on a growing instead of declining significance, and it has persisted to our own day in spite of their successes in the South in 1928, 1952, and 1956.

Because the South has been overwhelmingly Democratic since the Compromise of 1877, it has been assumed in many quarters that the Republicans, apart from Reconstruction, have never really been seriously active or interested in building a strong party in this section of the country. Among students of American politics there has been a widespread and persistent belief that with the withdrawal of the troops, the Republicans gave up the fight in the South as hopeless and unprofitable and wrote off this part of the country as a possible area to contend for, maintaining there only a skeleton organization composed almost entirely of federal office holders.[6] As a shrewd and highly competent observer of southern politics has recently written about the Republican party, " The national organization has been no more concerned than the patronage-minded state leader in building up the party in the South. It encour-

[6] E. E. Schattschneider, *Party Government* (New York, 1942), pp. 121-122; A. N. Holcombe, *Political Parties of Today* (2d. ed., New York, 1924), pp. 193-194; F. B. Simkins, *The South, Old and New, A History 1820-1947* (New York, 1947), pp. 226-229; Key, *Southern Politics*, pp. 277-285, 291, 292, 295, 296; Heard, *Two-Party South*, pp. 222-223; Myrdal, *An American Dilemma*, p. 477.

ages the state leaders to devote their energies to raising funds
to be spent in doubtful states. It does not treat the South as a
foreign mission. . . . Instead it milks the missionaries to help
maintain the mother church." [7] Another student of southern
politics has argued that " The inept Republican performance
in one state after another in the South [in the post-Reconstruction years] . . . led Republicans outside the South to conclude
that their southern party was hopeless." [8]

Such conclusions have helped to foster óne of the great
myths of American politics, for Republican lack of success
in the South has not been from a lack of effort. On the contrary Republican leaders have constantly worked to break up
the Democratic South and to rebuild their party in these states
on a strong and permanent basis.[9] They have had no intentions
of permitting the South to go Democratic by default, even
though this might appear to be the case. The Republicans
needed the South, and they needed it badly, if they ever wanted
to make their party the majority one in all of the major sections
of the country as they had been able to do in 1872, and if
they wanted to retain their grip on the federal government in
the very closely contested elections of the seventies and eighties.

Other notions, largely based upon faulty or erroneous history,
about the Republicans and the Negro and the South after
Reconstruction have grown up. Among these is the belief that
the disfranchisement of the Negro from 1877 on destroyed
Republican hopes about the South, and that the success of the
Democrats in performing this feat resulted in part from the
decision of the Republicans to give up the fight in this part of
the country.[10] Another is the conclusion that the only logical
policy for the Republicans in the South was the military enforcement of the Fourteenth and Fifteenth Amendments; that the
recall of the troops ruled out such strategy, surrendered everything the North had won at Appomatox, and facilitated the
consolidation of white supremacy in the South and northern

[7] Key, *Southern Politics*, p. 296.
[8] Heard, *Two-Party South*, pp. 222-223.
[9] Vincent P. De Santis, " Republican Efforts to ' Crack ' the Democratic
South," *Review of Politics*, XIV (April, 1952), 244-264.
[10] Schattschneider, *Party Government*, pp. 121-122; Holcombe, *Political
Partis of Today*, pp. 188-190.

acceptance of victory for the " Lost Cause." [11] Many of these viewpoints have survived because of the failure to subject them to adequate analysis, for while Republican activities in the South during Reconstruction have been pretty thoroughly scrutinized, those for the years that came after the removal of the troops remain in almost total obscurity.

This book has been inspired by the need to tell the story of Republican policy and strategy in the South for the years that followed the Compromise of 1877, and to clear up the misconceptions that have surrounded it. This volume covers the period from the restoration of " home rule " in the South through the election of 1896, when an entirely new era in national politics sets in. In these twenty years, which constitute a distinct and separate period in national and southern politics, the break with the old Republican policy in the South occurs, and the main patterns of the new one are firmly established to last to the present. The " lily-white " movements of the 1920's had their origins in the 1880's, and the Republican strategy to support Independents in the South in the congressional elections of 1954 had already been tried out on a large and successful scale by President Chester Arthur in 1882.

In the last quarter of the nineteenth century the Republicans talked a great deal about the Southern Question, and worked tirelessly to do something about it, for the rise of a strong Republican party in the South would have been a political development of the first rank. From it would have come new political alignments, new policies, and probably the end of Democratic supremacy and one party politics in the South. That the Republicans still have a Southern Question and are still a sectional party is quite evident from the presidential election returns since 1877. But because of the break through in the South by Herbert Hoover in 1928 and Dwight D. Eisenhower in 1952 and 1956, we can look for continued Republican effort and probably future successes of the Republicans in the South, and consequently a growing instead of declining importance of this political development.

[11] This point was made over and over again by Republican opponents of the policy to take the troops out of the South as chapter III shows. In our own day the same point has been made by students of the Negro like Logan, *The Negro in American Life*, pp. 12-13, 22, 29, 30, 35-37, 43-44 and Myrdal, *An American Dilemma*, p. 88.

It would be impossible to acknowledge adequately all the assistance I have received in this book, but a few persons deserve my special gratitude. I am especially obligated to Professor C. Vann Woodward of the Johns Hopkins University who introduced me to this subject in his seminar in southern history and who has aided and encouraged me in every step along the way. I am grateful to Professor J. Merton England of the University of Kentucky for editing and publishing portions of chapters II and IV in the *Journal of Southern History*. I am likewise grateful to the Reverend Thomas T. McAvoy, C. S. C., head of the history department at the University of Notre Dame for his personal encouragement and for his cooperation in freeing me of some of my teaching obligations at an important juncture in the writing of this book. I acknowledge my indebtedness to Watt P. Marchman, director of the Rutherford B. Hayes Memorial Library at Fremont, Ohio, who has never been too busy to lend an effective and willing hand. Finally my obligation to my wife Helene O'Brien De Santis is immeasurable for her inexhaustible patience with and tolerance of her husband during the course of composition.

I was assisted in completing research for this book by a grant from the American Philosophical Society.

VINCENT P. DE SANTIS

Notre Dame, Indiana
February, 1959.

TABLE OF CONTENTS

REPUBLICANS FACE THE SOUTHERN QUESTION—
THE NEW DEPARTURE YEARS, 1877–1897

CHAPTER I

SIGNS OF THE TIME

While the Republicans dominated the presidency in the generation that followed the election of Lincoln and appeared to have political supremacy, both in the national government and the country at large, their party, during most of these years, suffered from a sectional and minority status that seemed impossible to overcome. In the presidential election of 1856, the first one in which they participated, the Republicans captured only 33.1 per cent of the popular vote and 362 of the nation's 1772 counties, and they failed to win a single popular vote in the South. By 1860 the Republicans had picked up some strength when they took 39.8 per cent of the popular vote and 556 of the 1921 counties in the Union, and on this occasion they did gather some votes in the South—a total of 1,887, all of them in Virginia.[1] By 1860 Republican strength lay in New England, the Middle Atlantic, the East North Central, and the Pacific Coast states. But the slender percentage of the popular vote, the small number of counties won, and the failure to make headway in the South clearly revealed the sectional and minority character of the Republican party. Its majorities in key states like New York and Indiana were slim and could be offset by a unification and rejuvenation of the Democrats in the North. The Republicans needed a wider appeal and new recruits if they wished to become a majority party, and these new recruits could only be had either in the South or in the West.

In the congressional elections of 1860 the Republicans secured 106 of the 237 seats in the House and 31 of the 66 seats in the Senate, but if the South had not withdrawn from the Union, they would have been in a minority position in Congress. In fact, the Republicans never once during Lincoln's presidency had a clear majority of the membership of Congress. In the

[1] W. Dean Burnham, *Presidential Ballots, 1836-1892* (Baltimore, 1955), pp. 64, 76, 233, 252, 246-257.

19

elections of 1862 they did increase their numbers in the Senate to 36, but their strength in the House fell to 102. In 1864 the Republicans seemed to have a comfortable margin in an election for the first time with 55 per cent of the popular vote and 719 of 1991 counties, but one must remember that in 878 counties, most of which were in the South, there were no returns at all. Also a very close race developed in several states like Connecticut, New Hampshire, New York, Oregon, and Pennsylvania, which had been considered Republican strongholds, and in New England and the Middle Atlantic states as a whole, the Republicans won only after a narrow squeeze.[2]

But the election of 1868 showed quite clearly the grave problem of stability confronting the Republican party fourteen years after its foundation, when Grant, the most popular war hero in the North, had a plurality of only slightly more than 300,000 out of a vote that totaled 5.7 million. Even with a probable maximum Negro turnout in an occupied South, the Republican majority was surprisingly and uncomfortably narrow in many states and in all sections of the country. Out of the seven southern states which could vote two went overwhelmingly Democratic, and several of the other five were Republican only by a close margin. The only thing that " could possibly save any part of the South for the Republicans at this late stage was the unhampered but organized franchise of the ex-slave, which could only be maintained by the use of federal troops for an indefinite period," writes a recent observer of presidential elections. " The trans-Mississippi West was still so young and unpeopled that its effectiveness for a stable base for Republicans was still very much in doubt. As long as the Republican Party carried most of the powerful states it could win. . . . Nevertheless, in failing to have an effective Southern wing the G. O. P. was doomed to lead a somewhat harrassed life following Reconstruction. . . . The Democratic Party, burdened though it was with the stigmata of disunion and disloyalty, and with Republican control of the South, began to show strikingly that in a few years it was to revive its role of being the majority party in the country."[3]

---

[2] *Ibid.*, pp. 97-98; see also pp. 91-93, 97, 233, 246-257 for returns.
[3] *Ibid.*, pp. 107-108; see also pp .100-102, 106, 253-254.

In spite of the results of 1868, the corruption and scandals of the Grant administration, and the defection of the Liberal Republicans, the Republican party in 1872 reached the height of its supremacy when it carried every northern and western state along with eight from the South. In the North and West it gathered 57 per cent of the popular vote while in the South and the country at large it polled 55.8 per cent.[4] This was an all-time high for any party from 1836 to 1892, and the Republican party could no longer be tagged a sectional one, for it was now a majority one in all the major sections of the country as well as in the country itself.

But just when it appeared that the Republicans had taken a long lease upon the central government, their political prosperity came to an abrupt end, never again to reach the pinnacle of 1872. The political crash came in the congressional elections of 1874, when the Republicans lost control of the House and suffered a material reduction of their majority in the Senate. But more important than this one setback was the long period of party stalemate and equilibrium that set in in American politics following this election.

The next two decades witnessed a sharp contest between Republicans and Democrats to take over the government in Washington, and while each was strong enough to prevent the other from controlling it, neither could dominate it itself. In the five presidential elections between 1876-1892, the Republicans, while winning three of them, could not secure a majority of the popular vote in any one of them and gained a plurality only once. Throughout much of this period the Republicans depended for victory upon very small majorities they had in such key states as Indiana and New York, and they never won a plurality of the counties in the nation as a whole during the last quarter of the nineteenth century. In contrast, the Democrats, while electing a President on only two occasions, polled a majority of the popular vote in 1876 and a plurality in 1884, 1888, and 1892. Added to the struggle to win the presidency was the narrow margin of victory in the congressional elections. Between 1874-1896 the Democrats controlled the presidency and Congress at the same time for only two years, 1893-1895,

[4] *Ibid.*, pp. 109-110.

while the Republicans managed to do it for four years, once in 1881-1883 and again in 1889-1891. But only in the latter instance did they have a clear majority, for in the earlier period they had a margin of but one in the House, and only the vote of William Mahone, the Readjuster from Virginia, enabled them to organize the Senate.

The loss of the South by 1877, the presence of a large bloc of doubtful voters in some of the Eastern and Central states,[5] and the insecure hold the Republicans had upon the North are fundamental to the explanation for their failure to keep an uninterrupted grip upon the national government after their great victory in 1872. These developments along with the closely contested elections of the post-Reconstruction years produced a series of major efforts by Republican strategists to find more recruits for the party. In their attempt to gain a more secure footing in the North they intensified their waving of the bloody shirt, twisted the tail of the British lion to please the Irish-Americans, and ingratiated themselves with the northeastern business community through favorable legislation. To win votes in the doubtful states the Republicans made political concessions in the form of taking their presidential and vice-presidential nominees from these areas and by naming congressmen from these districts to important committee assignments. The Democrats matched them in their strategy in the doubtful states and among the business men.

But how to have political appeal in the South and to make their party strong in this section remained a major problem for the Republicans. During Reconstruction they had tried to solve it by enfranchising Negroes and disfranchising whites, a scheme, which had it worked out, might have allowed them to Republicanize the South and to establish their party firmly in control of the government at Washington for many years. Among the Radical leadership who dreamed up military Reconstruction was a variety of elements—the abolitionists who after the war demanded the political, social and economic equality for the Negro, the business man from the Northeast who championed the economic ideas of the Federalists and Whigs but who had been outvoted by the combination of southern and

---

[5] Conn., N. J., N. Y., Ohio, Ind., Ill.

western agrarians, and those Republicans who favored the idea of giving the Negro the vote and disfranchising the southern white merely to insure party success in the South. The cohesive force for all these groups was their intense desire to crush the political power of the old white ruling class in the South.

This was particularly true of the Radical leadership representing the business community of the Northeast, a section which felt it had been at a disadvantage since 1789, because the coalition of a planter South and an agrarian West had held the upper hand relative to matters of tariff and industry. The South had dominated this combination and in turn the national government through the Democratic party for a generation before the Civil War. This West-South alliance foundered over the issue of the war, and a new one between the Northeast and the West, with the former exercising the leadership, emerged. It was the economic and industrial factors of the Northeast that underlay much of the humanitarian idealism of the Radicals, and their two real aims—their economic motives and the securing of their party in power both in the South and at Washington—had to be clothed in the more appealing and more patriotic motives that they proclaimed during Reconstruction. How to keep the South safe for their party and from coming back to join hands with northern Democrats and the West to put the Republicans out of power became the number one problem for the Radicals.

Through a union of Negroes, Scalawags, and Carpetbaggers, the Republican party gained a temporary dominant political position in the South in the early phases of Reconstruction. This period of Republican power and strength in the South lasted in general from 1868, when the Radical state constitutions went into effect, until 1877 when the last of the federal troops of occupation were removed from this section. But in only three of the states—Florida, Louisiana, and South Carolina —did the Republicans remain in control that long. Counter-revolutions returned the Democrats to power in Tennessee by 1869; in Virginia, North Carolina, and Georgia by 1870; in Alabama, Arkansas, and Texas by 1874; and in Mississippi by 1875. And when Florida, Louisiana, and South Carolina reverted to the Democratic camp in 1877 the Republicans had been completely routed in the South.

Thus the loss of the South came as a bitter disappointment to the Republicans, for they were painfully aware of the severe handicap they had in the closely contested elections of the post-Reconstruction years when the Democrats had most of the ninety Representatives, all of the twenty-two Senators, and 112 electoral votes in the South. Not only was it nearly impossible to make sufficient gains elsewhere to compensate for this loss,[6] but it was illogical and poor strategy to allow the situation to continue without an attempt to remedy it. With their vote concentrated in the northern and western states, Republicans could expect to maintain their majority in the Senate. They could hope to battle for the presidency with the Democrats on fairly even terms, but without success in the South their prospects for winning complete control of the national government were exceedingly slim.

With all this in mind thoughtful Republicans, toward the end of Reconstruction, began to reexamine their policy in the South, and began to see what a dismal failure it had been and why there was such a pressing need for a new one. It had proved to be impracticable and impossible to maintain the Radical governments set up in the South. One by one they had fallen in spite of Force Bills and Grant's efforts to uphold them with the use of the military. Even the most vigorous wavers of the bloody shirt had come to realize this fact. " Gen. Grant held up the Southern Republican administrations by main force for more that four years, and they got no stronger on their legs, but rather weaker and weaker," explained the New York *Tribune.* " We cannot continue that policy after experience has so fully demonstrated its futility." [7] The *National Republican* stated that " The Republican party in the South has heretofore tried to rule by force of arms and Federal bayonets, and it failed." [8] The *Nation* pointed out that " Every Republican has become disgusted with military control of States, and thoroughly convinced that a State government which

---

[6] For example the Republicans in 1880 carried a larger proportion of congressional districts in the North and West than they had in 1860, and they had some support from the small farmers of the southern Appalachians, which they had lacked in 1860, yet they had only a margin of one in the House.

[7] New York *Tribune,* March 13, 1877.

[8] Washington *National Republican,* March 27, 1877.

cannot support itself should not be propped up by national soldiers," and *Harper's Weekly* felt that "Nobody can be justly reproached for saying that a policy which has lost to the Republicans every Southern State, which has not effectually protected the Negro, and which has embittered the jealousies of classes and of race . . . is not a wise permanent policy." [9]

The policy of imposing military rule and Negro suffrage upon the South had produced a deep-seated and undying antagonism among southern whites. The divisions over the Negro and politics in the Reconstruction era " went so far as to create a situation of almost permanent sentimental disaffection on the part of southerners," writes the most competent student of the processes of reconciliation between the two sections. " The injuries then experienced became a tradition. . . . The South had in fact suffered so much that from that day on a mark of a Southern man was his distrust of all who were not born below the Mason-Dixon line." [10] The *Nation* told its readers that " Gradually the errors and shortcomings of the Republican party in the treatment of the South, are, in one form or another, ' thronging to the bar, and crying all guilty, guilty!' We are learning little by little, that ' troops ' cannot save us, nor vituperation, nor the negro vote nor the ' party record.' " [11] Thus Reconstruction had a paradoxical effect. The Radicals had set out with the avowed purpose of dividing whites and removing race proscription in the South, and they wound up by uniting a divided people and by contributing much to race violence. The South had had a bi-partisan political record before the Civil War, but the "Solid South" had resulted from the program of the Radicals to insure political control of this section for their party. The issue of racial solidarity was raised to ally the upland and conservative Democrats of the South, and the lower class whites, already hating the Negro, followed the lead of the conservatives.

The old policy had not preserved or strengthened the Republican party in the South, nor had it apparently protected the freedman adequately or helped him to become a more respon-

---

[9] *Nation*, XXIV (March 29, 1877), 188; *Harper's Weekly*, XXI (March 31, 1877), 242.
[10] Buck, *Road to Reunion*, pp. 69-70.
[11] *Nation*, XXIII (November 16, 1876), 294.

sible citizen. " Let us face the truth," declared the New York
Tribune. " Our Southern policy has not only been a curse to
the whites, but it has been a curse to the freed people for whose
benefit it was adopted. It has not made them good citizens.
It has not taught them to use the ballot. It has introduced
among them a democratization more dangerous to the country
than the violence of the White League." [12] J. Willis Menard,
former Negro Congressman from Florida, in the summer of
1876, pointed out to the Republican nominee for the presidency,
Rutherford B. Hayes, " that inasmuch as troops and repressive
laws have failed to establish permanent peace between the two
races, we must seek elsewhere . . . for a remedy." [13] Electing
a Republican President, or keeping the Republican party in
power, did not of itself seem sufficient to mend matters at the
South. " We have had a Republican President and a Republican House and Senate for eight years, and yet the South is,
according to those who are most clamorous for a further trial
of the remedy, in a terrible condition," observed the *Nation*.
" Now if this is the result of eight years of Republican legislation and administration in time of peace, it is useless to urge
us to try four years more of it as a certain specific." [14]

To many Republicans the old policy in the South seemed
outdated and outmoded and quite out of step with Republicanism of the 1870's. By this date the Republican party had
been transformed from a group of radical crusaders to an
organization of conservative and respectable spokesmen for
big business. It was an incongruity for the Republican leaders
on the one hand to support a system of high tariffs, land grants,
subsidies, and special privileges for big business while on the
other hand to defend and even enforce with the use of federal
troops a Radical policy of Reconstruction in the South. The
Republicans began to see the southern problem with new eyes,
and the more they saw the more anachronistic seemed the policy
of Reconstruction. The Republicans had now become the party
of vested interests and big business; yet in the South it still
sought the votes of a " propertyless electorate of manumitted
slaves with a platform of radical equalitarianism. The con-

---

[12] New York *Tribune*, April 7, 1877.
[13] Washington *National Republican*, March 15, 1877.
[14] *Nation*, XXIII (July 27, 1876), 52.

tradiction was obvious." [15] While the Republican strategy of making concessions to business men seemed to have been a huge success, that of resorting to Radicalism in the South had been a enormous failure. Republicans clearly realized the serious mistake the party had made in adopting and clinging so long to a Radical policy in the South. Horace Maynard from Tennessee, whom Hayes appointed as David M. Key's successor as Postmaster General, observed about the South that " Things are not well there; they have been wretchedly managed; else it would not today present a solid Democratic vote. Naturally the Republicans should carry half the Southern States with as little trouble as Ohio." [16] Benjamin Bristow, the reformer in Grant's cabinet, wrote that " It was perfectly clear to me ten years ago that the unsteady and uncertain policy of the then President would lead to disastrous failure, in the business of reconstruction. A change of policy was demanded by the highest consideration of patriotism and the material interest of both sections." [17] Joseph Medill of the Chicago *Tribune* told Richard Smith of the Cincinnati *Gazette* that, " we have tried for eight years to uphold Negro rule in the South officered by Carpetbaggers, but without exception it has ended in failure." [18]

The conservative Republicans of the North were aligned with the Radical Republicans of the South, and party strategists began to look upon this as an unnatural and unwholesome combination. The natural allies of the northern Republicans in the South should have been conservative whites, especially those of Whig antecendents and traditions, but they had been alienated by the excesses of military Reconstruction. " The plan that has been adopted for the last 8 years to support governments composed of dishonest whites and ignorant blacks has proved as it must of necessity, a failure," wrote a Republican from New Orleans. " The mistake has been made, in

[15] C. Vann Woodward, *Origins of the New South, 1877-1913* (Baton Rouge, Louisiana, 1951), p. 28.

[16] Horace Maynard to Rutherford B. Hayes, June 26, 1876, in Rutherford B. Hayes Papers (Hayes Memorial Library, Fremont, Ohio).

[17] Benjamin H. Bristow to Carl Schurz, April 14, 1877, in Frederic Bancroft, *Speeches, Corerspondence and Political Papers of Carl Schurz* (New York, 1913), III, 412.

[18] Medill to Smith, February 17, 1877, in Hayes Papers.

not bringing in to the Republican Party the respectable portions of the white element, that *were Union before* and *through*
the conflict." [19] Republicans began to debate the idea of
dropping the Carpetbagger, placing the Negro under political
loyalty to his former master, and appealing to the latter along
the lines of old Whig conservatism. This was a revolutionary
proposal, and " The whole subject is a constant theme of
earnest talk in Washington," reported the New York *Tribune*
in January, 1877.[20]

This naturally led to a great deal of talk about the rejuvenation of the southern Whig party and the possibility of its joining
hands with the Republicans to gain control of the South.
William D. " Pig-Iron " Kelley told Hayes, " The old Whig
or Union party of the South should have been reinvigorated
as it could have been, and it and the colored people would
have given us clear majorities composed almost exclusively of
Southern people in the States south of Kentucky and Virginia."[21]
In any event if the Republicans ever hoped to redeem the South
for themselves they would have to change their policy and
would have to appeal to southern whites. " It is evident that
the Republican Party can no longer be maintained on past
issues," John Tyler, Jr., son of the former President, informed
Hayes, " and that a new line of policy must be adopted." [22]
Carl Schurz expressed the opinion that " Public sentiment is
indeed likely to force them [" force-bill and outrage " Repub-
licans] to give up their Southern policy—and they, or at least
most of them, will make that sacrifice, for that policy has always
been to them merely a means for partisan end." [23]

While there was considerable speculation in the mid-seventies
about a new Republican policy in the South there were sturdy
obstacles confronting the new venture. Southern white hostility
toward Republicanism and fear of Negro supremacy were
reluctant to give way before Republican blandishments. Republicans could afford to stand up for the rights and privileges

---

[19] J. D. Belden to Judge A. B. Sloanaker, April 23, 1877, *Ibid*.

[20] Woodward, *Origins of the New South*, p. 29.

[21] Kelly to Hayes, December 17, 1876, quoted in C. Vann Woodward, *Reunion and Reaction* (Boston, 1951), p. 37.

[22] Tyler to Hayes, February 17, 1877, in Hayes Papers.

[23] Schurz to Charles Francis Adams, Jr., July 22, 1875, in Bancroft, *Writings of Schurz*, III, 158.

of their southern brethren, but they could not afford to support their wrongs. In general the Carpetbagger-Negro governments had not won the respect of the country. " Carpet bag governments had not been successful," Hayes told Colonel W. H. Roberts, the managing editor of the New Orleans *Times* in December, 1876. " The complaints of the southern people were just in this matter." [24] A Republican from Louisiana in describing politicians of his own party wrote, " Our politicians are so bad that the North cannot realize or believe the infamies of our elections." [25] A Republican leader from Maine, Congressman William P. Frye, thought the Southern policy would have been solved long ago if political sagacity had been exercised in the matter of appointments in the South. " For this reason the Southern problem is to-day twenty times further from solution than it should be. Unfortunately, we have allowed political vagabonds, United States Senators and Representatives from the South, to hold patronage, and deliver it out among their miserable adherents. Hence the stigma ' carpetbagger ' falls on every Northern man in the South." [26] Jacob D. Cox, Republican leader from Ohio, told Hayes that " One of the most painful results of past faults in our party administration, is, that the character of many men in the South, claiming to be leaders of the party, is such that in every dispute over returns we are put upon the defensive. They have so often been wrong that even if right . . . a most important part of the Republican party North will hesitate to give them credit for honesty." [27]

Neither had these Radical governments in the South reflected a Republican sentiment based on a political conviction and sympathy growing among southern whites. In the main they had portrayed political shrewdness, skill in manipulating political machinery, and personal greediness. A " Hayes Republican " from New Orleans declared that Carpetbaggers under H. C. Warmoth in Louisiana had but two objects," to gather in the

---

[24] Woodward, *Reunion and Reaction*, p. 25.

[25] A Hayes Republican, New Orleans to the Editor of *Nation*, December 27, 1876, *Nation*, XXIV (January 11, 1877), 28.

[26] C. R. Williams, *The Life of Rutherford Burchard Hayes* (Columbus, 1928), II, 37.

[27] J. D. Cox, Toledo to Hayes, November 14, 1876, in Hayes Papers.

spoils and to perpetuate its own evil power," and that to all this " the northern people are wilfully blind, and . . . partisan spirit has led them into an endorsement of the greatest political infamy of the age." [28] The one fatal defect of Republican policy since the war, said the New York *Tribune* has been that it gave opportunity for " adventurers, who were utterly without standing or consideration in any Northern community, and who if not propped up by United States bayonets could not have been elected to any office by colored men of the South, to fasten themselves upon the party and the country as the representative Republicans of reconstructed States. All other blunders put together," continued the *Tribune*, " have not cost the Republican party as many votes as the single fact that it was represented and controlled in reconstructed States by unworthy men. To get rid of their incubus has been the one thing needful." [29] Grant's course had only served to increase this bitterness about Carpetbaggers, and Republicans found it extremely difficult to allay the fears of revived Carpetbagger-Negro rule in the South.

Factional disputes also interfered with the attempted rejuvenation of southern Republicans. The problem for the Republicans in the South after Reconstruction was to find a formula to bring together large numbers of whites and Negroes in the same party. But party factionalism and splits between " black-and-tan " and " lily-white " groups placed serious obstacles in the way of such a development. From the start of Reconstruction the coalition of Negro, Scalawag, and Carpetbagger was an uneasy one and had a great disadvantage, for the bulk of support had to come from the freedman. The Carpetbaggers had gerrymandered the voting districts in some instances to insure Negro majorities, and they had placed vast appointive powers in the hands of the governor to overcome opposition in counties with conservative majorities. But the combination of lower class whites and Negroes failed, because the farmer who had long fought the planter class also looked upon the competition of the colored man with fear. Besides, the Negro often found himself doing most of the voting and receiving

[28] *Nation*, XXIV (January 11, 1877), 27-28.
[29] New York *Tribune*, April 2, 1877.

few of the benefits of the Republican victory. The old planter class played upon this Negro jealousy and sometimes used the freedman against the Radicals. This was a fatal flaw in the alliance.

Republican cleavages also beset the Republican coalition in the South. Physical control of the state capitol and state arsenal usually meant power, and frequent struggles for this control occurred among Republicans in the South. The classic example took place in Arkansas with the Brookes-Baxter war. In these interparty fights southern Republicans frequently appealed to Washington for recognition and assistance, and Grant from time to time did intervene, even with the use of the military; a policy that offended many, both in the South and in the North. "How can this perpetual interference of the General Government in the affairs of the States . . . by the use of its military arm, be otherwise than prejudicial to all rights and interests, degrading to the public service, and dangerous to our liberties?" asked a New Yorker.[30] These feuds, instead of abating, widened and deepened after the troops left, and prevented the Republicans from effectively opposing the Democrats and on occasion resulted in national Republican administrations rewarding disreputable politicians in the South in an effort to secure party harmony. Factionalism, during and after Reconstruction, turned out to be the bane of southern Republicanism, and every Republican President from Grant on has wrestled with it.

Finally the ability of Democrats to keep southern Republicans from the polls or to nullify their vote, had sharply reduced Republican strength in all the southern states and had nearly eliminated it entirely in some parts. The success of the whites in excluding the Republican vote as an important factor in southern politics contributed significantly to national Democratic victories. As we shall see, such a development did persuade some northern Republican leaders to believe that it might be better to write off any chance of success for the party in the South, but they were in a minority, for Republican administrations in the years after Reconstruction worked to convince

[30] Howard Potter, New York City to the Editor of *Nation* October 23, 1876, *Nation*, XXIII (November 2, 1876), 270.

southern whites that the Republican party came as their friend and that they had wronged themselves and their state by voting Democratic. Republican strategists endeavored to bring southern whites into the party, for they ruled out the possibility of associating Republicanism in the South entirely with the Negro.

To coax southern Democrats out of their party and into the Republican fold involved a changeover from a policy of military interference to one of non-intervention in the South. Such a turnabout was a revolution in Republican policy, and the whole matter was debated privately and publicly in the winter of 1876-1877 and was eventually adopted. The removal of the troops which launched the new policy in the South incensed the Radicals who charged that the reversal came as a rude jolt and surprise to the North and to the rank and file of the party, and that it was part of a bargain to get Hayes into the White House. They accused Hayes of selling them out, of displaying a "base ingratitude" to "those that elected him," of misjudging his duty "shockingly," and of abandoning the Republican party.[31] Even Hayes seemed to agree with these accusations when he privately described his policy as a "total departure from the principles, traditions, and wishes of the Republican party."[32]

At first glance the evidence seems to support the charges of the Radicals. While the Republican platform of 1876 called for the "permanent pacification" of the South and the removal of "any just causes of discontent on the part of any class," it also demanded the enforcement of the Fourteenth and Fifteenth Amendments which in effect represented the policy of military Reconstruction. The platform was also a bloody shirt document since it associated the Democratic party with treason and warned the country not to turn over control of the national government to the traitorous Democrats.[33] While it

[31] John A. Logan to his Wife, March 8, 1877, in John A. Logan Papers (Division of Manuscripts, Library of Congress); B. F. Wade to Zachariah Chandler, August 9, 1877, in Zachariah Chandler Papers (Division of Manuscripts, Library of Congress); New York *Tribune*, August 9, 1877 for Ben Wade's interview.

[32] Rutherford B. Hayes Diary, October 24, 1877, Charles R. Williams, ed., *Diary and Letters of Rutherford Burchard Hayes* (Columbus, Ohio, 1929), III, 429.

[33] Kirk Porter, *National Party Platforms* (New York, 1924), pp. 94-98.

is true that Hayes' letter accepting the nomination in July, 1876, stressed the importance of reconciliation and assurance to the South, it, like the platform, called for the enforcement of the new constiutional amendements. Hayes believed that the South needed peace, but peace depended upon the supremacy of the law, and the South could not have an enduring peace if it habitually disregarded the constitutional rights of the Negro. " All parts of the Constiution are sacred and must be sacredly observed," wrote Hayes, " the parts that are new no less than the parts that are old." The South could advance its moral and material prosperity most effectively by a hearty and generous recognition of the rights of all by all—a recognition without reserve or exception. When the South accorded such a recognition, then it would be practicable for the national government to help it obtain the " blessings of honest and capable local government." Hayes desired this, and if elected, he considered it his duty to work for this end. He promised southerners he would " cherish their truest interests " and he pledged a policy " which will wipe out forever the distinction between North and South in our common country." [34] His running mate, William Wheeler of New York, pointed out how false it was to believe that it was possible to transform conditions in the South into those found in " model northern communities " in the course of ten or fifteen years. Such a change would only come with time, patience, gradual adjustment, and education, and in the process, the federal government would have to deal with much unavoidable friction. Thus the real problem remained in finding " our best and wisest statesmanship . . . to diminish the friction." [35]

Hayes was elected by a bloody shirt campaign which he himself encouraged. William E. Chandler, Republican leader from New Hampshire and one of the managers of the campaign stated that, " the bloody shirt, as it is termed, was freely waved, and Governor Hayes himself urged public men to put forward, as our best argument, the dangers of ' rebel rule and a solid South.' " [36] And that was exactly the case. From January until

[34] Williams, *Life of Hayes*, I, 462.
[35] Edward McPherson, *A Handbook of Politics for 1876* (Washington, 1876), pp. 214-215.
[36] Leon B. Richardson, *William E. Chandler, Republican* (New York, 1940), p. 212.

November the country was again flooded with sectional abuse. On the hustings Republicans laid each new outrage against the Negro in the South at the door of the Democratic party. Again and again the allegations were made that a Republican defeat would bring the leaders of the Confederacy into power, that the Negro would become a slave, that southern Republicans would be at the mercy of " rope clubs," and that the South would be compensated for the loss of its slaves.[37] Hayes promoted this type of campaign when he stated that the " main interest " of " a vast majority of the ' plain people ' " was that " A Democratic victory will bring the Rebellion into power," and that " the late Rebels " would " have the Government." This was the " true issue in the minds of the masses," who dreaded a victory for the united South. " They see in it continued trouble; nullification of the Amendments, Rebel claims and schemes, etc., etc., and I think anything which withdraws attention from this issue to merely personal matters is a mistake." Thus Hayes pointed out to Republican leaders that " Our strong ground is dread of a solid South, rebel rule, etc. It leads people away from hard times which is our deadliest foe." Even a Liberal Republican leader like Carl Schurz agreed with this strategy for as he told Hayes, " to the ' plain people ' who think that a Democratic victory would bring the Rebellion into power no other argument need be addressed." [38]

On election day Hayes wrote in his diary, " If we lose, the South will be the greatest sufferer. Their misfortunes will be far greater than ours . . . and the South will drift toward chaos again." On the day after the election, when he believed that the Democrats had won by a close margin, he told political friends and newspapermen, " I do not care for myself but I do care for the poor colored man in the South." Hayes felt more anxiety about the South—" about the colored people especially—than about anything else sinister in the result . . .

[37] Buck, *Road to Reunion*, p. 99; E. P. Oberholtzer, *A History of the United States Since the Civil War* (New York, 1931), III, 278-279.

[38] Hayes to Carl Schurz, August 9, 1876, to James A Garfield, August 12, 1876, to William Henry Smith, October 5, 1876, in Williams, *Diary and Letters of Hayes*, III, 340, 343, 365; Hayes to Garfield, August 6, 1876, in James A. Garfield Papers (Division of Manuscripts, Library of Congress); Schurz to Hayes, August 14, 1876, in Bancroft, *Writings of Schurz*, III, 286; Richardson, *Chandler*, p. 179.

the great injury is in the South. There the Amendments will be nullified, disorder will continue, prosperity to both whites and colored people will be pushed off for years." It seemed to him that he could do more "than any Democrat to put Southern affairs on a sound basis." Near the end of November in writing to an intimate and old friend in the South, Hayes expressed the feeling that a Democratic victory would prove "especially calamitous to the South—not to the colored people alone, but to the white people also," for Democratic success would drive off northern immigation and capital, both of which the South needed sorely.[39]

But these were campaign documents and speeches made in an effort to win votes, and the emotional reaction to an apparent defeat after a hard-fought contest. To what extent they reflected the honest opinions of Hayes and other top-drawer Republican leaders is open to question. But more importantly they did not represent public, and especially Republican, opinion in the North about Reconstruction, the South and the Negro. A changing attitude on the part of northerners toward the South and the freedman began to take place in the closing years of Reconstruction that helped to pave the way for a new Republican policy in the South. Gradually the more thoughtful northerners had become weary of the eternal Southern Question in politics and called for a halt to the discredited policy that employed federal troops to keep Carpetbagger governments in power. More and more, northerners had come to realize that reconstruction was primarily, if not entirely, a local problem, and that southerners would have to solve it themselves. As early as 1870, Horace Greeley, in the columns of the influential Republican paper, the New York *Tribune*, declared it was time to "have done with Reconstruction. The country is . . . sick of it. So long as any State is held in abeyance, it will be plausibly urged that the Republicans are afraid to trust the people. Let us give every State to herself."[40]

[39] Hayes Diary, November 7, 11, 12, 1876; Hayes to Guy M. Bryan, November 23, 1876, in Williams, *Diary and Letters*, III, 373, 374, 376, 377-378, 380; Williams, *Life of Hayes*, I, 493.

[40] New York *Tribune*, April 18, 1870, quoted in William Hesseltine, "Economic Factors in the Abandonment of Reconstruction," *Mississippi Valley Historical Review*, XXII (September, 1935), 201.

State governments propped up by federal bayonets could not go on forever. So the demand rose in volume, not only from southerners and Democrats, but from northerners and Republicans as well, for the removal of the troops from the South and for a complete cessation of federal interference in the domestic affairs of the states in this section. " The bulk of the people of the country North and South do not hate each other," stated the New York *Tribune*, " and it is a wretched piece of dishonesty on the part of politicians whose trade is loyalty to make them believe they do." [41] Only in this manner, argued such Republicans, could reconciliation between the two sections be speeded up and the party strengthened to deal with new and other questions. Otherwise the party faced destruction. *Harper's Weekly*, a most important Republican journal in the North, had predicted in 1871 that the party was doomed if it did not " promptly and decisively repudiate the thieving carpetbaggers," and after Hayes had recalled the troops, it maintained that the continuation of military Reconstruction " would have wholly overthrown the party within two years. There is no political fact plainer than this. Viewed partywise, the only hope lay in a bold and vigorous change of policy. Not to have made it would have been to destroy the party." [42] While the *Nation* may not have been entirely correct in concluding that " the great body of the Republican party is . . . opposed to the continuance at the South of the policy of military interference and coercion as pursued by General Grant," [43] there were many Republicans who wanted a different policy. But the sentiment for change was not unanimous, for there was an element in the Republican party, especially among its leadership, that still favored the old policy toward the South.

Northern opinion about Reconstruction and the South began to change sharply, at an early date, from what it had been in 1865-1867, as Greeley's statement in 1871 plainly reveals. What helped to influence the new northern attitude toward the South, and which were at the same time manifestations of it, were new studies about the southern states, a new reporting

[41] New York *Tribune*, April 18, 1870, quoted in Buck, *Road to Reunion*, p. 115.

[42] *Harper's Weekly*, XV (1871), 715; XXI (May 26, 1877), 402.

[43] *Nation*, XXIV (March 15, 1877), 156.

of the South, political events like the Liberal Republican Movement of 1872 and the congressional elections of 1874, a changing attitude on the part of much of the northern Republican press, and pressure from northern business men. All of these factors worked to produce in the minds of northerners by 1876-1877, a different impression about the South from what they might have had in the early years after the war. This change in tone on the part of northerners created a favorable climate for a new policy in the South and helped to sustain Hayes against the Radical attacks when he ended military Reconstruction.

There had been others besides Greeley who had called for a change of policy in the South. Jacob D. Cox, Grant's former Secretary of the Interior and a Republican leader from Ohio, in 1871 felt that Congress was following the wrong course. "Capital and intelligence must lead," wrote Cox. "Only Butler and W. Phillips would make a wilderness and call it peace." Cox advocated that the Republicans should organize and appeal to the "thinking and influential native Southerners," the "intelligent, well-to-do, and controlling class" of southern whites.[44] James Shepherd Pike, author of *The Prostrate State*, who had supported the Radical policy of Reconstruction at its outset, by 1870-1871 had become skeptical of the validity of such a policy, even as a party device. He also had doubts about universal suffrage and came to believe that the "nigger is a porcupine" who fills with quills everybody who undertakes to hug him." Pike felt Grant's program of reconstruction was a dismal failure and explained in 1871 that "the immediate cause of outrages in the . . . South is to be found in the unparalleled robbery and corruption practiced by the carpet-bag Government with the help of the Negro Legislatures." In the spring of 1872 he published an article, "A State in Ruins," concerning South Carolina, in the New York *Tribune,* in which he compared South Carolina in the days of her power when the "Dogmatic" but "high-toned aristocracy" ruled her, to her position of present tribulation when the state was governed by Negroes described as a "great mass of ignorance

[44] Cox to Garfield, March 17, April 1, 1871, in Hesseltine, "Economic Factors and Reconstruction," 202.

and barbarism," led by Carpetbaggers and a " few intelligent colored people " who were the miscreants and thieves.[45]

But the Liberal Republican Movement was the first great event which made an appreciable number of Republicans soften the harshness of their attitudes toward the South. Republicans like Carl Schurz, Greeley, George W. Julian, Charles Sumner, Jacob D. Cox, and Lyman Trumbull, whose loyalty and integrity were unassailed in the North now began to speak the language of harmony, to criticize the Carpetbag governments in the South, to abandon the bloody shirt, and to part with the Radicals over Reconstruction. The Liberal Republican Movement also brought into the same position the most powerful Republican journals and the ablest party editors in the North like Greeley's New York *Tribune*, Horace White's Chicago *Tribune*, Samuel Bowles' Springfield *Republican*, and Murat Halstead's Cincinnati *Commercial*. To have this group secede from the party and join a reform movement that stressed moderation toward the South was an important step toward a softer policy for this section.[46]

But the regular Republican party in 1872 vigorously fought the reform movement and rejected the " New Departure " Democrats from the South who made a point of accepting the war amendments and the Reconstruction Acts as accomplished facts and who insisted that bygones were bygones and instead emphasized the present problems. The regular Republicans resorted to the tactics of waving the bloody shirt, and *Harper's Weekly* accused Greeley of wanting to " undo as much of reconstruction as possible," and to let southerners " take care of the niggers." Thomas Nast conducted such a savage campaign against Greeley's reconciliation gestures and the " New Departure," that George W. Curtis, the editor of *Harper's Weekly*, whose language was not mild, protested, but Fletcher Harper, the owner, let Nast have his own way, and Mark Twain thought that in the campaign of 1872, Nast was working for " civilization and progress." Even Henry Adams and James Russell Lowell predicted that if Greeley won, " we should again witness that hideous uprising of exulting disloyalty and

[45] Robert F. Durden, *James Shepherd Pike, Republicanism and the American Negro, 1850-1882* (Durham, 1957), pp. 167-168.

[46] Buck, *Road to Reunion*, pp. 90-96.

violence which greeted the reactionary course of President Johnson." [47]

Thus Grant was chosen as the lesser of two evils, and his second administration demonstrated to both southerners and northerners who agreed with them, the futility of expecting a new policy for the South. The evil of Carpetbagger rule in the South seemed to grow worse, and the argument that " home rule " for the South was the only solution gained strength. Senator Matt Carpenter of Wisconsin, a long-time supporter of Radical Reconstruction, in May 1873 visited Louisiana with a congressional committee where he promised the people of New Orleans a better government and urged them to turn their energies from politics to trade and business, and Congressman Eugene Hale, presiding over Maine's Republican convention, stated that he was " tired and sick of the carpet-bag governments." [48] The Democrats, who supported the proposition of " home rule " for the South, gained strength in the years 1873-1876, and the Republicans, on the defensive now, more than ever had to use the weapon of the bloody shirt.

As the sentiment of opposition to the Carpetbaggers grew, there developed new hope that there would be a change of policy in the South that might encourage the migration of capital and manufacturing there. But blocking any change of policy were the stories of outrages in the South which the Radicals had exploited since 1866, and which for them, still remained a valuable source of campaign ammunition. But this received a serious blow in the congressional campaign of 1874 when the New York *Tribune* in September and October investigated the publication of a long list of murders and acts of violence in Alabama by a congressman from that state, and found no substantial basis for the charge. " Thereafter the accumulating atrocity stories were received dubiously by the northern people," writes a competent historian who has studied the problem.[49]

In 1874 there was a vast tidal-wave of popular feeling against the general course of the Republican party, and especially because of the never-ending, never-settled, and ever-disgraceful

[47] *Ibid.*, pp. 94-95.
[48] Hesseltine, " Economic Factors and Reconstruction," 207
[49] *Ibid.*, 208.

proceedings in the South. The policy of force and the use of
the bayonet to protect the Negro, who was never protected,
had become odious The cry for troops to put an end to outrages
which were constantly repeated despite the military occupation,
at least led many persons of all parties to the conviction that
either the outrages were inventions, or the use of the military
to protect the freedman was a glaring failure. The loudest and
most effective denunciation of the Republicans in the campaign
of 1874 was that they employed the army to bolster up state
governments in the South under the pretense of safeguarding
the Negro, and yet left the colored man exposed to all kinds
of mistreatment. In the elections of 1874 the Republicans were
defeated in such states as Massachusetts, Ohio, New York,
Pennsylvania, Wisconsin, and Illinois, and lost heavily in
Michigan, Iowa, and other Republican states. " The elections
of 1874 . . . clearly ended the era which the elections of 1866
had as clearly begun," writes a standard authority on Reconstruction. " With the Democrats controlling the House of
Representatives and near to control of the Senate, the radical
policy toward the South was doomed to early disappearance." [50]

When the Democrats gained control of the House in 1874,
Republicans began to take inventory of their policy in the
South. Commenting on the Carpetbaggers, Marshall Jewell,
the Postmaster General under Grant, wrote, " We have got a
hard lot from the South, and the people will not submit to it
any longer, nor do I blame them." Jewell was of the opinion
that the Carpetbaggers did not have " Among them one really
first class man." A consul in Germany thought it was " too
d——d bad that our party should be ruined and have to go
the wall through the careless labors of such cattle " as the
Louisiana Carpetbaggers. But the people were " tired out with
this wornout cry of ' Southern Outrages!!! Hard times and
heavy taxes make them wish the ' nigger,' ' everlasting nigger '
were in —— or Africa. . . . It is amazing the change that has
taken place in the last two years of public sentiment." George
F. Hoar, Republican Senator from Massachusetts, admitted that
the character of the Carpetbaggers was such that they would

---

[50] William A. Dunning, *Reconstruction Political and Economic,* 1865-1877
(New York, 1907), p. 251.

not have been tolerated in the North, and Senator Timothy Howe, Republican from Wisconsin, lamented about the failure of Republican hopes in the South and quite bluntly said that the war had not been " fought for the nigger," and that the freedman was not " the end and aim of all our effort." By 1874 even Vice-President Henry Wilson had reached the conclusion that the Republican party would have to change it policy, and on a trip through the South he had observed that business conditions had picked up and a spirit of industry seemed to be spreading among southern whites.[51]

There were new studies and a new reporting about the South in the 1870's that helped to change the northern opinion about this part of the country. Edward King's " The Southern States " published serially in *Scribner's Monthly Magazine* during 1873 and 1874 and in book form in 1875 put forth the theme that if the South were fairly treated by the North " prosperity would speedily return to a region of vast material resources." King found southerners " as loyal to the idea of the Union today as are the citizens of New York." Chapter by chapter this report piled up an overwhelming mass of evidence pointing to the evil results of Reconstruction. James S. Pike, with the background of a Radical and abolitionist, had visited South Carolina and watched the legislature in session, and from this came his book in 1874, *The Prostrate State: South Carolina under Negro Government*. As Paul Buck has observed, Pike's book " caught a vivid picture of radical Reconstruction at the moment and in the place of its grotesque flood tides of corruption . . . it did present a selection of facts freshly witnessed so colorfully as to fix permanently its picture as the one most remembered of all that have emerged from Reconstruction literature. The ' Africanization of South Carolina ' as the acme of misgovernment, corruption and injustice became a tradition, carrying with it the conclusion Pike suggested,—' Is it not time to bring to an end the punishment of the innocent many for the crimes of the guilty few.' " Charles Nordhoff, a strong Unionist and an advocate of Negro betterment, and Washington editor of the New York *Herald* from 1874-1890, in 1876 published *The Cotton States in the Spring and Summer of 1875* which forecast

<hr>

[51] Hesseltine, " Economic Factors and Reconstruction," 207, 209.

an optimistic social and economic future for the South and which undermined the necessity for the use of bloody shirt.[52]

" These . . . studies of the South were the most influential of the period," concludes the leading authority on reconciliation of North and South. " They commanded the widest reading public and they were treated with greatest respect by reviewers. There was in none of their pages the expression of any sentiment which did not tend to soften the Northern attitude toward the South and thus make for a better understanding. What was true of them was generally true of the great mass of material which found its way into print. *Harper's*, *Lippincott's*, *Appleton's*, and the *Atlantic* vied with *Scribner's* in reporting Southern scenes. The net result of this activity was to convey a new impression of the South to the North. In general it was maintained that Southerners were amicably disposed to the Union and that sectional biterness was declining rather than increasing." When one contrasts the journalism of 1865-1866 with that of the 1870's, " it can be appreciated that something of a revolution had been accomplished in this reporting of the South. The earlier reporters had considered it ' news ' to describe a South that was disgruntled, rebellious, and unregenerate. The Negro had been the hero and the Southern white the villain. But while white Republican orators still played these themes, the editors of newspapers and magazines apparently sensed among northern readers a demand for narratives which sympathetically portrayed the Southern white society in its efforts to achieve a richer participation in the national life." [53]

This changing attitude of the North toward the South was reflected and also influenced by the changing attitude of important Republican newspapers and periodicals in the North. The *National Republican* thought there was " sufficient justification for remonstrance by the South against governments originally established by military power, and since kept in being by a union of objectionable elements, unknown in former days, and representing no substantial interests, or but in small proportion to the whole party of the States concerned." The people of the

---

[52] Buck, *Road to Reunion*, pp. 130-133.
[53] *Ibid.*, pp. 132-134.

North have " long felt the injustice of these governments . . . and the occasion for their encouragement had disappeared." There is " the positive conviction in the public mind of the impolicy of upholding unnatural power in the face of protest of those who in reality constitute the State . . . there are no considerations which should induce Federal aid, and no authority to warrant it." The " great majority of the party is . . . convinced that whatever reasons have heretofore existed for sustaining these governments, they exist no longer." Self-government for the South did not mean any abandonment of party friends which was not demanded " by every interest of the country . . . for certainly no one will contend that any possible good can result from further exasperating the Southern people by forcing them to submit to these governments." [54]

The New York *Tribune*, which had furiously waved the bloody shirt throughout the campaign of 1876, now discovered that " the fatal fault of the Repubican policy hitherto was that it always relied upon force, and not upon the willing support of Southern white citizens." This was a " system of despotism which not only ' crushes ' the community immediately subjected to it, but undermines the whole fabric of American liberty. Some way or other we must come to the principle that the Federal military cannot hold up any State governments." [55] The Chicago *Tribune*, which in nearly every editorial from July, 1876 through election day referred to the dangers of a " Rebel " and Confederate victory and which printed numerous alleged outrages in the South, reversed itself after Hayes had assumed office and called for an end to the Carpetbaggers and the use of federal troops to maintain state governments in the South.[56] " It is simply impossible to sustain by negro support a State Government to which the whites, as a class, should refuse obedience," argued the *Tribune*. " The social pyramid at the South cannot be kept in any one of the States resting artificially on its apex, propped around with bayonets . . . intelligence and property must be allowed to rule, whatever the question of numbers may be. . . . The blacks must consent to recognize this, and then Republican friends must undeceive

---

[54] Washington *National Republican*, March 1, February 28, 1877.
[55] New York *Tribune*, March 20, 29, 1877; see also March 14, 26, 28, 31.
[56] Chicago *Tribune*, March 8, 10, 22, 24, 26, 27, 28, 30, 1877.

them, and advise against a black color-line." [57] The New York *Times* concluded that "The reason for frankly and fearlessly amending the policy pursued toward the South . . . is found in the failure of that policy. . . . To close one's eyes to the fact of failure would be absurd. . . . If reconstruction were a success, its fruits would vindicate it." [58]

E. L. Godkin in the *Nation* made most effective thrusts against Republican policy in the South. He began his attack before the Greeley campaign, but it " grew in volume as events in the South confirmed the accuracy of his trenchant observations and dire predictions." Because of the years of emphasis Godkin " built up a complete dogma of the folly of Republican rule in the South and applied it to every episode that raised the Southern issue." His central theme was that the evils in the South were not curable by legislation that came from the outside, for these were evils that could only disappear under the influence of a general improvement of southern society. Radical interference, selfishly motivated, acted only as an irritant.[59] Throughout the 1876 campaign the *Nation* hammered away at the "Republican knaves" who clung to the bloody shirt pointing out that if Hayes were elected on that theory, " we are delivered bound hand and foot to the disreputable gang for whose overthrow we have been so long laboring." [60] The *Nation* felt that the Radicals should not have attempted " the insane task of making newly-emancipated field hands, led by barbers and barkeepers, fancy they knew as much about government and were as capable of administering it, as the whites." It was a complete failure to give " the blacks the same political weight as the whites. . . . It was . . . a silly attempt, doubly silly when made through the use of troops. If it had succeeded it would have proved not only that the lessons of history were all false, but that civilization was a mere dream." Immediately following the election of 1876, Godkin set forth a new Republican creed which he wanted exacted of every party member. For the South it should mean

[57] *Ibid.*, April 2, 1877.
[58] New York *Times*, March 13, 1877.
[59] Buck, *Road to Reunion*, p. 97.
[60] *Nation*, XXIII (August 3, 1876), 66; see also July 27, August 10, 17, 24, October 19, 1876.

the application of the " old American method of conciliation and confidence and the abandonment of the old Austrian notion that whole communities may be made up of devilish persons insensible to reason and justice, and only manageable by brutal force and denunciation. . . . Let us now hear the last of it, and go forward on the nobler and more excellent way." What enthusiasm was possible for the Republican party, asked Godkin, "whose only missionaries to the dark places of our soil were carpetbaggers, and whose sole remedy for the horrors of a social revolution have been ' troops ' and vituperation? Let us now look for better work. Do not let us hear any longer from American lips that fellow-citizens must repent and ask pardon before you will help them, and when they complain of the bitterness of the medicine you offer them, that it is twice too good for them and that you wish it was bitterer." [61]

While *Harper's Weekly*, the mouthpiece of the regular Republican party in the North, also waved the bloody shirt, and exclaimed, " no greater evil could befall us than to suffer weariness of the Southern question," it did ask who would defend a policy that created state government of the " freed slaves . . . so repugnant and odious to the white population that they could be maintained only by the military power of the Union?" [62] Charles A. Dana, editor of the New York *Sun*, originally a Radical, became a Democrat and made " No force bill! No Negro domination!" the constant cry of his newspaper throughout Grant's second administration.[63]

Reaching a wide public these influential newspapers and journals played a most important role in softening the attitude of northerners toward the South and in preparing the climate necessary for a new policy. But an equally influential pressure for a change came from the business community. Here was an interest group that the Republican party could ill afford to ignore. Businessmen seeking profits in the South soon discovered that military Reconstruction blocked their efforts for economic exploitation of this section. They wanted more

[61] *Ibid.*, XXIII (August 24, 1876), 114; (October 26, 1876), 246; (November 9, 1876), 280-281.

[62] *Harper's Weekly*, XX (November 4, 1876), 886; XXI (February 17, 1877), 122; see also (March 17, 1877), 202.

[63] Buck, *Road to Reunion*, p. 97.

security and settled conditions in the South, and they wanted stable southern governments which they felt could be organized if the troops and Carpetbaggers left and the "best" white men returned to power. "Every consideration of national interest and national pride requires the prosecution of a more generous policy" of Reconstruction, wrote the editor of *Hunt's Merchant's Magazine*, "in order that we may develop the wealth of the South." But business men wanted more security, and while "The South has required a large amount of merchandise . . . and Southern merchants have shown some anxiety to open credits . . . as a rule," said the same editor, "our merchants have not deemed it prudent to extend credit to that section until political affairs become more settled." [64] Marshall Jewell, former member of Grant's cabinet, a Connecticut business man and a future Republican National Chairman, spoke for many of his class, when he told Hayes, "Our business interests greatly need . . . the rehabilitation and building up of the South," [65] and the New York *Times* felt "If there were no other reasons for deprecating a renewal of partisan strife in the disputed Southern States, the urgent needs of the business and industrial interests of the country alone would be sufficient." [66]

"All the sober, substantial men" of New York, St. Louis and Washington, supported Johnson's policy of Reconstruction, wrote Grant's aide-de-camp in the fall of 1865, and as early as that year, the leading business journals of the day like *Hunt's Merchant's Magazine* and the *Commercial and Financial Chronicle* urged a policy of rapid conciliation between North and South as the best way to restore trade between the two sections.[67] In supporting Johnson's plan of Reconstruction, *Hunt's Merchant's Magazine* placed "great confidence in the President's views . . . and we believe that every consideration of national interest and of national pride, require the prosecution of the more generous policy. . . . The most important

[64] *Hunt's Merchant's Magazine* (New York), LIV (1866), 170-172; LV (1866), 309-310; see also *Commercial and Financial Chronicle* (New York), III (1866), 42.

[65] Marshall Jewell to Hayes, February 22, 1877, in Hayes Papers.

[66] New York *Times*, April 11, 1877.

[67] Adam Badeau to E. B. Washburne, October 20, 1865, in Hesseltine, "Economic Factors and Reconstruction," 192; Buck, *Road to Reunion*, p. 6.

consideration of public interest demand this . . . in order that we may develop the wealth of the South, all political questions must be settled, so that peace and security may become universal." The South had lost its capital and the only way to attract capital was "by ensuring large profits; and this can only be by . . . giving to capital the security of a civil government." Capital could not be attracted to the South and neither could its industry and wealth be developed so long as this section was "under semi-military rule." [68]

The *Commercial and Financial Chronicle*, also a supporter of Johnson's policy, soon discovered that the Radical attack upon the President and the Supreme Court and congressional reconstruction were "paralyzing all industries . . . and a deep feeling of impatience is becoming well nigh universal under the prolonged incubation." The South was fast sinking into a state of "utter prostration," and the North was daily becoming more hopeless under a wider suspension of activity. This journal also warned that if Negro majorities controlled the state legislatures, capital would stay out of the South. The time had come to devise some plan not only to restore confidence in the South, "but among the capitalists and manufacturers and merchants of the whole country." The continued agitation and the prolonged "suspended animation" in the South imposed an "incubus upon the whole capital and industry of the entire country," and "probably the most forcible reason for the speedy and effectual settlement of our Southern difficulties lies in the necessity to the nation of a revival of business." [69]

As military Reconstruction wore on, the business journals maintained that ," All men are weary of this. The commerce, the industry of the entire people languish." Military control of the South was the "worst possible condition for social and industrial progress . . . and it is opposed to the wishes of the white population." Business men contended that political conditions in the South were not such as to encourage enterprise in that section, that the uncertainty and suspense had deadened trade, had produced great distress, and threatened much more. The *Commercial and Financial Chronicle* received letters from

[68] *Hunt's Merchants' Magazine*, LIV (1866), 169-174.
[69] *The Commercial and Financial Chronicle*, VI (1868), 70-71.

manufacturers and their agents that urged the necessity for an immediate settlement, "while from all parts of the country there are evidences of great disappointment and discouragement." [70] This, the leading business journal of the country, consistently called for a policy of moderation and leniency toward the South. It attacked Radical Reconstruction and reported conditions in the South in a manner that contradicted Radical propaganda. The more vocal groups of northern business men favored moderation as the best means of bringing about a rapid economic recovery of the South. This was particularly true of merchants, cotton manufacturers, financiers, and railroad executives. The cotton brokers of New York and Philadelphia and the cotton manufacturers of New England wanted, most urgently, to restore friendly relations with the South.[71] The Boston *Evening Transcript* reported that Boston merchants and business men wanted "cordial relations" between North and South, and the Albany *Argus* insisted that business men of the North would resent the attempt to organize the Republican party on the basis of hatred for the South.[72]

There appeared to be a fundamental difference between Radical politicians and northern business men about the South. The former sought to exploit this section for political advantage, and the latter regarded it an area for economic expansion.[73] An exchange of letters in the New York *Tribune* in the winter of 1869 between Greeley and Benjamin F. Butler clearly reveals these divergent views. Greeley pointed out that Radical Reconstruction had retarded business. In reply, Butler declared that Greeley's course had encouraged the rebels to defy the Republican party, and conditions would have been better "if a half dozen leading rebels had been hung at the end of the war." [74] During his campaign in 1872, Greeley had charged that "had it not been for carpetbag mismanagement" the South "today would be filled with millions of Northern or foreign yeomanry carving out farms, or working in . . . iron, copper, coal, and marble." But the Radicals disagreed with this con-

---

[70] *Ibid.*, 263, 583, 166; XXIII (1876), 585; XXIV (1877), 3.
[71] Buck, *Road to Reunion*, pp. 154-155.
[72] Logan, *Negro in American Life and Thought*, pp. 18, 34.
[73] Hesseltine, "Economic Factors and Reconstruction," 197-199.
[74] *Ibid.*, 199-120.

clusion, and the New York *Times* even felt that their policy held out "every encouragement . . . to Northern and foreign capitalists." [75] While Greeley lost the election his southern program left a deep impression on the voters. The idea that Radical Reconstruction drove out industry from the South had received much publicity in the North. In the years that followed the election so much of the northern press proclaimed the horrors of carpetbaggism that business became convinced that only by its removal could there be any economic expansion into the South.

After Greeley's death the New York *Tribune* continued to point out the close connection between military Reconstruction and the "economic derangements attendant upon carpetbag governments." Added to this was the fear from the danger involved in the rising movement of the lower income groups in the country. Some made the connection between the Granger movement in the West assailing strongholds of private monopoly and the "bottom rails" who had gotten on top in the South. In 1871, an observer had noticed that there were six thousand white adult males in Georgia "who cannot read or write, and if to them were added the whole bulk of the negro population, so vast a mass of ignorance would be found that, if combined for any political purposes it would sweep away all opposition the intelligent class might make. Many thoughtful men are apprehensive that the ignorant voters will, in the future, form a party by themselves as dangerous to the interests of society as the communists of France." Another thing that bothered business men and property holders in the North about the poverty of the South, which they had come to ascribe to the villainies of the Carpetbaggers, was the "withdrawal of taxes" which the South might have paid under more favorable circumstances. This "throws just that additional burden upon the tax-paying property of the North," announced the New York *Tribune* in 1873.[76]

The North had also significantly changed its mind about the Negro. Except for the Republican party interest in the Negro vote, there was not much concern among northerners for helping

[75] *Ibid.*, 203-204.
[76] *Ibid.*, 205-207.

the freedman. After 1877 northerners were, for the most part, in substantial agreement that the Negro was not prepared for equality and that the South should be allowed to deal with him in its own way. The North now believed that the elimination of the Negro from politics must be recognized to give more meaning to the reunion of North and South. Northerners were coming to regard the Negro as a thorn in their flesh, and as standing in the way of a return to national solidarity and a development of trade relations between the two sections. They were coming to look upon the Negro as the American peasantry, and as being inferior in race stamina and race achievement, and they were coming to believe that the true interests of both races required that the control should be placed in the hands of the whites, and that the only hope for good government in the South rested upon the assured political supremacy of the white race.[77]

Even in the early years after the Civil War there was considerable northern opposition to Negro equality and suffrage,[78] and as Reconstruction progressed, some of the great northern champions that the Negro originally had, began to reverse their opinion. Godkin in the *Nation* in 1874 asserted that the average intelligence among most Negroes was " so low that they are slightly above the levels of animals," and he asked how long it would take to change the " once ' sovereign State ' of South Carolina into a truly loyal, truly Republican, truly African San Domingo." At the same time Godkin also concluded that the Negro, as a legislator, was " merely a horrible failure." By 1877 the *Nation* felt that the Negro had all the usual guarantees of citizenship under our Constitution. He could vote and hold office " on the same terms as the white man," and he had " equal standing in the courts. When all this had been done for a man in the United States, what more can be done? What more are we prepared to do?" By the spring of that year the *Nation* had assumed the position that " The negro will disappear from the field of national politics. Henceforth the nation, as a nation, will have nothing more to

[77] Myrdal, *An American Dilemma*, pp. 226, 738-739; Buck, *Road to Reunion*, pp. 283, 296; Simkins, *The South, Old and New*, p. 229.

[78] Leslie H. Fishel, "Northern Prejudice and Negro Suffrage, 1865-1870," *Journal of Negro History*, XXXIX (January, 1954), 8-27.

do with him." [79] The New York *Tribune* had reached the conclusion that "after ample opportunity to develop their own latent capacities," Negroes had only proved that "as a race they are idle, ignorant, and vicious." [80] *Harper's Weekly* observed that there were Republicans who seemed to suppose that without armed occupation of the South "there can be no security for the negro. But it will be found that his condition is most satisfactory where the military arm is weakest," and that the danger of the Negro being "reduced to a condition little better than slavery . . . has in great measure passed away." [81]

As a careful and recent student of the Negro in America in the last quarter of the nineteenth century has shown, "the Northern press was not reluctant to sacrifice the Negro on the altar of reconciliation, peace and prosperity," and that attitudes of the northern press and magazine "endorsed the policies and approved the events that steadily reduced the Negro to a subordinate place in American life. On this point American thought generally conformed to American life." [82] Northern literary magazines like *Harper's, Scribner's, Atlantic, North American Review* and *Forum* contributed not only to the fixing of the stereotypes of the Negro, but also to the interpretation of events that was sympathetic to the "Lost Cause." Most of the books and volumes of poetry about the Negro that northerners read were by southerners, and with the exception of George Washington Cable, they developed stereotypes, marked either by exaggeration or omission, and all agreed in emphasizing the Negro's divergence from an Anglo-Saxon norm to the flattery of the latter. Both Social Darwinism and the Social Gospel, rampant after the War, contributed to the concept of the inferiority of the Negro. This was especially true of the writings of William Graham Sumner who argued that the question of whether or not the Negro was the equal of a white man was not an essential question, for since the

[79] *Nation*, XVIII (April 16, 30, 1874), 247-248, 282; XXIII (September 7, 1876), 145-146; XXIV (January 11, April 5, 1877), 22-23, 202.
[80] New York *Tribune*, April 7, 1877.
[81] *Harper's Weekly*, XXI (April 14, March 31, 1877), 282, 242.
[82] Logan, *Negro in American Life and Thought*, pp. 159, 216.

South regarded the Negro as inferior, the only practical question was how to deal with that opinion.[83]

Some historians contend that northern newspapers frequently repudiated the application of the American creed to the Negro, because they were the creatures of Big Business, the principal engineer of the Compromise of 1877 and the subsequent determination to leave the South alone.[84] Whatever the reasons, the northern press had greatly changed its attitude toward the freedman, as it had toward Reconstruction, and the South, and in that change, it had created a new climate of opinion in the North. " It is time," announced the Chicago *Tribune* " to seriously consider the protection which the colored people find under home rule, such as has been established in Georgia and Arkansas, from which there has been no complaining for years of bulldozing or outrages." And when the troops finally left Louisiana in April, 1877, the *Tribune* sighed that, " For the first time for a third of a century, it may be considered that the black population of the United States have ceased to be the overwhelming and engrossing subject of American politics . . . now, in 1877, the long controversy over the black man seems to have reached a fiinality. . . . The colored men have nothing more to ask: there is nothing which national politics can give them as a class." [85]

Grant recognized the changed attitude toward the South and the Negro that had set in in the North, when in the closing days of his presidency, he reversed himself on his earlier policy of intervention in the South. When S. B. Packard, Carpetbagger claimant for governor in Louisiana, asked for federal troops to settle the disputed election in this state, Grant turned him down, pointing out that public opinion would no longer support the maintenance of a state government by the use of the military, and that " he must concur in this manifest feeling . . . and under the remaining days of his official life they [the troops] will not be used to establish or to pull down either claimant for control of the State." [86] Earlier Grant had told Garfield that Packard could not be sustained but would

[83] *Ibid.*, pp. 251-256, 162, 165-168.
[84] *Ibid.*, p. 170; Oberholtzer, *History of United States*, II, 541.
[85] Chicago *Tribune*, March 10, April 24, 1877.
[86] *Nation*, XXIV (March 1, 1877), 124; New York *Times*, March 3, 1877.

be driven from the state as soon as the electoral vote was decided. Packard had such little force that he feared a collision would wipe him out before Grant could rescue him, and the President did not feel that he should move from "apprehension merely." [87] As for the contest in South Carolina, Grant was of the opinion that it had assumed such a phase that "the whole army of the United States would be inadquate to enforce the authority of Governor Chamberlain." In an interview with the Associated Press, Grant stated that "the entire people are tired of the military being used to sustain a State Government. If a Republican State Government cannot sustain itself," he added, "then it will have to give way. If a remedy is required, let Congress, and not the President provide it." [88] Grant "had many advisers against, recognizing the last carpetbag governments," Alphonso Taft, the Solicitor General, informed Hayes. "One consideration has had some weight with him and that is, that he was not so well sustained by the Republican Party when he recognized and upheld [William Pitt] Kellogg as he expected." [89]

Grant's decision to forego intervention helped to prepare the way for a new Republican policy in the South, and his action kept pace with the changing opinion that had developed in the North and among the rank and file of the party by 1877 toward the South. By this date Republicans in all parts of the country were not only demanding a change from military Reconstruction but were proposing how to do it. One has but to read the vast number of letters that poured in upon the national Republican leaders throughout the two decades after Reconstruction to appreciate the tremendous support that Republicans gave to the efforts to redeem the South for their party. Hayes' letter of acceptance, in which he held out to the South, the hope of early "home rule" led many Americans, and especially Republicans, to believe he had blueprinted a new policy for the South, and from every section of the country they pressed and encouraged him to take the step. Here was the beginning of a flood of demands and proposals for a change of policy in

[87] Garfield Diary, January 20, 1877, in Garfield Papers; William E. Chandler to Hayes, January 13, 1877, in Hayes Papers.

[88] Nation, XXIV (March 1, 1877), 127, 124.

[89] Alphonso Taft to Hayes, February 14, 1877, in Hayes Papers.

the South that continued to roll in throughout the remainder of the nineteenth century.

The amount of advice showered upon Hayes from the moment he received the nomination for President in June, 1876 until his letter of acceptance appeared on July 8, can hardly be overestimated. Some of it was obviously contradictory. His running mate, Wheeler, recommended that he should not say much on the southern problem for " your views as illustrated on the battle field on that question ought to suffice." [90] But Charles Nordhoff, a leading journalist in Washington, to whom Hayes had written for suggestions, advised him to say that federal interference in the South should be avoided, " except when the clearest and extremist necessity demanded it." [91] Carl Schurz wanted Hayes to declare that " the Constitutional rights of local self-government must be respected," but Hayes objected to the phrase " local self-government." It seemed to him " to smack of the bowie knife and revolver. ' Local self-government ' has nullified the Fifteenth Amendment in several States, and is in a fair way to nullify the Fourteenth and Thirteenth. But I do favor a policy of reconciliation based on the observance of all parts of the Constitution—the new as well as the old." [92] Hayes stuck to this and promised the South " honest and capable local government," free of federal interference—a statement which southerners regarded as a pledge and for which they looked to Hayes to fulfill. But he had promised this only upon the condition of southern whites recognizing the political and civil rights of the Negro, a condition that the white South would not tolerate and which it ignored contrary to the assurances it gave to Hayes.

Hayes felt that he had prepared " a bold and honest Letter of Acceptance," that would " offend some and cool the ardor of others, but it is sound and I believe will be strong with the people. At any rate," he concluded, " it is the true course." He told an intimate friend in the South, Guy Bryan of Texas, that he would see in the letter " the influence of the feelings which our friendship has tended to foster. It will cost me

[90] William A. Wheeler to Hayes, July 1, 1876, *Ibid.*

[91] Charles Nordhoff to Hayes, June 28, 1876, *Ibid.*

[92] Schurz to Hayes, June 21, 1876, in Bancroft, *Writings of Schurz*, III, 251; Hayes to Schurz, June 27, 1876, Williams, *Diary and Letters*, III, 329-330.

some support," Hayes added. "But it is right, I shall keep cool, and no doubt at the end be prepared for either event." He explained to George William Curtis, the editor of *Harper's Weekly* that he had wanted " to talk of the rights of the colored man and at the same time to say what I could for the interests and feeling of the well disposed white man." [93]

Hayes had no illusions over the resistance the Radicals would put up to any change of policy in the South, but he was determined to maintain " the firmest adherence to principle against all opposition and temptation . . . I shall show a grit," he noted in his diary, " that will astound all who predict weakness." He promised Bryan that he would " stand by the paragraph on the South in my letter. The more sinister the reports, the more I am convinced that I hit the true and only solution," and he maintained that his " general views on the Southern question were given authoritatively and correctly in my Letter of Acceptance." Southerners were anxious to know whether Hayes would take the troops out of the South, but he was unwilling to elaborate upon his July statement and was unwilling to write anything on the subject for the public.[94]

But the letter made a most favorable impression upon the country at large. From Washington, Nordhoff announced that the letter was an eminent success. " The best men in Congress speak the most highly of it," reported Nordhoff, " as honest, frank, square, and in every way strong and satisfactory." William Dean Howells wrote, " I can't forbear telling you how much I like your letter of acceptance. It's the manliest thing done in politics since the Declaration, on which it's an improvement in some respects." [95] A former Republican governor of New York felt " confident now that we shall get some of the southern states," and a party leader from Maine thought the letter would " help us everywhere with good men, and is

[93] Hayes Diary, July 8, 1876, Williams, *Diary and Letters*, III, 333; Hayes to Guy M. Bryan, July 8, 1876, in E. W. Winkler, ed., " The Bryan-Hayes Correspondence," *Southwestern Historical Quarterly*, XXVI (1922-1923), 294; Hayes to George William Curtis, July 10, 1876, in Hayes Papers.

[94] Hayes, Diary, September 24, 1876; Hayes to Bryan, October 24, November 23, 1876, in Williams, *Diary and Letters*, III, 363, 380; Winkler, " Bryan-Hayes Correspondence," 310.

[95] Williams, *Life of Hayes*, I, 465-466.

what we can stand or fall with honor." [96] Among the reform element in the Republicans there was great joy about Hayes' letter. Horace White of the Chicago *Tribune*, called it the "most encouraging political document promulgated since the war," and Whitelaw Reid of the New York *Tribune* felt if it had been specially designed to enable the *Tribune*, "and those for whom it speaks to make their support of you effective, it could not have been better accomplished for the purpose." George William Curtis regarded it as the work of a very different person, and he told Hayes, "All good men owe you an incalculable debt." Wayne MacVeagh linked equal rights and honest government for the South as issues "fully worthy of the Centennial canvass." [97] From the South, a Republican county chairman, disclosed to Hayes that the letter gave "universal satisfaction here among Republicans. . . . I know a number of heretofore Democrats who will support you. I know no Republicans who will not." [98]

Among members of Congress, Hayes' letter proved to be "decidedly popular." Here and there were expressions of personal dissent, but on the whole the letter was acceptable to Republicans, and Democrats admitted that it was bold and manly. [99] Leading northern newspapers and journals warmly praised what the letter said about the South. "It is a model letter of its kind," exclaimed the Chicago *Tribune*. "The utterances concerning . . . the Southern States are those of a statesman and patriot who knows neither sect nor section." [100] The New York *Times* contended that Hayes' views on the South would receive general approval; the *National Republican* called it "frank and fearless," and the New York *Tribune* thought it embodied "the strongest desires of all honest and thinking American citizens." [101] *Harper's Weekly* was overjoyed

[96] E. D. Morgan, New York to Hayes, July 11, 1876; Eugene Hale, Maine to Hayes, July 17, 1876, in Hayes Papers.

[97] Horace White to Hayes, July 12, 1876; Whitelaw Reid to Hayes, July 21, 1876, George William Curtis to Hayes, July 13, 1876; Wayne MacVeagh to Hayes, July 10, 1876, *Ibid*.

[98] J. R. Dillon, Davidson County, Tennessee, to Hayes, July 13, 1876, *Ibid*.

[99] New York *Times*, July 11, 1876.

[100] Chicago *Tribune*, July 10, 1876; see also July 11, 1876, March 6, 1876.

[101] New York *Times*, July 10, 1876; Washington *National Republican*, July 10, 1876; New York *Tribune*, July 10, 1876; see also New York *Times*, July 11, 1876 for favorable comments from other northern newspapers.

that Hayes' views on the South were "the precise positions" that it had steadily maintained, but the *Nation* found the language on the Southern Question "too vague to be reassuring, Hayes was not sufficiently explicit as to the proper remedies for the Southern disease, but simply talked of his desire for peace and conciliation in general terms," and that observed Godkin, "may cover almost any kind of policy." [102]

But Republicans in all parts of the country quickly responded to Hayes' leter with suggestions on how to rejuvenate their party in the South. Native white Republicans in the South were perhaps the most vigorous and vociferous advocates of a new policy. Sharply protesting against military Reconstruction, this element of Republicanism called for a new departure that would remove the troops and kick out the Carpetbagger. *"I am confident you will obtain the support of the whole people in every Southern State,"* a Republican from New Orleans told Hayes, "if you will keep the military away from them and let the military go after the Mexicans and Indians." [103] A Virginian and a son of a former President advised Hayes to "avoid the carpetbaggers . . . and address yourself to the material and Industrial interests of the South," and the Democratic party in this section would disappear. [104] Native white Republicans also clamored for greater recognition from Washington and for control of the patronage in their states. They complained that Grant had appointed too many Carpetbaggers and Democrats to office in the South, and they pleaded with Washington officials not to judge all southern Republicans by the "specimens" who lived in the nation's capitol, for they only "hang around the White House for crumbs" and "are generally a lot of bums who shift with the wind and who have no weight or control at all." [105] Finally, they asked Washington to stop the practice of rewarding defeated Republican candidates in the South, for this had "proved absolutely destructive to the Party everywhere in the South," and had "operated as a bonus to the vilest and most depraved wretches in the Party

---

[102] *Harper's Weekly*, XX (July 29, 1876), 610; *Nation*, XXIII (July 13, 27, 1876), 17, 52-53.
[103] Forrester Do Chonde to Hayes, March 1, 1877, in Hayes Papers.
[104] John Tyler, Jr. to Hayes, February 17, 1877, *Ibid*.
[105] L. A. Sheldon, New Orleans to Garfield, March 1, 1877, in Garfield Papers.

everywhere in the South." Such a policy was "utterly degrading to the character of the Party," and was driving out of it "men of decency and self-respect, of culture and ability." Nearly every Republican in the South "of mark and true worth," had been compelled "to abandon his Republican attitude, to escape from the assaults made upon his fair name and fame with all the filth and garbage raked out of Sewers and Cap pools." [106]

If native white Republicans in the South complained, they also proposed how to rebuild their party in their states. One from Georgia, after canvassing many former Whigs, informed Hayes that it was "*impracticable to get any considerable following under any specific organization or name at present,*" but that "a large following independent of party" and "*at first under the name of independant Democrats* could be gathered together. Such an independent movement would provide the best means "*to destroy the democracy and build up a good strong party* that will fall in line and assist in electing the *republican candidate for President in 1880.*" [107] Others favored the strategy of sharing the patronage in the South with conservatives now acting with the Democratic party as the best course for conciliating and dividing southern whites. [108] Another plan envisioned a revival of the Whig party in the South and its coalition with Republicans. "I greatly desire to see a *union* of the *Old Whigs* and *Republicans* in this State and city," wrote a business man from Richmond. [109] Republicans who argued for this plan pointed out that the Whigs provided the only source of new recruits for the party in the South, and that the Whigs had become restive within the Democratic party and could be weaned away with federal offices and favors. [110]

But some southern whites balked at the idea of conciliating conservatives and former Whigs in the South, on the grounds

[106] John Tyler, Jr. to John Sherman, June 27, 1880, in John Sherman Papers (Division of Manuscripts, Library of Congress).

[107] Foster Blodgett, Atlanta to Hayes, May 25, 1877, in Hayes Papers.

[108] Lewis Hanes, North Carolina to Hayes, February 14, 1877; J. A. McDonald, North Carolina to Hayes, January 1, 1877; W. F. Cole, Grenada, Mississippi to Hayes, March 8, 1877, in Hayes Papers; John Tyler, Jr. to Sherman, June 24, 1879, in Sherman Papers.

[109] George A. Hundley to Hayes, April 24, 1877, in Hayes Papers.

[110] John Tyler, Jr. to Hayes, March 12, 1877, *Ibid.*; Jno. Bowles to Sherman, March 14, 1877, in Sherman Papers.

that southern Bourbonism was too hard to eradicate, and that the old line Whigs were too few in number and too aristocratic to lead the white southern masses into the Republican party. Instead, effort should be made to bring the self-working whites, who had not held slaves, into the party. This element should be encouraged and fostered for its own sake and should not be subordinated to the Negro. A white farmer from South Carolina pointed out that his class, who lived mostly in the swamps, backwoods, and mountains, must not be confused with the " so-called cracker population," and for " every Negro vote lost we can gain a white vote." Many of the white independent farmers were saying, " let us get rid of the rule of the negro first, beat the vicious ring, and then we will get rid of the aristocrats who dragged us into the rebel armies to fight for them." [111]

Republicans outside the South called for a new policy in equally strong terms. The Secretary of the Republican National Committee summed up a large segment of party sentiment when he told Hayes that " the people want a new administration in every sense of the word." [112] A Republican from Chicago suggested smoothing over the animosities of the past and educating the Negro, and an Ohio friend wrote to Hayes, " Rutherford take a friends advice and kill our southern brethren with kindness." [113] The Liberal and reform elements in the party felt that Grant's course had divided and almost ruined the party, and they pleaded for a new departure that would ingratiate the party with the white South. [114]

General Grenville M. Dodge of Iowa, who played a key role in the Texas Pacific Railroad bargain of 1877 that helped to put Hayes in the White House, recommended a policy of granting national aid for internal improvements in the South, as a means of building a strong Republican party there. Such a result could be achieved, wrote Dodge, without " turning

[111] J. P. M. Epping to J. J. Patterson, United States Senator from South Carolina, March 10, 1877, in Carl Schurz Papers (Division of Manuscripts, Library of Congress).

[112] Richard McCormick to Hayes, February 14, 1877, in Hayes Papers.

[113] O. Bensen to W. K. Rogers, Hayes' Private Secretary, March 8, 1877; J. B. Way to Hayes, March 8, 1877, *Ibid*.

[114] James B. Belford to Hayes, February 9, 1877; Wayne MacVeagh to Hayes, February 10, 1877; Jno. D. Defrees to Hayes, February 11, 1877, *Ibid*.

our backs upon, or abandoning any of our friends, white or black." [115]   Two Republican leaders in the House, Garfield and Charles Foster, both from Ohio, agreed with Dodge on this proposition, and in fact they regretted that the Republican party was so squarely committed against further subsidies as to prevent them from advocating the building of the Texas Pacific Railroad by the help of Congress. They thought that a large following might be gained for the Republican party in the South, and that Texas might be made a Republican state, by the party favoring this project. Both had no doubt of being able to build up a strong southern following for a Republican administration by advocating such southern public improvements that had been granted to the North during and after the War. [116] But Carl Schurz, an influential adviser of Hayes, opposed the idea of attempting to gain the favor of the South by such a bid and recommended not referring to the matter of internal improvements at all. " If nothing is said about it," he cautioned Hayes, " nothing will be missed. . . . Your good will toward the Southern people can be set forth strongly in many other ways." [117]

Important Republican editors also pressed Hayes on a new policy. Whitelaw Reid hoped for " a policy that may retrieve the error and disgrace of Republican dealings with the South— precisely in accordance with the admirable tone of your letter of acceptance," and " we hope," Reid told Hayes, " to see your administration totally disassociated from the mistaken policy and ruinous leaders that have brought this party . . . to the verge of defeat." Murat Halstead of the Cincinnati *Commercial* recommended the strategy of trying to win white support in the South and that of dealing liberally with the South by the national government, and the *National Republican* wanted a policy that would use the old Whig-Union element in the South as a nucleus for a strong and respectable Republican organization in this section. The Cleveland *Leader*, the New York *Times*, and the *Nation* wanted the " political adventurers " removed from office in the South, and the federal offices to be filled " wisely, with men of suitable character, ability and

[115] G. M. Dodge to Hayes, February 15, 1877, *Ibid*.
[116] James Comly to Hayes, January 8, 1877, *Ibid*.
[117] Schurz to Hayes, February 2, 1877, *Ibid*.

standing," identified " by solid and permanent interest . . . by birth and social and other ties with the South. They were not to be office seekers and were not to be dependent on their appointment for a living." [118]

Even among some of the Republican leaders who had helped to launch the party upon a program of military Reconstruction and who later attacked the new departure taken by Hayes, there were supporters for a change of policy in the South. During the 1876 campaign, Hayes in conferring with James G. Blaine, in Ohio, discovered that the Maine leader had " almost precisely " his views and hopes as to the South. " By conciliating Southern whites, on the basis of obedience to law and equal right," Blaine hoped to " divide the Southern whites and so protect the colored people." Later in a long talk with Garfield, Blaine voiced the opinion that the time had come for the Republican party to stop keeping state governments in power by the use of troops.[119] Roscoe Conkling, Republican boss from New York, told a reporter for the New York *Herald* that no considerable element of the Republican party objected to the removal of the troops, and that he did not protest on that score.[120] Garfield informed Hayes that the South could not ask for " a more liberal and generous policy than is set forth in your letter of acecptance; and that all who know your character and spirit will feel assured that you will carry out the programme, set forth in your letter, faithfully and fearlessly. Not that I hope the day will soon come, when parties in the South shall not be divided on the color line; but when the constitutional rights of the negro may be as safe in the hands of one party as the other—and that thus, in the South, as in the North, men may seek their party associations on the great commercial and industrial questions, rather than questions of race or color." [121] John Sherman fully concurred with Hayes'

[118] Whitelaw Reid to Hayes, February 21, 1877; Murat Halstead to Hayes, February 11, 1877, in Hayes Papers; Washington *National Republican*, March 23, 1877; Edwin Cowles, of Cleveland *Leader* to Garfield, March 3, 1877, in Garfield Papers; New York *Times*, February 26, 1877; *Nation*, XXIV (March 15, 1877).

[119] Hayes *Diary*, October 4, 1876, Williams, *Diary and Letters*, III, 364; George F. Hoar, *Autobiography of Seventy Years* (New York, 1903), II, 12.

[120] Washington *National Republican*, November 10, 1877.

[121] Garfield to Hayes, December 12, 1876, in Hayes Papers.

wish to demonstrate to the South his desire for " Peace, conciliation, and fraternity," and if Hayes did this, he would start
with " the best prospects for a successful administration." [122]

No sane Republican leader could ignore this widespread
party demand and support for a new policy in the South, nor
could he disregard the sentiments of the business community.
The unstable Carpetbagger governments were considered posi-
tively harmful to important northern business interests, and
following the Panic of 1873 it became increasingly difficult to
have northern capital come into the South or to persuade
economic Carpetbaggers to push forward and complete the
plans and developments they had launched in more prosperous
days before the crash. By 1876-1877, the depression had
deepened and widened, and northern business men had, for
the most part, discontinued or given up their southern operations and were attempting, in their home areas, to salvage what
they could from the ruins of the depression. The Philadelphia
Times declared that " Republican capitalists would today withdraw their investments if they apprehended a restoration of the
only Republican authority that the South could furnish." [123]
This seemed to be the case, for a St. Louis business man
informed Hayes, during the election crisis, that " the business
community is almost unanimous against trouble and I think
that Southern men generally are so inclined." [124] Abram Hewitt,
Democratic National Chairman in 1876, who had at first denounced the Electoral Commission, which decided the disputed
presidential election, as a fraud, late in February, 1877 called
for a halt to the filibuster and asked for a completion of the
count. What impressed the New Yorker was a flood of petitions from business interests asking relief from the political
crisis that had brought business to a standstill. Hewitt himself
wrote that business had been arrested, " the wheels of industry
ceased to move, and it seemed as if the terrors of civil war
were again to be renewed." [125]

" The business men of today are *sick* of the politicians and

[122] Sherman to Hayes, February 10, 1877, *Ibid.*
[123] Woodward, *Origins of the New South*, pp. 113-114; see also his *Reunion and Reaction*, pp. 54-55.
[124] George H. Shields to Hayes, December 28, 1876, in Hayes Papers.
[125] Woodward, *Reunion and Reaction*, pp. 7, 190.

want real Reform," a business man from New York City told
Hayes. "If the country cannot have this change soon it will
see a greater panic than 1837-1857 or 1873." [126] A boot and
shoe company in Boston hoped Hayes would end military
Reconstruction and abandon the Carpetbaggers; the President
of the Chicago and Paducah Railroad Company wanted Hayes
to return the best white men to power in the local governments
in the South; a New York banker asked that men of "influence
and position" occupy the federal posts in the South; and the
President of the Mobile and Montgomery Railway Company
argued that the only way for a respectable Republican party to
grow in the South was to give to the old line Whigs exclusive
control of the patronage. The present Republican leaders in
the South were too corrupt and unscrupulous and all they
wanted from the Negro was his vote. But the Whigs represented the best elements in the South, they were restive and
dissatisfied, and they could rally the freedmen to support the
Republican party.[127]

The two elements of the Republican party most affected by
any change of policy in the South were the Negroes and Carpetbaggers. The latter faced political extinction when Hayes
recalled the troops and gave up the policy of federal intervention. They complained that northern Republicans had not
and never would comprehend their "situation," and that native
Republicans of the South were unfitted for the task of southern
regeneration. They opposed any kind of a Republican alliance
with southern Democrats, and they wanted Hayes to pursue
a course that would convince southern Democrats "that the
Reconstruction Acts are a finality." They argued that it was
unjust for Washington to abandon them, and they implored
Hayes to demand his rights "in truly Grant and Jackson style,"
for it was their "only salvation," and if he failed them their
liberties were gone.[128]

[126] Henry E. Bowen to Hayes, March 7, 1877, in Hayes Papers.

[127] Everett Lane, Boston to Hayes, February 10, 1877; Dan Tyler to Senator
J. R. Hawley, March 12, 1877. in Hayes Papers; Ralph Plumb to Garfield,
March 2, 1877, in Garfield Papers; R. F. Wilson to Wm. E. Chandler, March 3,
1877, Wm. E. Chandler Papers (Division of Manuscripts, Library of Congress).

[128] George E. Spencer to S. W. Dorsey, February 19, 1877; Thomas B. Keogh,
North Carolina to E. F. Noyes, February 16, 1877; W. W. Holden to Hayes,
January 1, 1877, in Hayes Papers; J. C. Winsmith, South Carolina to Sherman,
March 2, 1877, in Sherman Papers.

Five Carpetbaggers still sat in the United States Senate,[129] and they fell into an ugly mood when they heard of Hayes' plan to repudiate them. Dismayed and angered by the turn of events they went about Washington lamenting their fate, charging Hayes with treachery, predicting the overthrow of the Republican party, and threatening to desert it. They met informally from time to time to air their grievances and to plot their strategy. This latter entailed mostly an attempt to salvage something from the wreck and to vote with the Democrats, if necessary, for as one of the Carpetbaggers remarked they had been made " cat's paws of long enough; now they are going to make the best terms they can for themselves." [130] But such bluster failed to cover up the apprehensions of the Carpetbaggers, for a close friend of Hayes reported that they were " dreadfully afraid " of him. " Moralists and modern reformers are making them believe that they are to be left to the tender mercy of the gentle *bull dozer*." [131]

While it was natural for the Carpetbaggers to urge Hayes to sustain them, there were also others who advised letting them down gently. " As a class they ought to retire," wrote one of Hayes' most active white supporters in the South, " but the wholesale removal of them would be unjust." [132] From Virginia came a report that the Democratic leaders in the state did not want the Carpetbaggers to go until arrangements were made to fill the posts vacated by them.[133] But it became more imperative for the Republican party to drop them when one of their northern champions, William E. Chandler, admitted that they had no future in the South and that " all they (selfishly) hope for is what consideration and patronage the Administration may give them." [134] Thus the Carpetbaggers, while crying out against the changeover, had also reached the conclusion that Hayes meant to surrender the remaining Republican governments in the South. " It seems to me the tendency of public

[129] George Spencer of Alabama, Stephen W. Dorsey and Powell Clayton of Arkansas, John J. Patterson of South Carolina, and Simon B. Conover of Florida.
[130] New York *Times*, March 13, 1877; New York *Tribune*, April 5, 1877.
[131] Thomas C. Donaldson to Hayes, February 25, 1877, in Hayes Papers.
[132] Andrew J. Kellar to Wm. Henry Smith, February 16, 1877, in Wm. Henry Smith Papers (Hayes Memorial Library, Fremont, Ohio).
[133] Robt. Bolling to Hayes, May 3, 1877, in Hayes Papers.
[134] Chandler to Hayes, January 13, 1877, *Ibid*.

opinion is that way," wrote a former Carpetbagger governor of Florida to the original head of the Freedmen's Bureau in that state, " and we may look for the warm and loving embrace of the southern whites by the next [Hayes] administration." [135]

The great mass of the Republican party in the South, the Negroes, showed more concern about the protection for themselves than they did in a new policy to rebuild their party. Yet one of their leading newspapers did express the belief that the troops would not be recalled. The New Orleans *Republican* called it an insult to Hayes to think that he would " abandon his political friends and supporters in the South for the personal advantage he would be likely to derive from the conciliation of his utterly routed enemies," for even if Hayes wanted to, he could not " ignore the fact that his title to the Presidency rests upon precisely the same basis as Mr. Packard's to the office he holds." [136] Ever mindful of Negro support for the Republican party, Hayes conferred with two northern leaders of the race, James Pointdexter, Ohio legislator, and Frederick Douglass, and learned with satisfaction that they approved his new policy. In fact Douglas gave him many useful hints about the whole subject.[137]

The evidence is quite clear that northerners and Republicans, in all parts of the country, had become weary of military Reconstruction, and that they wanted a new and more moderate policy in the South. Southerners and northern Democrats had long clamored for a change, but Republican leaders could more easily ignore such demands until they rose in volume from their own party. Thus the stage had been set for a new attempt to Republicanize the South. Great odds and difficulties awaited the new efforts, but Republican leaders, and especially the Presidents, between 1877-1896, were confident they could reach this goal.

---

[135] Marcellus L. Stearns to Thomas Osborn, February 21, 1877, *Ibid.*
[136] New Orleans *Republican*, February 28, 1877.
[137] Hayes Diary, February 18, 1877, Williams, *Diary and Letters*, III, 417.

CHAPTER II

HAYES TRIES CONCILIATION

" The pacification policy still gains," wrote President Hayes to an Ohio newspaper friend in the spring of 1877. " I am confident it will secure North Carolina, with a fair chance in Maryland, Virginia, Tennessee, and Arkansas, and I am not without hopes of Louisiana, South Carolina, and Florida." [1] Such was the optimism of Hayes as he launched his southern policy—a policy which has been obscured since 1877 by the attention given to the removal of the troops. For Hayes had greater ambitions than to end military Reconstruction and to restore " home rule " to southern whites. He dreamed of building a strong Republican party in the South that would no longer depend upon the Negro for its main strength and that could command the esteem and support of southern whites. While this meant splitting the white vote in a section where men had come to divide almost solely on the race question, Hayes firmly believed he could do this, and his faith and courage seldom deserted him in his valiant try.

Historians have portrayed Hayes as a respectable mediocrity with an average capacity and an impeccable public and private life. True, he lacked brilliance, but he had such a determination and steadfastness of purpose about his plans for the South that he eventually frustrated even his bitterest foes. During the campaign of 1876 he had confided to his diary, " If elected, the firmest adherence to principles against all opposition and temptations is my purpose. I shall show a grit that will astonish those who predict weakness." [2] And he did show a grit, for the most part, concerning his policy in the South. In the face of violent attacks upon his program by Carpetbaggers and Stalwarts he pushed it to the end, always certain of its righteousness and believing throughout that a large majority of the " best people " backed him.

---

[1] Hayes to Wm. D. Bickham, May 3, 1877, in Hayes Papers.
[2] Hayes' Diary, September 24, 1876, Williams, *Diary and Letters*, III, 363.

Hayes became the first Republican President to experiment with the plan of appointing regular Democrats to important posts in the South in the hope of gaining Republican success there. But he seldom received credit for any honest motives, for the public in 1877, and for a long time to come, had the impression that this was part of the bargain that made him President. Hayes' experiment was an extremely important one because of its sharp departure from the strategy of the Radicals during Reconstruction, and had it worked successfully, his prediction to his Ohio friend on the outcome of the 1880 election in the South might well in part have materialized. Because the experiment failed, successive Republican Presidents stayed away from it until the time of William Howard Taft. Of course orthodox Democrats continued to receive appointments in the South, because political and social conditions demanded that this be done, but Republican Presidents after Hayes and down to Taft did not seriously believe that this patronage would help to break up the Democratic South.

Hayes had been in Congress (1865-1867) at a time when the most important task for the national legislators was to formulate a Reconstruction program for the South. While he believed that the class of men placed in charge of the freedmen were " not very likely to be correct in conduct," for they were " weak men of small experience, or corrupt men in too many instances," he did tell a close southern friend that the congressional plan of Reconstruction contained " the best terms you will ever get—and they should be promptly accepted . . . you must adopt it, if you regard your own welfare . . . don't be deceived by Andy Johnson," Hayes added. " Johnson and his office-holders will be ' a mere snap—a flash in the pan.' . . . My last word is, don't let Andy Johnson deceive you. He don't know the northern people." [3] While not in sympathy with the uncompromising bitterness of a Radical leader like Thaddeus Stevens, Hayes did support the Radical plan of Reconstruction put through by his party in Congress. When he ran for governor of Ohio for the first time in 1867, he was nominated on a platform that fully endorsed congressional Reconstruction, and he conducted a campaign based on the strategy of waving

[3] Hayes to his wife, May 16, 1866, and to Guy M. Bryan, October 1, 1866, *Ibid.*, 24, 32-33.

the bloody shirt, although he did feel that preventing the South from participating in the national government was a " plain and monstrous inconsistency and injustice," and that " no such absurdity and wrong can be permanent." [4]

Hayes looked upon Grant's election in 1868 as " a happy thing," and as having a good effect in the South and everywhere. Before the Ohio Republican State Convention in June, 1869, which had renominated him for governor by acclamation, Hayes stated that he was " fully warranted in saying that General Grant has begun the work of reconstruction in a masterly way and with marked success." By 1871 Hayes was convinced that the South was the most important political question of the day, that " the Administration is right on the South and the Democracy wrong," and that Grant had been " faithful on the great question of the rights of the colored people," even though the personal affairs of the administration had been " badly managed in many instances." It was Grant's quarrel with Senator Charles Sumner over Santo Domingo and not the ills of military Reconstruction that first raised doubt in Hayes' mind about Grant's renomination. Hayes was also uncertain about the sincerity of the New Departure Democrats. They were not sound and they were not to be trusted he thought, and he agreed with the comment of the Albany *Evening Argus* that " The voice is the voice of Jacob but the hand is the hand of Esau." [5]

But Hayes began to change his mind about the South and Reconstruction. Ever since the close of the war, he had kept up a constant correspondence with his college classmate, Guy M. Bryan, of Texas, who throughout these years urged a more moderate and a more lenient policy toward the South. Particularly did Bryan press for local self-government in the South and he predicted that if Hayes advocated such a course he would be " most gratefully remembered by the South. . . . You can make not only a good name," wrote Bryan, " but be regarded as a benefactor to your country." [6] Bryan's letters

[4] Williams, *Life of Hayes*, I, 277-280, 292-327, 318.

[5] Hayes to his Uncle, S. Birchard, November 11, 1868; Hayes to Charles Nordhoff, March 13, 1871; Hayes Diary, March 16, June 12, 1871, Williams, *Diary and Letters*, III, 56, 133-134, 135-136, 147; Williams, *Hayes*, I, 336-337.

[6] E. W. Winkler, ed., " The Bryan-Hayes Correspondence," *Southwestern His-*

were an important influence that conditioned Hayes' attitude toward the South, and Hayes acknowledged this when he told Bryan, "you will see in my letter of acceptance, I trust, the influence of the feeling which our friendship has tended to foster." [7]

By 1872 Hayes had become a Liberal Republican but had remained regular instead of taking a walk. On amnesty for the South he was with Greeley, but he preferred to carry on the fight within party ranks. By 1875 he was not in sympathy with "a large share of the party leaders. I hate the corruptionists of whom Butler is leader," he confided to his diary. "I doubt the ultra measures relating to the South." In the same year he had come full circle from his support of congressional Reconstruction when he believed, "As to Southern affairs ' the let-alone policy ' seems now to be the true course." [8] Then came his letter of acceptance in 1876 in which he held out to the South hope of an early return to local self government, free of federal interference.

During the disputed presidential election of 1876 when there was pressure from all sides for agreements and details, Hayes refused to make any public declarations of policy until the final result was announced. He constantly maintained that he was absolutely free from commitments as to his policy. He listened respectfully to those who came to see him, and he talked quite freely up to the point of his letter of acceptance, but he had no private assurances for any of his visitors. He meant to keep himself "free as long as practicable, and to hear in a friendly way all that may be offered." To all who came he made it clear that he stood on his Letter. "That as to Southern affairs it plainly indicated what I thought desirable. That the Southern people must obey the new Amendments and give the colored men all of their rights." [9]

torical Quarterly, XXV-XXIX (1921-1922—1925-1926), XXVI, 157-159 for quotation; Robert C. Cotner and Watt P. Marchman, eds., "Correspondence of Guy M. Bryan and Rutherford B. Hayes: Additional Letters," Ohio State Archeological and Historical Quarterly, LXIII (October, 1954), 349-377.

[7] Hayes to Bryan, July 8, 1876, "Bryan-Hayes Correspondence," XXVI, 294.

[8] Hayes Diary, March 28, 1875; Hayes to Bryan, July 27, 1875, Williams, Diary and Letters, III, 269, 286.

[9] Hayes to John Sherman, December 16, 17, 1876; to Wm. Henry Smith, December 16, 1876; to J. A. Garfield, December 16, 1876; to Wm. Dennison, December 17, 1876; Hayes Diary, December 17, 1876, Ibid., 389-392.

As the critical days of the political crisis of the winter of 1876-1877 wore on, Hayes expressed hope that a wise and liberal policy would allow the Republicans to divide the southern whites, and he began to think about what he would say in his inaugural address. He felt he must " urge a liberal policy toward the South especially in affording facilities for education and encouraging business and immigration by internal improvements of a national character." Carl Schurz thought that the letter of acceptance " would be the best text " on the Southern Question in the inaugural, and by February, even Hayes believed that his " anxiety to *do* something to promote the pacification of the South is perhaps in danger of leading me too far. I do not reflect on the use of the military power of the past," he wrote to Schurz. " But there is to be an end to all that, except in emergencies which I can't think of as possible again. We must do all we can to promote prosperity there [South]. . . . But the more I think of it the more I see in what you say. We must go cautiously and slowly. . . . You will see from what I write you," he told Schurz, " that the South is more on my mind than anything else. Perhaps we must be content to leave that to time—taking care not to obstruct time's healing processes by injudicious meddling." Hayes felt the South could be made prosperous by a " cheerful acquiescence " in the results of the war, by peace, by education and by improvements, and he thought that he should " profess a desire to so appoint as to aid in good local government." [10]

About two weeks before he assumed the presidency, Hayes noted in his diary that his course would be " a firm assertion and maintenance of the rights of the colored people of the South, according to the Thirteenth, Fourteenth, and Fifteenth Amendments, coupled with a readiness to recognize all Southern people, without regard to past political conduct, who will now go with me heartily and in good faith in support of these principles." Nearly a week later, a newspaperman, after spending several days in Columbus, Ohio talking with Hayes and his advisers and friends, reported in the press that Hayes had come to the conclusion that there must be two new

[10] Hayes Diary, January 5, February 9, 1877, *Ibid.*, 400, 414; Hayes to Carl Schurz, January 4, February 4, 1877, Schurz to Hayes, January 25, 1877, Bancroft, *Writings of Schurz*, III, 355, 374-375, 387-388.

parties in the South separated by a political rather than a color line. His policy would be an attempt to divide the native white vote in the South—throwing the hardshell "rebel" vote with the ignorant Negro into the Democratic party and the old Union Whigs and intelligent Negroes into a new Union or Republican party. Then he proposed to withdraw the troops and permit each party to take care of itself. A few days later the *National Republican*, a Radical newspaper, quoted Hayes as saying, "Assure any of our Southern friends that I am impressed with the necessity of a complete change of men and policy. I shall stand by the ideas uttered in my letter last summer." According to the *Republican*, "This, more fully interpreted means, not only the entire right of self-government, but also a large and liberal policy in respect to matters of internal improvement." [11]

In his inaugural address, Hayes again spoke to the South and reiterated many of the sentiments he had expressed in his letter of acceptance. He reassured southerners that he would "regard and promote their truest interests," and pledged himself to destroy the color line and the distinction between North and South. Permanent pacification of the country was supremely important but only upon principles and measures which guaranteed the full protection of all citizens in the free enjoyment of their constitutional rights. The South still lacked local self government, and Hayes believed the time had now arrived when such government was the "imperative necessity required by all of the varied interests, public and private of these states." Yet this local government had to be one which guarded the interests of both Negroes and whites, and it had to submit "loyally and heartily to the Constitution and the laws." [12]

From all sides letters poured in upon Hayes endorsing his remarks in the inaugural about the Southern Question, urging him to stand firm in the course that he had charted for the South, and telling him that the "better class of men" supported him. "Your course is what we expected and heartily approve,"

[11] Hayes Diary, February 18, 1877, William, *Diary and Letters*, III, 417; Louisville *Courier-Journal*, February 24, 1877; Washington *National Republican*, February 28, March 1, 1877.

[12] James D. Richardson, *A Compilation of the Messages and Papers of the Presidents* (Washington, D. C., 1911), VI, 4394-4396.

wrote James Russell Lowell, Henry W. Longfellow, Charles W. Eliot, and C. E. Norton. " All good men heartily cooperate and sympathize with you. God will sustain you and guide you," a Boston correspondent told Hayes. From Ohio came the admonition to " Never forget that *you are Captain*," and from Pennsylvania the advice to " *Stand firm*. Your policy meets the approbation of the people. They demand and will have it." From Georgia came the information that it " is universally believed in the South that your policy toward our section will be conciliatory." From our Minister to England came the report that " No message of a President to the people has ever been received with such universal favor on this side the Atlantic as the late inaugural. It seems the harbinger of peace and union and prosperity in the future." [13]

Hayes' inaugural address also won the support of the influential newspapers and periodicals in the North. The New York *Tribune* declared that " neither the Ku Klux nor the carpetbagger will find comfort in the new President's language, but the real South will take heart in hearing it, and honest Republicans at the North . . . will hold their heads in the dawn of a nobler day. . . He means to cause a genuine peace and reconciliation at the South, and for ten years the country has needed nothing more." The Chicago *Tribune* stated that Hayes " clearly proposes to be Right, and to follow the Right to all its logical conclusions under all circumstances." The *National Republican* was sure that Hayes desired " to see in the South local governments of Southern creation and support, and not local governments erected and maintained by strangers to the soil." The *Nation* thought that since the inaugural in the main was an amplification of the letter of acceptance, it must had had the charm of novelty for the Republican managers, " as none of them during the canvass seemed to have any recollection of the letter or its contents." The *Nation* regarded the inaugural address as " a clear, modest, and sensible document, which promises nothing which reasonable men may not hope

[13] Lowell, Longfellow, Eliot, Norton to Hayes, March 9, 1877; W. W. Kimball, Boston to Hayes, March 9, 1877; W. W. Sloan, Port Clinton, Ohio, to Hayes, March 11, 1877; J. W. Gillespie, Harrisburg, Pennsylvania, to Hayes, March 12, 1877; Herschel Johnson, Sandy Grove, Georgia, to Hayes, March 10, 1877; Edwards Pierrepont to Hayes, March 10, 1877, in Hayes Papers.

to see performed, and leaves nothing untouched of which mention was desirable." *Harper's Weekly* was happy about the fact that the fiery partisan contest of the last nine months had ended in the accession of a President whose first words tended to allay fury and placate passion. "The general policy indicated . . . is unquesionably that which is approved by the intelligence and patriotism of the whole country . . . [and] the President may count upon the support of the mass of his countrymen." Even the New York *Times* had to admit that "It is impossible not to admire the spirit of this position [about the South] of the President's message. It is perfectly patriotic; it is free from narrowness and partisan bias; it is enlightened, and it is independent." [14]

Hayes had come to feel that military Reconstruction had only served to thwart Republican chances of success in the South, and the surviving Republican leaders who had helped to fasten this program upon the South would have reluctantly had to agree with this conclusion. In fact Hayes was so gloomy and pessimistic about the prospects of Republicanism in the country that he considered the party to be nearly dead and badly in need of some revitalizing force. Above all he believed that the party had to be national instead of sectional; it had to have an appeal in the South as well as in the North and West. But before it could have an appeal in the South it had to be rejuvenated, for it had been thoroughly discredited there by military Reconstruction.

To make southern Republicanism more respectable and thus more appealing, Hayes resolved to reduce, and if possible eliminate, Negro and Carpetbagger leadership in it and to conciliate southern conservative whites. This decision immediately brought the charge from the Stalwart Republicans that Hayes was casting aside loyal party members and organizations, but the President did not forsake the Republican party in the South. In his attempt to reorganize it, he did abandon the Negroes when he recalled the troops, and he did try to drop those Republican leaders in the South who had no following save the federal officeholders who clustered about them. Hayes

[14] New York *Tribune*, March 6, 7, 1877; Chicago *Tribune*, March 6, 1877; Washington *National Republican*, March 6, 1877; *Nation*, XXIV (March 8, 1877), 139; *Harper's Weekly*, XXI (March 24, 1877), 222.

was of the opinion that enough good sense existed among the intelligent people of the South that he could exploit it to the point of developing a real two party system there. For this reason he turned to the most responsible and influential classes in the South for support, never imagining that he could do this in a few weeks by passing around the sugar plums of office, but satisfied that he could accomplish the task by pursuing a steady policy of friendship and non-intervention. In short, Hayes keyed his attack to the objective of breaking up the Democratic South by enhancing the character and strength of southern Republicanism.

Before Hayes could hope to convert southern Democrats he had to win their confidence, and the presence of troops in the South, however small the number, made this indeed a difficult task. But he moved swiftly and forcefully to break down some of the barriers that stood between southern whites and the Republican party. He brought David M. Key, a southern Democrat and a former Confederate officer into perhaps the most important patronage dispensing position in the government, that of Postmaster General. He withdrew the federal troops from their last garrisons in the South and restored "home rule" to southern whites. With these two spectacular moves, and courageous ones, too, in view of the attitude that the Stalwarts had toward the South, Hayes set out to rejuvenate southern Republicanism.

While these first steps to bring about a political revolution in the South have been thoroughly explained,[15] a few observations might be made. Hayes had wanted a southerner in his cabinet since such an apopintment might help to reconcile the North and South and to mitigate southern white hostility toward Republicanism. At first he looked around for a native white Republican and did consider three of them—John M. Harlan from Kentucky, Thomas Settle from North Carolina, and James L. Alcorn from Mississippi. At one point he had settled upon Harlan for his Attorney General, but abandoned the idea at the request of Senator Oliver P. Morton, Republican boss from Indiana, although Hayes never knew why Morton protested.[16]

[15] Woodward, *Reunion and Reaction.*
[16] Hayes Diary, January 17, 1877; Hayes to Carl Schurz, February 2, 1877;

Then Hayes toyed with the idea of filling a cabinet seat with a southern Democrat. " I would like to get support from good men of the South," he confided in his diary. " How to do it is the question. I have the best disposition toward the Southern people, Rebels and all. I could appoint a Southern Democrat in the Cabinet. But who would take it among the capable and influential good men of these States? General Joseph E. Johnston occurs to me. I must think of this." [17] John Sherman and Stanley Matthews, Republican leaders from Ohio and persuasive advisers of Hayes, tested reaction in Washington to the proposal of a " Rebel " heading an executive department and came up with strong recommendations for such a move. Sherman reported the general feeling in the capital favored the inclusion of " one and perhaps two " southern Democrats in the cabinet. Matthews informed Hayes that a southern Democrat " well posted and in communication with the leaders " had suggested " the names of suitable gentlemen from the South [Governor J. C. Brown of Tennessee, General Edward C. Walthall of Mississippi and John Hancock of Texas] to go in, upon the basis of a policy directed to the disintegration of the Democratic party." [18]

James Garfield, another of Hayes' Ohio friends, appeared to be more cautious and suggested taking only " the greatest " or " no rebel " at all, since such a step could either be a " disastrous failure or a great success," but Garfield feared Hayes was " not quite up to this heroic effort." [19] The New York Times, a leading exponent of Stalwart Republicanism in 1877, reminded Hayes that it would only accept an influential southern Democrat, while Carl Schurz, Liberal Republican leader, thought the appointment of a southern Democrat " might be a good stroke of policy if the right man can be found." [20]

Finding a capable and leading Democrat from the South

Conversation between Hayes and William Henry Smith, general agent of Western Associated Press, August 9, 1890, Williams, Diary and Letters, III, 402, 412, 426-427.

[17] Hayes Diary, February 17, 1877, Ibid., 416-417.

[18] John Sherman to Hayes, February 17, 1877; Stanley Matthews to Hayes, February 13, 1877, in Hayes Papers.

[19] Garfield Diary, March 6, 1877, in Garfield Papers.

[20] New York Times, March 4, 1877; Carl Schurz to Hayes, January 30, 1877, in Hayes Papers.

for a cabinet post proved to be no easy task for Hayes. In addition to Johnston he seriously considered former Governor Gilbert C. Walker of Virginia and Key, whom the Tennessee Governor had appointed in 1875 to fill out the unexpired Senate term of former President Andrew Johnson. William T. Sherman, then the Commanding General of the United States Army, thought the selection of Johnston would be unwise and protested against it, and Ben Hill, Democratic leader from Georgia, objected to Walker for not being a native southerner. In the end the President picked Key, and Hayes later explained to a personal friend, " But a place for some Southerner was in mind. Johnston was not preferred and Key was. This is all there is of it. But I beg you to let it rest." [21]

Yet certain factors had helped Key. Andrew J. Kellar of the *Memphis Avalanche*, a leading figure in the negotiations for the presidency in 1876-1877, had strongly recommended this appointment because it would aid him in rounding up southern Democratic support for the administration. " Were Key in the cabinet," Kellar pointed out, " I could take the aggressive and warmly [work] with Governor Hayes to lead the conservative and national citizens of Tennessee, Arkansas, and Texas to a higher platform and to a better era in politics." [22] As for Key, he had written a significant letter to a personal friend in Febraury, 1877, which Hayes had read, and which in part stated that " If I were to become a member of the administration, I should . . . feel bound to build it up and strengthen it in the hearts of the people. . . . If, as I hope and believe, the administration will develop a broad and liberal policy toward the people of the South, I would not hesitate to incorporate my fortunes and self with it." [23] But Hayes still hesitated and did not officially offer the post to Key until after the latter

[21] Hayes Diary, February 17, 1877; Hayes to Wm. Henry Smith, January 27, 1881, Williams, *Diary and Letters*, III, 416-417; Washington *National Republican*, March 5, 1877; James Ford Rhodes, *History of the United States Since 1850* (New York, 1916), VIII, 6.

[22] A. J. Kellar to Wm. Henry Smith, February 19, 1877, quoted in Dorothy Ganfield Fowler, *The Cabinet Politician; the Postmasters General* (New York, 1943), p. 163.

[23] New York *Tribune*, March 8, 1877; Louisville *Courier-Journal*, March 8, 1877.

had come to Washington from Tennessee and had conferred at length with the President on the evening of March 6.[24]

Hayes hoped and Republican and Democratic leaders believed that Key's appointment would increase southern white support for the Republican party. A Democratic Senator from Pennsylvania expressed the opinion that Hayes had picked Key to initiate a new appointment policy in the South, and William Henry Smith, general agent of the Western Associated Press, flatly stated that if Hayes gave Key " a wide and wise discretion " he could organize affairs in the South to increase Republican sentiment there. " The same rules of Civil Service cannot be applied to the South at present as to the North," wrote Smith. " There must first be an adjustment to the new order of things. Wholesale changes are not necessary. But a weeding out of disreputable and objectionable men *at once* seems to be desirable to prepare the way. Key must know how—he certainly can get the men to search out reputable and conservative citizens for the places. Post offices conferred on country merchants and on country editors would improve the services and put citizens in better humor." [25]

Key quickly demonstrated his desire to see Hayes achieve success with his southern policy. Within a week after taking office he stated in an interview that he had been invited to a cabinet seat to represent the South and to " give personal attention to that matter," and he promised to weed out all the incompetent officials there and to choose men without regard to politics, with the only requisite being ability and the capacity and disposition to aid Hayes in reconciling the North and South. When the President traveled though the South in 1877, Key accompanied him and made speeches pleading for reconciliation of North and South, and in 1878, when the Democrats again raised the question of the validity of Hayes' election, the Postmaster General sprang to the defense of his chief. Key addressed an open letter to southern Democrats, urging them to have nothing to do with such a maneuver as the " question of title was irrevocably settled by the last Congress " and

---

[24] New York *Times*, March 7, 1877; New York *World*, March 7, 1877.

[25] Albert V. House, Jr., " President Hayes' Selection of David M. Key for Postmaster General," *Journal of Southern History*, IV (1938), 91; Wm. Henry Smith to Hayes, March 22, 1877, in Hayes Papers.

reminding them of how often northern Democrats had betrayed them.[26]

While Key remained in the Cabinet hundreds of southern Democrats requested postmasterships, and Senator Augustus Merriman of North Carolina asked whether they would be eligible for patronage from the Post Office department. Key's answer disclosed an important part of Hayes' strategy to win Republican votes in the South. The Postmaster General explained that in all his southern appointments he would favor Republicans, all other things being equal, but in case of a contest for the office or in the event no Republican met the approval of a large majority of the people having business with the office, then Key would select someone oustide his rule and one who would satisfy the business interests of a community.[27]

Toward the end of his term Hayes rewarded Key with a lifetime position, a federal judgeship for eastern Tennessee. Key probably left the Cabinet, because his appointment had not conciliated enough southern whites. In fact, many southern Democrats had looked upon it with much skepticism and came to regard it as an effort by Hayes to receive some endorsement of legality from Democrats in Congress. At times southern Democrats heaped abuse upon Key when they called him the " Uriah Heep of the South " and " a trick mule brought forward toward the close of entertainment, for the special delight of the audience." Many Democrats in the South agreed with the observation of the Charleston *News and Courier* that Key fell short of being a southern Democrat of an unimpeachable record. " As an essay at conciliation, the appointment was a dead failure," concluded the New York *Times*. " The Southern Whites thought no more of the President, and less, if possible, of Mr. Key." On the other hand, a Negro Republican leader of Mississippi, with national connections, viewed Key's appointment as a " crushing blow to southern Republicanism. It was the straw that broke the camel's back." [28]

[26] New York *Times*, March 12, 1877, June 1, 1878; *Nation*, XXVI (May 30, 1877), 349.

[27] New York *Times*, March 20, 1877; Louisville *Courier-Journal*, March 20, 1877.

[28] Wilmington, North Carolina *Post*, August 31, 1877; New York *Times*,

The removal of the troops posed greater problems and created wider repercussions than the appointment of Key, and in this Hayes moved more slowly and cautiously. Reluctance to offend any supporters and an unwillingness to cast aside votes he might again need played an important role in Hayes' decision. In public and private statements he had expressed a desire to restore " home rule " to the South, but political consideration stayed his hand for over a month following his inauguration. Fulminations of northern Stalwarts who raised the cry about the sin of abandoning loyal party members in the South served as one deterrent. Possible defection of southern Republicans in Congress caused equally important reflection for Hayes. Those in the House threatened to bolt the party caucus for organizing that chamber should Hayes withdraw the troops.[29]

Such blustering made Hayes pause, for he faced a dilemma. In spite of a Democratic majority in the House in the Forty-fifth Congress (1877-1879) he hoped to organize it for the Republicans by electing Garfield Speaker. This maneuver called for the aid of southern Democrats, and some basis existed for believing they would cooperate with him. When Wade Hampton came to Washington to discuss the disputed state election in South Carolina, he conferred with Stanely Matthews upon the possibility of choosing Garfield Speaker through a coalition of Republicans and southern Democrats. H. V. Boynton, Washington correspondent of the Cincinnati *Gazette* and a chief negotiator between Hayes and Tom Scott in 1877, informed Garfield of Hampton's willingness to help Hayes organize the House, but Garfield had little faith in the scheme and wrote in his diary, " It will . . . be a test of the sincerity of the Southern Democratic supporters of Hayes' policy to know whether they will give him an administrative House. If they do, he may succeed. If not, his friends north will not tolerate continuance of his southern scheme." [30] Hayes was caught on the twin horns of a dilemma: if he failed to recall the troops

October 31, 1881; John R. Lynch, *The Facts of Reconstruction* (New York, 1913), p. 180.

[29] New York *Times*, March 3, 1877; New York *Sun*, March 3, 1877.

[30] Washington *National Republican*, April 2, 1877; Garfield Diary, March 21, April 6, 1877, in Garfield Papers.

he faced the loss of potential southern Democratic support; if he removed them, southern Republican insurgency faced him. Torn between avoiding one or the other he delayed his decision.

So long as southern Republican threats appeared to be real, Hayes held back from recalling the troops. How southern Republicans would feel about such a move concerned him. After all, he was a practical politician, and although he wanted to purge the party of its Carpetbagger and Negro influence, he had to let these two elements down gently. Hayes took pains to keep their voting strength in line, and he went out of his way to allay their fears. For instance when it became apparent that the President would take the troops out of the South, he invited the Carpetbagger Senator from South Carolina, John J. Patterson, to the White House and asked him to tell Republicans in this state that the administration had no intentions of deserting them.[31]

Complicating the question of removing the troops were the disputed elections in Louisiana and South Carolina where the last two federal garrisons of occupation remained, and where two Carpetbaggers, Packard and Chamberlain, were claimants for the governors' seats. To settle the dispute by giving the electoral vote of these two states to Hayes and yet denying victory to Packard and Chamberlain, seemed like a glaring inconsistency to many Republicans. Whether it bothered Hayes' conscience is not known, but it did cause some concern to other party leaders and even to friends of Hayes who negotiated for his victory. William E. Chandler thought that such a solution to the dispute would be a misfortune, and Garfield did not see how Packard could be overthrown "without destroying the authority which gave the electoral vote" of Louisiana to Hayes.[32] "You cannot dismiss those gentlemen [Packard and Chamberlain] with a wave of the hand," wrote William Henry Smith, one of the key figures in the Compromise of 1877. "They deserve the serious thought of our best men, and when settled they must be determined by considerations other than those of mere party expediency. Unless the decision shall be based upon Justice and truth it cannot stand. General Sheridan

[31] New York *Tribune*, April 5, 1877.
[32] Chandler to Hayes, January 18, 1877, in Hayes Papers; Garfield Diary. January 19, 1877, in Garfield Papers.

says it will be a fatal mistakle to let the State Govts. pass beyond Repub^n control," Smith warned. "At least we must have security for the future." [33]

According to John Sherman the great problem of the Hayes administration was the disputed election in Louisiana, and on this "there is much diversity of opinion. I see no way," Sherman told Hayes, "but the recognition of the Packard government followed by the utmost liberality to the South. I wish sincerely *that* question was settled by *this* [Grant] Administration." But Hayes learned from a high official in the Grant Administration that the President had decided to leave Louisiana and South Carolina in status quo until Hayes took office. Originally Grant had intended to wait until Hayes was declared elected and then recognize Packard and Chamberlain, but now that it was near to the close of his presidency, Grant was determined not to take a step that was not in accordance with Hayes' views. Carl Schurz thought the whole matter was a "very delicate business . . . especially as it may become of great importance with regard to your Southern policy. I think I see a way out," he told Hayes, "but it will be open only when you have a good hold on the confidence of the Southern people." [34]

If Hayes remained silent on the disputed election in the South, such was not the case of some of his most intimate friends. Stanley Matthews, a lifelong friend and relative of Hayes, made it clear to the Carpetbagger claimants that federal force would not maintain them in power. "Without reference to the rightfulness of the origin of your title of Governor," he told Packard, "I am of opinion that circumstances are such that it will be out of the question for the Republican Administration to maintain it, as it must necessarily do, by force of federal arms." In a letter, endorsed by William E. Evarts, Hayes' Secretary of State, Mathews suggested to Chamberlain that an "accomodation" be reached through Chamberlain's concurrence and cooperation that would remove the necessity of federal troops sustaining either government in South Carolina and "leave that to stand which was best able to stand of itself."

[33] W. Henry Smith to Richard Smith, February 19, 1877, in Hayes Papers.
[34] John Sherman to Hayes, February 13, 1877; Alphonso Taft to Hayes, February 19, 1877; Carl Schurz to Hayes, February 20, 1877, *Ibid.*

Such a course would relieve Hayes of making any decision between the claims of the rival governments and would entitle Chamberlain to the gratitude of the Republican party and the country. To Hayes, Matthews communicated his fear of delays in the Louisiana business, " lest they create new difficulties, without removing old ones. Public opinion is enthusiastic and united in favor of the new policy, but it may grow cold and lose heart," wrote Matthews. " Boldness is sometimes most prudent and I think the present an occasion for cutting the knot, instead of waiting to unite it. There is great apprehension in the public mind lest the good intentions of the Inaugural may be frustrated. My fear is, lest by delay we may lose the fruit to be gathered by their prompt realization." [35]

Samuel Bowles of the Springfield *Republican* considered " The Louisiana steal " as " a dreadful one, but if the Republican party can follow President Jackson's example and get religion, they may yet cheat the devil." On the other hand the New York *Herald* underscored the necessity for recalling the troops when it declared that, " No intelligent man, who is politically sane and has watched the situation in the South, can have any sort of doubt that the Packard and Chamberlain governments would dissolve like the baseless fabric of a vision and vanish into thin air as soon as the federal authority should declare that it would no longer protect them." Yet the New York *Times* asserted that there was no way out of the impasse in the South except by some form of federal interference.[36]

Hayes' apparent procrastination in removing the troops raised doubts in the minds of southern Democrats over the sincerity of his intentions to restore " home rule." They were afraid that he had changed his mind, and L. Q. C. Lamar, Democratic leader from Mississippi, writing to Hayes several weeks after the inaugauration reflected the apprehensions of many of his associates in the South. " It was understood that you meant to withdraw the troops from South Carolina and Louisiana," Lamar told Hayes. " All that was required was an order to withdraw the troops. . . Upon that subject we thought you

[35] Williams, *Hayes*, II, 41; New York *Times*, March 11, 1877, for letter to Chamberlain; Matthews to Hayes, March 3, 1877, in Hayes Papers.
[36] Bowles' statement, in Bancroft, *Writings of Schurz*, III, 408; *Herald* quoted in Williams, *Hayes*, II, 40; New York *Times*, March 8, 1877.

had made up your mind, and indeed you so declared to me
. . . but the delay so far has encouraged the hope that possibly
the policy of the Inaugural will be abandoned. . . . If you
would achieve what you have begun you must do as you said
you would." [37] But a more optimistic note came from Schurz.
" Hayes makes haste slowly but surely," he wrote. " You will
soon wake up and see things done. Hayes is a general like
old Thomas; wants to have his wagons together when he
marches, but loses no battles. You need not be anxious." [38]

Hour upon hour in the spring of 1877 Hayes and the men
around him wrestled with the problem of the disputed elections
in Louisiana and South Carolina. They studied various solu-
tions which had been offered such as holding new elections
in the states, recognizing the lawful action of the legislatures,
acknowledging Packard and Chamberlain, and leaving them to
their own state remedies, and recalling the troops and leaving
events to take care of themselves. Within the Cabinet all
but Charles Devens, the Attorney General, " seemed indisposed
to use force . . . and he is not decidedly for it." Evarts was
of the opinion that the military could not be used to sustain one
government against another in case of contested elections, and
that the states must take care of those matters themselves." [39]

Hayes thought that the public would not sustain the policy
of upholding a state government against a rival government by
use of federal force. If this led to the overthrow of the *de jure*
government in a state, the *de facto* government had to be
recognized. His policy was " trust, peace, and to put aside the
bayonet. I do not think the wise policy is to decide contested
elections in the States by the use of the national army," Hayes
wrote in his diary. To him local self-government meant the
determination by each state for itself of all questions as to its
own local affairs. " The real thing to be achieved," as Hayes
saw it, was " safety and prosperity for the colored people.
Both houses of Congress and the public opinion of the country
are plainly against the use of the army to uphold either claimant
to the State Government in case of contest. The wish is to

[37] Lamar to Hayes, March 22, 1877, in Hayes Papers.
[38] Schurz to W. M. Grosvenor, March 29, 1877, Bancroft, *Writings of Schurz*,
III, 410.
[39] Hayes Diary, March 16, 20, 1877, Williams, *Diary and Letters*, III, 428.

restore harmony and good feeling between sections and races. This can only be done by peaceful methods. We wish to adjust the difficulties in Louisiana and South Carolina," added Hayes, " so as to make one government out of two in each State. But if this fails, if no adjustment can be made, we must then adopt the non-intervention policy, except so far as may be necessary to keep the peace." [40]

To counsel him in these difficult hours, Hayes asked his college classmate, Bryan, to come from Texas to Washington, saying, " You can help me." Bryan was Hayes' guest at the White House for over three weeks during the settlement of the Louisiana and South Carolina troubles, and Hayes confided in him and trusted him and explained that it was not the President's duty, but that of the legislature of each state to determine questions, " which circumstances bring here to me for my action. I am determined," Bryan quoted Hayes as saying, " that the legislature shall not be trammeled by the military, for the troops shall be removed as soon as I am informed the legislature is organized." [41]

‹ Hayes seemed happy and confident about results in the South once he had ordered the troops away. " Now I hope for peace, and what is equally important, security and prosperity for the colored people," he remarked privately. " The result of my plan is to get from those States by their governors, legislatures, press and people pledges that the Thirteenth, Fourteenth and Fifteenth Amendments shall be faithfully observed; that the colored people shall have equal rights to labor, education, and the privilege of citizenship. I am confident this is good work. Time will tell." [42]

While Hayes recalled the troops primarily for political reasons—as a move to rejuvenate the Republican party in the South, he was motivated by other factors which historians have only recently come to appreciate. He wanted to restore harmony and good feeling between the North and the South and between Negroes and whites. He was also influenced by the overwhelming demand of Republicans and of the business

---

[40] *Ibid.*, March 20, 14, 23, 1877, 428, 427, 429.
[41] " Bryan-Hayes Correspondence," *Southwestern Historical Quarterly*, XXIX (1925-1926), 302-303.
[42] Hayes Diary, April 22, 1877, Williams, III, 430.

community for a change from military Reconstruction. His decision also came from necessity. Republican state governments in the South had steadily lost so much strength through their defects and objectionable features that they had become entirely unable to sustain themselves, even by force. Finally, Grant had in a sense initiated the action that led to the withdrawal of the troops when he reversed his earlier policy of intervention in the South and refused aid to Packard and Chamberlain.

While Hayes had removed the troops, he would not yield the right of interference given to him by the Enforcement Acts of 1870-1871. His reluctance in this matter came out in the struggle he had with Congress over this issue. The Forty-sixth Congress (1879-1881) having Democratic majorities in both the House and the Senate, made this enforcement legislation one of the chief points of its attack. Southern Democrats objected in particular to those provisions which gave federal deputy marshals and supervisors the power to regulate elections and to appeal to the courts in the event of fraud. Democrats in Congress sought to nullify the Enforcement Acts by attaching riders to Army appropriation bills aimed at removing federal supervision of elections. In 1877 a Republican Senate refused to accept such a bill coming from a Democratic House, and the Army went without funds for some time. Between 1879-1881 a Democratic Congress pased eight bills in an attempt to eliminate the use of federal deputy marshals in elections, but Hayes vetoed all of them, and Congress lacked enough votes to override him. Not until the 1890's were the Democrats able to eliminate the Enforcement Acts through Supreme Court decisions and legislation.

Hayes fought the repeal of the Enforcement Acts, because it would have placed him under the " coercive dictation " of a " bare " majority in Congress. Furthermore, he disliked the idea of removing any legislation designed to protect elections and to secure the sanctity of the ballot. But of greater importance he took exception to the various Democratic amendments on the grounds that they were an unconstitutional and revolutionary attempt to deprive him of one of his most important prerogatives by forcing him to approve a measure which he in fact did not favor. Thus he looked upon the Democratic proposals as an encroachment by Congress on the powers of the President. He recoiled from the idea of using the military at the polls; there was now and there had recently been no such use, but he refused to surrender the federal right to intervene. If the need arose, he would intervene in the North as well as in the South to secure honest results in congressional elections. Hayes argued that the use of the Army was a general and well established executive prerogative, at all times in all parts of the country, which he would not surrender " on certain days and at certain places." [43]

By his persistent vetoes of bills aimed at repealing election laws, Hayes puzzled southerners, for his action in this respect did not seem consistent with his new policy.. After recalling the troops, why should he resist attempts to repeal laws sanctioning the use of the military in the South? Such a stand won him some measure of popularity with the Stalwart element of the party, but how many white converts to Republicanism in the South it gained is open to question.

Hayes had the insight to realize that conciliation of the white South called for more effort on his part than the removal of the troops and the selection of a former Confederate for the cabinet. Besides, he wondered whether these two moves had ingratiated himself and the Republican party with the white South. Friends and newspapers seemed to think this was the case. " You will carry with you by steady adherence to your policy the South," wrote Bryan. " I know you are growing rapidly in their confidence and affection. My brothers are your warm supporters, and thousands whom I met at the State Fair last week commend and support you." [44] But only a personal jaunt through the South would answer many of Hayes' questions and would also enable him to make a direct appeal to the whites in these states. Hayes' two trips to the South in 1877 turned out to be a novel spectacle. Lincoln had been the last President to visit this section, but he had gone as a conqueror. Hayes went as a conciliator bringing with him his wife and members of the cabinet and leading southerners

[43] *Ibid.*, April 2-13, 1879, 529-547; Richardson, *Messages and Papers*, VII, 493-495, 531-547, 591-598.

[44] Bryan to Hayes, May 22, 1877, " Bryan-Hayes Correspondence," *Southwestern Historical Quarterly*, XXVII (1923-1924), 65.

like Wade Hampton. Through Louisville, Atlanta, Lynchburg, Richmond, and Charlottesville he traveled pleading for union and conciliation, and prominent white southerners sitting on the same platform with him echoed his sentiments. All this immensely gratified the *Nation* especially to see the President who had been elected by the " bloody shirts " within one year " traveling triumphantly through the South pleading before joyous multitudes for union and conciliation." [45]

The hospitality and turnouts in the South dazzled Hayes and dumbfounded his critics who never dreamed that the President would talk in such plain terms to southern whites. But more importantly, Hayes concluded that his new policy had been responsible for the hearty reception he had received. " I am very happy to be able to feel that the course taken has turned out so well," he noted in his diary. Republican friends, North and South, agreed with him. William Henry Smith called the trips " the most pleasant surprise of the year. . . The implacable are at last dumbfounded. They never believed that you would talk plainly to the Southern people of the Constitutional Amendments and education as you did. Let them pass. They are now powerless for evil." A Carpetbagger leader and iron manufacturer from Alabama had watched the reaction of southerners to Hayes and reported that he had made a " host of friends in the South among the people but the politicians among the Democrats hate him worse for so doing." [46]

Encouraged by the hearty reception the South had given him, Hayes set out to divide the Democratic vote there on economic rather than on race lines through a program of national aid for internal improvements. This would appeal to former Whigs whose party in the past had championed a similar scheme and to dissatisfied southern Democrats who believed their northern associates had abandoned them on this issue. On several occasions before his inauguration Hayes, in private statements, had favored national aid for internal improvements, and shortly

[45] *The Nation*, XXV (September 27, 1877), 191. For a fuller discussion of Hayes' trips to the South see Logan, *The Negro in American Life and Thought*, pp. 21-29.

[46] Hayes' Diary, September, no date, 1877; Wm. Henry Smith to Hayes, September 27, 1877, Williams, III, 443; Willard Warner, Tecumseh Iron Works, Tecumseh, Alabama, to John Sherman, September 26, 1877, in Sherman Papers.

after taking office he told Garfield he intended to propose such a program for the South, if it would bring enough southern support to the administration to make it worth while.[47]

Newspapers aided Hayes in his campaign to win southern votes on economic issues. The Louisville *Courier-Journal* carried a story written by its Washington correspondent to the effect that Hayes very decidedly favored a system of internal improvements that would benefit and develop the South, and that he lamented the impoverished conditions of this section and the failure of the national government to come to its aid. In an interview the President gave to the Philadelphia *Times* he spoke of his plans to encourage the development of industries in the South as far as such action lay within the powers of the national government.[48]

Stimulated by these reports, eager southern Democrats in Congress brought forward schemes for internal improvements in their various states. In Virginia they wanted a tunnel through the Allegheny mountains and the completion of the James River and Kanawha Canal projects. Florida Democrats considered the construction of a canal across the state from the Atlantic Ocean to the Gulf of Mexico as a gesture of conciliation. North and South Carolina desired an inland waterway from Pamlico Sound to the channel behind the Sea Islands. Perhaps the most promising measure from a conciliatory point of view embraced the construction of a canal by way of the Tennessee River through Alabama and Georgia. Many conventions and commercial bodies in the South had urged the passage of such a measure, and the United States engineers had elaborately examined location for the canal. Most important of all the plan involved the spending of many millions of dollars in the South. These represent only a few of the proposals in the wake of Hayes' declarations. From October to December in 1877, southern Democrats introduced forty bills in the Senate and 267 in the House asking for federal funds for projects in their respective states.[49]

[47] Hayes' Diary, January 5, 1877, February 9, 1877; Hayes to Carl Schurz, January 29, 1877, Williams, *Diary and Letters*, III, 400, 410, 414.
[48] Louisville *Courier-Journal*, April 26, 1877; New York *Tribune*, May 19, 1877.
[49] New York *Tribune*, March 4, 1879.

On an earlier occasion Hayes had successfully exploited the cleavages between northern and southern Democrats over the issue of national aid for internal improvements. His assurances to Tom Scott, President of the Pennsylvania and Texas Pacific Railroads, of aid from the national government for the completion of the latter line had, in large part, enabled the Ohioan to enter the White House under peaceful circumstances.[50] In the fall of 1877 Hayes hoped to repeat his earlier performance by turning a Democratic majority in the House to his advantage in organizing this body for the Republicans, and his prospects for accomplishing this appeared to be bright. The press reported that most of the Democratic congressmen from Louisiana, Mississippi, Arkansas, and Tennessee stood ready to support a candidate for Speaker who favored national aid for internal improvements, and that they planned to vote for a Republican if their party caucus refused to endorse the Southern Pacific Railroad Bill and the Mississippi levee measure.[51]

Although dissatisfied southern Democrats threatened to bolt their party they remained steadfast and turned their back on Hayes' proffer of cooperation. Samuel J. Randall, Democratic chieftain from Pennsylvania, fresh from a state convention that protested against " subsidies, land grants, loans of the public credit, and the appropriation of the people's money to any corporation," [52] defeated Garfield and became the new Speaker of the House.

Following this setback, Hayes expressed grave doubt of the wisdom of granting government aid for internal improvements in the South. He objected in particular to subsidies for the Texas Pacific Railroad for fear that this line sought excessive funds which might result in another Credit Mobilier.[53] Thus Hayes reversed an earlier attitude he had held on this subject and ignored the assurances he had given to Tom Scott. If any southern Democrats seemed willing to cut themselves loose from their party over the issue of national improvements, they lost their enthusiasm in light of Hayes' change of heart.

All of Hayes' efforts in the South had been directed toward

[50] Woodward, *Reunion and Reaction.*
[51] New York *Tribune,* March 30, 1877.
[52] Louisville *Commercial,* August 24, 1877.
[53] New York *Tribune,* December 22, 1877.

eliminating the ill will that military Reconstruction had developed among southern whites, but much work remained to be done if the Republican party hoped to detach any southern state from the Democratic column. Hayes knew southern Democrats to be just as restive under Negro and Carpetbagger office holders as they had been under federal soldiers. Grant's appointment policy in the South had made the Republican party there pretty largely an organization of federal officials and this situation made it diffcult to win additional recruits from among southern whites. Fully alive to this problem, Hayes launched a new appointment policy in the South which he developed in connection with his, and the Republican party platform, pledge on civil service reform during the campaign of 1876. This became his most important effort to win the support of southern whites.

In the South the Carpetbaggers for the most part, had controlled the patronage during the Grant administrations in order to keep themselves in power and to take controlled delegations to the Republican national conventions. These conditions prevented " respectable " southern whites from joining the Republican fold even if they had wanted. This disturbed Hayes no end, and he hoped to persuade the southern whites that a better political future lay in store for them. When he accepted the nomination in 1876, he had underscored his " inflexible purpose " not to be a candidate for reelection, an assertion that enabled him to act without an eye to the 1880 national convention. His letter of acceptance and his inaugural address contained a blunt declaration in behalf of civil service reform which was to be " thorough and complete " for as he put it, " he serves his party best who serves his country best." [54]

Hayes, by his own example, planned to make efficiency the test for holding public office, and the brother-in-law and other relations which had brought charges of nepotism upon Grant would not discredit the new administration.[55] In several meetings with the press shortly after he took office, Hayes quite frankly declared that he had little or no place for the Carpetbagger in the South. As for the native white and Negro

[54] Williams, *Life of Hayes*, I, 462; Richardson, *Messages and Papers*, VI, 4394-96.
[55] Williams, *Life of Hayes*, II, 74, 75.

elements of the party he proposed to let them down more
gently. They both needed to meet certain requirements in
order to be eligible for a federal post. Simply being a Republican was not enough. The native white had to be a conservative, and the Negro had to be qualified for the position. In
addition both had to command the respect of their communities
and had to possess character and ability. If he failed to find
Republicans in the South who could measure up to these
standard, Hayes planned to turn to southern Democrats.[56]

But he fell short on performance because politics entered
the picture. He granted federal posts to all members of the
Louisiana Returning Board, which in no small fashion had paved
the way for his election, to some of their relatives, and to their
secretaries. He gave offices to the forty-seven Negro members
of the Louisiana legislature when the Democrats turned them
out in 1877. He sent Packard, the Carpetbagger claimant for
governor in the disputed state election in Louisiana in 1876,
as Consul to Liverpool, a position regarded in 1877 as the
most lucrative spot in the federal service and one whose fees
amounted to a larger salary than that of the President.[57] All
this added up to a glaring inconsistency in Hayes' anxious
efforts to conciliate southern Democrats, and it forcefully
pointed up his reluctance to repudiate entirely the old and
tainted leadership of the Republican party in the South. But
consistency means little in practical politics, and Hayes was a
practical politician. Yet in all fairness it should be noted that
he clearly and early recognized this shortcoming in his policy,
and he deplored his " mistakes." He had appointed "wrong
men " but would try to make amends in the future.

And Hayes did make amends as his campaign to lure
southern Democrats away from their party swung into full
action, a campaign that brought a wave of resentment from
Republican leaders as they helplessly watched the patronage
slip away from their hands. Everywhere in the South they
bitterly assailed this strategy, and everywhere in the South
Hayes gambled on the patronage to coax southern whites into

[56] New York *Tribune*, June 19, 1877; Washington *National Republican*, April
14, 1877.
[57] H. J. Eckenrode, *Rutherford B. Hayes, Statesman of Reunion* (New York,
1930), pp. 221-226, 247; Oberholtzer, *Hist. of U. S.*, III, 345-346.

the Republican camp. In Georgia he took the advice of two Democratic leaders, Alexander H. Stephens and John B. Gordon, on patronage matters. In South Carolina he brushed aside the Republican state chairman, Robert B. Elliott, a Negro, who not only had no patronage to dispense but had to appeal to Washington for a post for himself to earn a living in order to continue to be a Republican in the state. Ostracized, he could not make a living through his law practice, and he reported that Hayes had filled the greater part of the federal offices in the state with Democrats and "mere nondescripts" and men from other states.[58]

Even in a Republican stronghold such as east Tennessee, Hayes provoked the charge from party leaders that he had allied himself with "rebel" Democrats and fair weather Republicans and a warning that "unless there is a change, you cannot hope for any support from those of us who bore an active part in the campaign of '76." [59] Democrats in Arkansas twitted Republicans of that state about Hayes' failure to find capable and honest men among them to fill the federal offices. From Virginia and Florida came anxious queries from Republicans as to why Hayes permitted the Democrats to grab off the richest plums of office, and from Mississippi came the lament of a national committeeman that Hayes' course had humiliated Mississippi Republicans and advanced the cause of the opposition. When disgruntled Republicans from Alabama protested to Hayes about the lack of patronage, he brusquely informed them that by putting Democrats into office he had increased Republican sentiment in the state.[60]

In Texas Hayes "studiously ignored" Edmund J. Davis, Reconstruction governor, and his faction, and preferred Democratic advice, and in Louisiana, Republicans accused the President of frittering away the patronage in a vain attempt to control the Democratic party in that state. While Republicans

---

[58] New York *Tribune*, December 3, 1877; Robert G. Elliott to John Sherman, June 23, 1879, in Sherman Papers.

[59] L. C. Houk to Sherman, August 5, 1879; A. M. Hughes to Sherman, May 10, 1879, in Sherman Papers.

[60] A. L. Hill to Wm. E. Chandler, March 21, 1878, in Wm. E. Chandler Papers; John Tyler, Jr. to Sherman, January 12, 1880; James T. Magbee to Sherman, January 10, 1880; George M. Buchanan, to Sherman, November 17, 1879, in Sherman Papers.

in North Carolina received some of the local offices, they complained of not being able to obtain any out of the state. As one of them, the United States District Attorney for the eastern district of the state, put it, they wanted an equal chance for the " honors and emoluments of the Government" otherwise what inducement " has a southern man to be a Republican? The question is not one to be answered by the sordid reply that all we think of is the loaves and fishes. There is a principle in it which is the test of mankind and self respect." [61]

Hayes' political strategy in the South created a furor, and daily rumors swept Washington that he would be forced to call a halt to it, but the President vigorously denied these reports and in fact pursued his course with greater enthusiasm than before. " It is not correct that no *heretofore* Dems. will be appointed," he wrote to Bryan. " I appointed two last week— P. M. at Memphis and Petersburg . . . and others." Then in the manner of clothing his policy in a conundrum, Hayes added, " Of course I shall appoint Republicans generally, but & & you understand me." [62] The fact is that Hayes never did let up in putting southern Democrats into office. A leading Republican daily in the South estimated that he had given Democrats one third of the posts in the South in the first five months of his administration.[63] To the very end of his presidency Hayes favored Democrats for office in the South, for as he told Bryan in his last year in the White House, "(By the way I have appointed in the last four months over forty Southern Democrats—notably Trescott of South Carolina to China)." [64]

While Hayes was optimistic about wooing southern whites away from their Democratic loyalties, he wanted only those who had something in common with the conservative Republicans of the northeast. "What we wish is to combine, if possible, in harmonious political action the same class of men in the South as are Republicans," John Sherman, Hayes' Secretary of the Treasury, told a Republican leader in Louisiana,

---

[61] R. M. Moore to Sherman, December 3, 1879; D. M. A. Jewett to Sherman, November 19, 1879; J. W. Albertson to Sherman, May 1, 1880, in Sherman Papers.

[62] Hayes to Bryan, June 13, 1877, in Hayes Papers.

[63] Louisville *Commercial*, August 21, 1877.

[64] Hayes to Bryan, March 28, 1880, in Hayes Papers.

"that is the producing classes, men who are interested in
industry and property." To a Republican leader in Virginia,
Sherman pointed out, " We cannot hope for permanent success
in New Orleans until we can secure conservative support
among white men, property holders, who are opposed to
repudiation and willing to give the colored people their constitutional rights." [65]

In his great anxiety to win over southern conservative whites,
Hayes rejected tempting offers of coalitions with the Independent Democrats in the South, because to him they smacked of
repudiation and radicalism. This was especially true of the
Readjusters in Virginia. This movement grew out of the controversy over the settlement of the public debt in Virginia,
contracted almost entirely through the active promotion of a
system of public works by the state in helping to construct
canals, turnpikes, and railroads, and it got under way in 1878
with William Mahone, a former Confederate General, as its
leader. In the beginning the entire issue centered around the
question of the state meeting its obligation to the bondholders,
and since the Mahone forces favored a readjustment of the
debt, they received the label of repudiators from their opponents, the Funders. In the state election of 1879 both sides
worked to win the votes of the Negro, and the Readjusters,
in winning, gained the support of both the colored and white
Republicans of the Tidewater and the Southside.[66]

Since the Funders represented principally the regular Democratic element in Virginia, some Republican leaders looked
upon Mahone's victory as a means of detaching the state from
Democratic control. John Tyler, Jr., son of the former President and Inspector of Customs at Richmond, sprang up as a
leader in the movement to effect a closer relationship between
the Republican party and Mahone. Immediately following the
election, Tyler addressed letters to the Hayes administration
and to Republican leaders in Virginia in which he urged that
a " thorough and cordial understanding" be established be-

[65] Sherman to Robert O. Hebert, June 19, 1879 and to John Tyler, Jr., June 9,
1879, in Sherman Papers.

[66] For a full discussion of the Readjuster movement see Charles Chilton
Pearson, *The Readjuster Movement in Virginia* (New Haven, 1917), and Nelson
M. Blake, *William Mahone; Soldier and Political Insurgent* (Richmond, 1935).

tween Mahone and "ourselves" which in turn could achieve the "Salvation" of the Republican party in Virginia.[67]

The rise of Mahone sharply divided Republicans in Virginia. There were those who felt that the Readjuster movement was, "A protest against the despotism of the Conservative partisan ring," and not one of repudiation, and that the Republicans would be better off helping Mahone than in opposing him.[68] Other Virginia Republicans wanted Hayes to strengthen the regular party in the state and under no circumstances to assist Mahone.[69] The Republican state chairman, Major B. W. Hoxey, urged his followers to support Mahone and declared that the Readjuster's program amounted to nothing more than Republicanism.[70]

Then some of the national Republican leaders, like Simon Cameron of Pennsylvania, got behind the project for a coalition with Mahone. But the decision had to be made by Hayes, and he frowned upon the idea. Tainted with repudiation, Mahone shaped up as an opponent of orthodox Republicanism and southern conservatism, both forces which Hayes was striving to link together. To have embraced Mahone, even to capture Virginia, would have endangered Hayes' plan for winning the conservative white south over to the Republican party, and he promptly turned down the proposed union with the Readjuster leader. Hayes publicly took issue with the Readjusters and rebuked Republicans in Virginia who had taken sides with Mahone. Above all, Hayes hoped that the Negroes would not be misled by the appeal of demagogues and vote against the Funders whom he called the party of honesty and right.[71]

In spite of all this, an oddity and an omen of what was to come did crop up during the 1879 campaign in Virginia. The Treasury department, publicly announced that the administration, informed of a revenue official at Petersburg favoring

[67] John Tyler, Jr., to Hayes and Sherman, November 8, 1879, quoted in Blake, *Mahone*, p. 156 Tyler's letter was sent to prominent Republican leaders in the states, *Ibid.*, pp. 197-198.

[68] R. W. Hughes to John Tyler, Jr., November 7, 1879; S. M. Yost, editor of Staunton *Valley Virginian* to Hayes, December 2, 1879, in Hayes Papers.

[69] James D. Brady, Petersburg, Virginia, to Hayes, December 2, 1879; T. Spicer Curlett, Litwalten, Virginia to Hayes, December 2, 1879, *Ibid*.

[70] Wilmington, North Carolina *Post*, December 7, 1879.

[71] Louisville *Commercial*, November 1, 1879; New York *Tribune*, November 22, 1879.

Mahone, had ordered the office holder either to abandon his views or give up his position. " Sound Money " Americans in all parts of the country acclaimed this action. But the Petersburg collector turned out to be a Funder and a stiff Readjuster opponent. On the other hand the Collector of Customs at Norfolk owned and edited the Norfolk *Day Book*, which advocated " forcible readjustment'" and the administration never disturbed him.[72]

If Hayes turned his back upon Mahone, he also turned it on other Independent movements in the South. Several of them put in an appearance in the last years of his administration and rose out of the Greenback issue and discontent with the conservative control of the Democratic party. While southern Democratic leaders and press appealed for unity and harmony, many Republicans, North and South, strongly urged Hayes to merge with the Independents. But there were too many economic radicals among their ranks to win any endorsement from Hayes. Again Sherman clearly expressed the President's policy when he wrote to a native white in Georgia, " I have but little confidence in anyone who does not openly and manfully assume the Republican name and principles. Independent movements in a state like Georgia," added Sherman, " when successful only lead to more extreme conduct by Independents in order to maintain their relation with the old party." [73] In the summer of 1879, the Buffalo *Commercial* reported that " Not much is said now about the independent political organization which was to be developed at the South under the invigorating influence of the new departure. The old Whigs failed to come to time, and the Democrats had no idea of wandering off into strange paths." [74]

Hayes also backed away from the proposal to establish a new party in the South or to revive the Whig party in that section. There was considerate speculation about these moves, and rumors concerning these two possibilities filled the press as Hayes unfolded his policy. Many people who talked with the President in the spring of 1877 came away with the impres-

---

[72] William L. Royall, *History of Virginia Debt Controversy* (Richmond, 1897), pp. 34-36.

[73] Sherman to John Conley, October 16, 1879, in Sherman Papers.

[74] Quoted from Toledo *Commercial*, August 10, 1879, clipping in Hayes Papers.

sion that he was planning to build a Whig-Republican party in the South. Newspaper stories actually had a well organized movement under way made up of conservative and moderate men of both major parties and appealing to voters under the name of the National Union Party. There appeared to be such a groundswell for this development that prominent political leaders from many parts of the country descended upon Washington in the spring of 1877 to talk to Hayes and his cabinet about the matter.[75] But Hayes never gave any encouragement to the idea, for he refused to give up the name and principles of the Republican party. He had come away from his trip to the South with the belief that "thousands of intelligent people" in the South had no real Democratic loyalties and yearned to unite with the conservative Republicans of the North.[76] To bring about such an alliance became one of his great dreams. As for the former Whigs, Hayes hoped that they would come into the Republican party and share the leadership of it in the South with the Douglas Democrats, but he had no intentions of organizing the Whigs into a separate party despite a flood of rumors that he would do so.

As has been pointed out, Hayes launched his southern policy with great optimism—an optimism that seldom deserted him in his vain struggle over four vexatious years to redeem the South for the Republican party. Writing to Bryan in 1880 Hayes boasted that he was "not without pride in results obtained" and that he no longer needed to speak of the "Southern Question."[77] Several months after he had left office Hayes, reviewing his administration, recorded in his diary that he had found the country "divided and distracted and every interest depressed" but that he had left it "united, harmonious, and prosperous." When he had entered the White House "the South was solid and the North divided. At its close the North was united and solid and the South was divided." At the outset the Stalwarts had "reviled" his southern policy, but "now" Hayes observed, "all are silenced by the results. Their President [Arthur] utters not a word on the subject. His silence

[75] New York *Tribune*, March 18, 1877; Washington *National Republican*, May 28, 1877; see also Woodward, *Reunion and Reaction*, Ch. 2.
[76] Hayes Diary, November 3, 1877, Williams, *Diary and Letters*, III, 450.
[77] Hayes to Bryan, March 28, 1880, in Hayes Papers.

is the most significant proof of the wisdom and success of my policy." [78] What were these results that Hayes took so much pride in, which led him to write off the " Southern Question " as being solved, and which had silenced the opposition? What had this strategy accomplished politically in the South? His aim had been to destroy the Democratic supremacy in the South? That he failed even to dent it was quite evident from the easy fashion in which the Democrats won all of the southern states in 1880. But such an important and radical departure from military Reconstruction deserves a deeper and more pentrating analysis before one can assess Hayes' optimism over the results.

In the spring of 1877 the New York *Tribune* sent one of its men into the South for several months to study the immediate effects of Hayes' policy. Everywhere this reporter went he found a radical enough division of opinion among the whites to result in party cleavage, but vital concern for the safety of their local interest required them to continue to act together. While many whites had become restive under Democratic leadership and had become pleased with Hayes they had not yet reached the point where they would support him. It was still too early for them to decide. They wanted to know whether this was just a passing fancy with Hayes or whether he would push on with it. Would his own party sustain him in his effort or would it seek again to organize the Negro for use in political campaigns in the South? Southern whites waited for answers to these and other questions before leaving the Democratic party. In North Carolina and Tennessee where the white vote prevailed and where a large Republican element existed, Hayes' policy had strengthened the Republican party. In South Carolina, Mississippi, and Louisiana where the Negro vote could dominate, the *Tribune* man found voters willing to help Hayes against the Stalwart attacks. In these three states whites cared little about party names. Local self government and protection against federal intervention occupied their minds. In Georgia and Alabama, where Negroes and whites nearly balanced one another, the Democratic party appeared more solid than anywhere else in the South. Here, rarely could

[78] Hayes Diary, December 29, 1881, Williams, *Diary and Letters*, IV, 58-59.

a politician be found advocating the idea of a divided white vote. The reporter concluded that the old Republican party of Reconstruction days was dead and offered the opinion that any Washington effort to resurrect it meant failure. The new policy had completely demoralized the Negroes in Florida, South Carolina, and Louisiana. Their Carpetbagger leaders had fled to the North, and Washington had vetoed the idea of sending troops. Outside of Kentucky, Tennessee, and North Carolina, this northern traveler met few white Republicans save federal office holders and their dependents. But when these party members lost their jobs they began to abuse Hayes and either changed their politics or left the state.[79]

The acid test for Hayes' policy came in the elections of 1878 and 1880, and it is only after an analysis of these that one can reach any satisfactory conclusions on Hayes' optimism. In the 1878 contest southern whites turned their backs on Hayes' conciliatory gestures. They rejected all Republicans for governor and drastically cut back Republican strength from the South in Congress from ten to three members.[80] But Hayes had had other things in mind. He wanted to maintain his party's majorities in the Black Belts while making gains in the white counties, for if he could do this then he was on his way to breaching the Democratic South. Thus the real clue to the success or failure of Hayes' policy lay in the answer to these two vital questions. Had his shift from appeals to Negroes to appeals to southern conservative whites caused the Republican party to gain in the white counties and to lose in the Black Belt? Had his neglect of the Negro permitted the Republicans to hold their Reconstruction majorities in the Black Belts while making gains in the white counties?

Any attempt to answer these questions immediately raises other questions and knotty problems. One is that of determining what proportion of Republican strength in the Black Bets represents white voters and what proportion represents Negro voters. Another is that of tabulating the voters in the white counties. Does a larger Republican vote in the white counties in 1878 and 1880 over that of 1876 indicate that more southern whites had voted Republican because of Hayes' policy,

[79] New York *Tribune*, June 1, 1877.
[80] New York *Tribune Almanac for 1878*, pp. 56-57; for 1879, pp. 53-54.

or does it mean that they voted Republican for some other reason? Likewise, does a falling off of Republican votes in the Black Belt reflect Negro dissatisfaction with Hayes' policy or does it signify southern white success in keeping Negroes away from the polls? It is practically impossible to answer these questions, but in all fairness they must be raised before an analysis of the vote in the Black Belts and white counties can be made.

Compared with the election returns of 1876, Republican strength took a nose dive in both white counties and the Black Belts in 1878. Out of the 293 counties with 50 per cent or over Negro population, only sixty-two gave Republican majorities in 1878 as compared to 125 counties in 1876. Of the 154 counties with less than 5 per cent Negro population, nine returned Republican majorities in 1878 as contrasted with twelve counties in 1876.[81] The whites of both areas had remained true to their Democratic loyalties and had not swung over to Republicanism. Hayes had not expected this to happen in the white counties, where because of relatively few Negroes, southern whites could afford the luxury of voting outside the Democratic party. One might have expected the whites in the Black Belts to remain steadfast to the Democratic party out of fear of Negro supremacy, but many former Whigs lived in these counties, and Hayes had hoped that they would shove aside the race question and vote their convictions on matters of protective tariffs and national aid for internal improvements.

The 1878 election returns dismayed Hayes, and he reluctantly but openly admitted to the press that his strategy to win the

---

[81] *American Almanac for 1879*, pp. 350-403. The selection of counties with 50% or more Negroes and those with 5% or fewer Negroes is not an arbitrary one. *The Negro Population in the United States, 1790-1915* (Washington, D. C., 1918), p. 125 uses the 50% or over figures for classifying Black Belt counties in the South. As for the figure 5% or less, one can hardly dispute the fact that such a county is predominantly white which can act politically without fear of Negro supremacy. It is true that the use of the 50% and 5% figures presents a broad division between white and black counties and probably conceals gradation of correlation, as well as exceptions. But for the purpose of this study an examination of the counties in the South at the extreme ends of the racial spectrum furnishes sufficient evidence of the success or failure of Republican policies to win additional southern white recruits while holding the Negro in line. A study of the counties between the two extremes might prove interesting, but it is doubtful if it would change the general conclusions.

south had not paid off. " I am reluctantly forced to admit that the experiment was a failure," he hold a reporter.[82] Such a statement to the press served the purpose of softening the blows against the new policy and erasing the fears of the Stalwarts. Privately, though, Hayes had different ideas. Continuing to recognize that the South still was substantially Democratic, he also concluded that the Democratic vote had been light and that the Republicans had suffered from a lack of organization.

The election of 1880 ended all doubts of the success or failure of Hayes' experiment. In 1876 under Military Reconstruction, the Republicans had taken three southern states, all on the basis of disputed returns. With the troops gone and with the new policy in effect for nearly four years, Garfield failed to carry a single southern state. His popular vote in the South fell behind that of the Republicans for 1876, but his proportional vote was just slightly higher, and the number of counties he carried was about in the same proportion as that of Hayes. In the South in 1876 the Republicans polled 740,708 popular votes or 40.34 per cent of the total cast and carried 201 of the 928 counties. In 1880 they gathered 671,826 popular votes or 40.84 per cent of the total and captured 206 of the 943 counties.[83]

In the congressional elections of 1878 the Republicans had lost ground in both the white and Black Belt counties. Almost the same trend continued in the 1880 presidential election, as compared with that of 1876, in which again the Republicans lost strength in the Black Belts, although they did fare better here than they had in 1878, while they kept even in the white counties. Garfield won 133 of the 293 Black Belt and thirteen of the 154 white counties in contrast to the 141 and thirteen Black and white counties respectively that Hayes had taken.[84]

In 1880 the three southern states with the highest proportion of Negroes in their population were South Carolina, Mississippi, and Louisiana in that order. In all three a noticeable

[82] New York *Tribune*, November 13, 1878; Washington *National Republican*, November 13, 1878.

[83] Burnham, *Presidential Ballots*, pp. 252-255, 237-243.

[84] *Ibid.*, pp. 165-225. This figure for white counties may be larger. In Texas where there were 98 white counties according to the 1880 Census, only 45 in 1876 and 52 of them in 1880 reported election returns.

decline in Republican strength occurred in 1880. On the other hand in Georgia, which had the largest Negro population and greatest number of Black Belt counties of any southern state, the size of the Republican vote in 1880 increased substantially. Moreover the number of Republican Black Belt counties in Georgia rose from seven in 1876 to seventeen in 1880. In Arkansas, Tennessee, and Texas where whites made up about 75 per cent of the population, Garfield had a higher popular vote than Hayes, although in Arkansas and Texas the Republicans actually received a small proportional vote in 1880 than in 1876. Further examination of the election figures amply sustains the general conclusion, with few exceptions, that Garfield polled his lowest percentages of the total vote in those southern states with the highest proportion of Negroes in their population and his highest percentages in those states of relatively few Negroes.[85]

	% of Negroes in population	Rep. % of Pres. Vote, 1876	Rep % of Pres. Vote, 1880
South Carolina	60.7	50.24	33.96
Mississippi	57.5	31.92	29.70
Louisiana	51.5	51.64	36.40
Alabama	47.5	40.01	37.09
Georgia	47.0	28.00	34.42
Florida	47.0	50.21	45.88
Virginia	41.8	40.40	39.39
North Carolina	37.9	46.37	48.15
Arkansas	26.3	39.86	38.97
Tennessee	26.2	40.22	44.26
Texas	24.7	29.72	23.77

Hayes' optimism and pride in the " results obtained " are hardly justifiable by the elections returns of 1878 and 1880. The high hopes that he had for capturing more than half of the southern states in 1880 were all dashed to the ground. The South was more Democratic than ever. Nor were Hayes' observations about the disappearance of the " Southern Question " hardly in tune with political realities, for it continued to remain both a pressing and vexatious problem for the Republican party—lasting even into our own day. But while

[85] Negro Population, 1790-1915, p. 51; Burnham, Presidential Ballots, pp. 252-255.

Hayes had failed to convert southern whites to Republicanism, he had committed his own party to the strategy of redeeming the South. His policy had broken sharply with the Republican tactics of Reconstruction, and it was a starting point in a new direction. Whether his policy would be carried out, repudiated in part or entirely, varied or added to by succeeding Republican administrations and leaders responsible for making policy remained to be seen, but one thing was certain; the Republicans had no intentions of giving up the South by default, no intentions of writing it off as hopeless and unprofitable. They were greatly alarmed and fully alive to their handicap in the South, and they meant to do something about it.

CHAPTER III

REPUBLICAN DISSENSIONS

While there had been a widespread demand for an end to military Reconstruction, the new Republican venture in the South came under a scorching attack by certain elements in the party and caused such a serious split to develop within its ranks that for a while it seemed as though it might suffer the same fate of the Whigs. The Carpetbaggers and Stalwarts could not reconcile themselves to the effort to conciliate the southern whites, and in their eyes Hayes had betrayed the party in an outrageous fashion. Hayes " has sold us all out," wrote John A. Logan, Stalwart leader from Illinois, to his wife from Washington only a few days after the inauguration, " And the base ingratitude shown by Hays [sic] to those that elected him has disturbed all here." [1] Simon Cameron, Stalwart boss from Pennsylvania, thought Hayes' policy was a more ungrateful betrayal of his party than that committed by either John Tyler or Andrew Johnson.[2]

Stunned by the turn of events in the spring of 1877, the Carpetbaggers lashed out at Hayes because he had sounded the death knell of their checkered political careers. Two of them from South Carolina, Senator John J. Patterson and former Governor Daniel H. Chamberlain, led the bitter attack of the Carpetbaggers upon Hayes. Patterson declared the new policy would kill the Republican party in the South, and when asked what he intended to do about the matter he replied, " I tell you what we carpetbaggers ought to do. Why d – – – it, we ought all to resign." Patterson never took such drastic action, but he did continue to strike back, and late in 1877 on the floor of the Senate he bitterly accused Hayes of abandoning those who had elected him." [3]

While Packard received the lucrative post of Consul at Liverpool, Chamberlain went unrewarded. Joining a law firm

[1] John A. Logan to his Wife, March 8, 1877, in John A. Logan Papers.
[2] New York *Tribune*, December 25, 1877.
[3] *Ibid.*, April 11, 1877; *Congressional Record*, 45th Congress, I Session, pp. 774-778.

in New York he became, in the beginning at least, a harsh critic of the policy that had led to his downfall in South Carolina. Before a Fourth of July audience at Woodstock, Connecticut in 1877 Chamberlain insisted that Hayes' statements before he entered the presidency had never foreshadowed the removal of the troops, and he called the President's action unconstitutional, revolutionary, and false to every dictate of " political honor, public justice, and good morals." Later in the year he tried to persuade the Stalwarts to drive Hayes over " neck, heels, and boots to the Democracy than that he should remain where he is nominally, while really serving Gordon, Hill & Co." The first necessity, warned Chamberlain, was to drive out traitors. " If we can't win without them we certainly can't with them." [4] But within a few years Chamberlain would change his mind and call for pretty much the same policy in the South that he was now assailing. And twenty-four years after the troops were recalled, Chamberlain in an article for the *Atlantic Monthly* for April, 1901, wrote, " The overthrow of Republicanism or negro rule in South Carolina was root-and-branch work. The fabric so long and laboriously built up fell in a day. Where was fancied to be strength was found only weakness," and " there was no possibility of securing permanent good government in South Carolina through Republican sources." [5]

The Stalwarts fought Hayes for several reasons. In the Congress a group of arrogant leaders had dominated the national government since 1867. They had pretty largely made the Republican party what it was by 1877, and in a certain sense they were the party. They had overthrown Johnson, gained nearly complete possession of Grant, and they intended to put Hayes at their mercy. In 1877 and for almost two more decades the seat of power in the federal government lay not in the presidency but in Congress. The intense and heated struggle between the chief executive and the Congress that had spectacularly begun with Johnson and the Radicals had far from died down. As far as the Stalwarts were concerned Hayes had gotten off to a poor start when he ignored all of

[4] New York *Tribune*, July 5, 1877; D. H. Chamberlain to Wm. E. Chandler, December 29, 1877, in Wm. E. Chandler Papers.

[5] Williams, *Hayes*, II, 53-54.

the big Republican bosses, except Oliver P. Morton of Indiana, in making up his cabinet. This snub along with Hayes' plans for civil service reform had incensed the Stalwarts, and they declared war on the President using his southern policy as a pretext to cover up the real reasons for the attack. For example four of the most influential Stalwarts in the Senate, Roscoe Conkling of New York, James G. Blaine of Maine, Cameron and Logan, combined forces to prevent the confirmation of Key for the cabinet, and Hayes might have been greatly embarrassed at the very outset of his administration, had not southern Democrats like John B. Gordon and Benjamin Hill from Georgia and L. Q. C. Lamar from Mississippi come to his aid.[6]

Then there were those Republicans who had labored, sincerely or otherwise, to find a place for the Negro in politics, and they believed that in any settlement which reconciled North and South, " all parts of the Constitution, the new as well as the old, must be sacredly observed," as Hayes had put it in his letter accepting the nomination. These Republicans felt that Hayes had all too quickly, and in a cowardly fashion, surrendered these fundamental demands, and that in removing the troops he had contemptuously exposed the Negro to his life-long enemies and had forever given up hope of enforcing the Fourteenth and Fifteenth Amendments in the South.

Wendell Phillips thought the new policy was " a surrender of what Grant gained for us at Appomattox," and he called Hayes a " political Rip Van Winkle, an old-fashioned Northern snob-that class which, before the war, believed all the honor and all the gentlemen resided in the south." [7] Ben Wade, the old Radical leader from the President's home state, in a public letter, said that he had been " deceived, betrayed, and even humiliated by the course he [Hayes] has taken to a degree that I have not language to express. . . . No doubt he meditates the destruction of the party that elected him. A contemplation of all this fills me with amazement and inexpressible indignation." Some months later, Wade told Zachariah Chandler, the Republican National Chairman, that " Hayes has gone further south than Johnson at the same period of his administra-

---

[6] Hayes Diary, March 14, 1877, Williams, *Diary and Letters*, III, 426-427.
[7] New York *Tribune*, March 28, November 24, 1877.

tion, he seems to have abandoned the Republican party. I do not know of one principle or practice of the old Republican party that he [Hayes] is not now at war with," lamented Wade." But what can we do? " [8]

In spite of the newspaper reports that Conkling did not object to the removal of the troops, an interview which he publicly and categorically denied had ever taken place, Hayes southern policy was completely at variance with the reconstruction measures that Conkling had supported, and he had no sympathy with the new departure in the South. When the New York Republicans met in convention at Rochester in the fall of 1877, George William Curtis offered a resolution commending the new southern policy, but Conkling spoke so strongly against the resolution that it was defeated by a margin of nearly three to one. Two of Conkling's henchmen at the same convention excoriated Hayes' policy in caustic terms. Thomas C. Platt charged the President with supplanting sterling Republicans in office by rabid Democrats which had destroyed the party organizations in the South, and Martin I. Townsend asked why the federal troops had not been withdrawn from Sitting Bull's territory at the same time they had been taken out of the South. Townsend accused the administration of " trying to force the Millenium & that they are looking for perfect men—altogether better than we have had on Earth for some time." [9]

Other Republicans complained about the new southern policy. One from Wisconsin " cursed the weakness of President Hayes and the folly of his policy. I look upon him as a very weak second edition of Andy Johnson; as though he had robbed the grave of Andy's mantle, after it had become mildewed and rotten." [10] The Republican state chairman in New Hampshire regarded Hayes' action as " a great embarrassment to us. Nothing has ever so much astonished and grieved me." [11]

[8] New York *Times*, April 23, 1877; Wade to Chandler, August 9, 1877, in Z. Chandler Papers.

[9] A. R. Conkling, *The Life and Letters of Roscoe Conkling* (New York, 1889), pp. 550-551; 537-538; Washington *National Republican*, October 13, November 10, 1877; T. C. Platt, *Autobiography* (New York, 1910), pp. 91-93; *Nation*, XXIV (April 26, 1877), 244; George B. M. Cartee, Salem, New York to Wm. E. Chandler, August 24, 1877, in Wm. E. Chandler Papers.

[10] New York *Tribune*, April 30, 1877.

[11] Richardson, *Chandler*, p. 207.

The Republican state chairman in Pennsylvania, newly elected to Congress, reasoned that the logical result of the new policy demanded that he vote for a Democrat, rather than a Republican, for Speaker.[12] An "average Republican" from Pennsylvania told Hayes that "all honest Republicans have been betrayed—sold out—by your friends," and a Republican from Vermont thought that the party was attempting to carry water on both shoulders, an almost certain sign of disruption.[13] Hamilton Fish, Grant's Secretary of State, was reported as saying that had he been in Hayes' place, he would have cut off his right arm before he would have taken the presidency on the electoral vote of Louisiana, without the recognition of Packard.[14]

Many Republicans in Ohio, the President's own state, were unhappy about the new policy. Some feared that while it might split the Democratic party in the South it could at the same time wreck the Republican party in the North.[15] "Many of our people were hurt over the President's policy toward the South," wrote Garfield to a friend after the Ohio Republican Convention of 1877.[16] There was much anxiety among Ohio Republicans concerning the solution to the Louisiana and South Carolina difficulties. Anything in reason to reconcile the South which did not leave southern Republicans "to the tender mercies of the White Leaguers," would be accepted by Republicans, wrote the editor of the Marion *Independent*, but if abandonment did occur, a great deal of "reconciliation" would be necessary to keep Ohio Republican in 1877.[17]

While leading Republicans in Ohio avoided any public condemnation of Hayes' policy and even denied being critical of it, they revealed their rancor in private. "I have not taken pains to conceal my disapproval of the course of Pres. Hayes toward the republicans of S. C. & La.," wrote Alphonso Taft to William E. Chandler. "But I ought not to be in the papers

[12] New York *World*, April 6, 1877.
[13] Robert Morton, Philadelphia to Hayes, May 18, 1877, in Hayes Papers; J. N. Balestier, Brattleboro, Vermont to Wm. E. Evarts, March 7, 1877, in Wm. E. Evarts Papers (Division of Manuscripts, Library of Congress).
[14] Thomas C. Donaldson, *Memoirs*, p. 21, copy in Hayes Papers.
[15] W. M. Farrar to Garfield, March 21, 1877, in Garfield Papers.
[16] T. C. Smith, *The Life and Letters of James Abram Garfield* (New Haven, 1925), II, 655.
[17] George C. Crawford, to John Sherman, March 22, 1877, in Sherman Papers.

as personally unkind or hostile to Hayes, as I do not wish to occupy that position." Taft had asked Chandler to return the letter or a copy of it to him, "which was a true expression of my views, right or wrong, then, and now." [18]

Garfield, another Ohio Republican chieftain and minority leader in the House, was not at first critical of the new policy. Being a close associate of Hayes he hoped the President's course would have a fair trial, and as he told an intimate friend, the President of Hiram College, " It is due to Hayes that we stand by him and give his policy a fair trial." A few days after the inauguration at a social gathering at the home of George M. Robeson, former Secretary of the Navy, Garfield heard the general situation " quite fully discussed with many criticisms upon the policy of the President." It was " quite clear that below the surface of approval" there was " much hostile criticism and a strong tendency to believe that Hayes' policy will be a failure. Blaine thinks the differences between North and South are too deep to be bridged over by the proposed methods. I insisted," Garfield tells us, " that we should give the policy a fair trial and have said so to all who have spoken to me on the subject." [19]

As time went by Garfield became more critical of the new policy and feared a fatal split would develop in the party. Two days after the troops left South Carolina he confided to his cousin, Dr. Silas Boynton, that " in the main the President's purposes " were right but that he was " going a little faster than our people will sustain him. I see signs already of an outbreak in our own ranks." By the summer of 1877 Garfield no longer credited Hayes for initiating the new policy and told a reporter that Grant's course in the South had made it inevitable. That fall he spoke " very plainly " to Hayes about his southern policy and told the President that the flaw in his program was that he assumed to act as though southern conciliation was his own personal doing. " He thus made his friends fear and his political enemies hope that he was acting as though he were not in alliance with his party," Garfield wrote about Hayes. " It would have been more just and more politic to

[18] Taft to Chandler, April 24, 1877, in Wm. E. Chandler Papers.
[19] Garfield to Burke A. Hinsdale, March 10, 1877, Smith, Garfield, I, 648; Garfield Diary, March 11, 1877, in Garfield Papers.

have associated his party with his proffers of good will." By 1878 Garfield had reached the conclusion that Hayes was no longer " master of his administration," that he had " completely . . . lost his hold upon his party," and that his election had been " an almost fatal blow to his party." [20]

The Ohio Republicans did endorse the new southern policy in their platform for 1877, but they lost the state to the Democrats by more than 20,000 votes whereas in 1876 Hayes had won it with around a 5,000 majority. While the New York *Tribune* concluded that Communism had captured Ohio and saw no connection between the defeat here and Hayes' southern policy, Garfield believed that discontent with the new departure in the South contributed to the Republican setback.[21] Warner Bateman, prominent Cincinnati lawyer, and John Sherman's campaign manager for the presidential nomination in 1880, backed up Garfield on his observation on the Ohio election. " The President's Southern policy was distasteful to many Republicans and some openly voted the Democratic ticket in expressing their disgust," wrote Bateman to Sherman. " This condition was aggravated by a half-hearted defense of it by some of our speakers, and by a general ignoring of the question on the stump by most of them." [22] Bateman's charge is borne out by the action of Taft, who while willing to campaign in Ohio in 1877, would not speak in behalf of Hayes' southern policy. Taft, during the hustings, had at no time concealed his disappointment in and disapproval of the policy, and his position was well understood throughout the state.[23]

The Ohio showing failed to shake Hayes' complacency, and Garfield was satisfied that " six months administration have partially blinded the President to the dangers and criticism of his course. It seems to be impossible for a President to see through the atmosphere of praise in which he lives," concluded Garfield. Before 1877 was out, three Republican state con-

[20] Smith, *Garfield*, II, 653; *Ohio State Journal* (Columbus, Ohio), July 18, 1877; Garfield Diary, October 26, 1877, January 19, March 2, 3, 4, 1878, in Garfield Papers.

[21] New York *Tribune*, October 11, 1877; Garfield Diary, October 10, 1877, in Garfield Papers.

[22] Bateman to Sherman, October 11, 1877, in Sherman Papers.

[23] Taft to Wm. E. Chandler, August 6, 1877, in Wm. E. Chandler Papers.

[24] Garfield Diary, October 13, 1877, in Garfield Papers.

ventions had failed to commend the new policy for the South. The Iowa convention actually condemned Hayes' action in South Carolina and Louisiana. The Maine convention, on Blaine's motion, tabled an endorsement of the new policy, and the New York convention, under pressure from Conkling, crushed any sentiment for Hayes.[25]

But it was two of the most influential Republican leaders of the period, William E. Chandler of New Hampshire and James G. Blaine of Maine, who led the uncompromising attack upon Hayes' policy. Chandler had perhaps done more than anyone else to engineer the returning board counts for Hayes from the three disputed southern states in 1876, and Blaine had surely earned the title of " Mr. Republican " for this era, but they could not stomach Hayes' particular methods to rejuvenate southern Republicanism. Chandler waited throughout most of 1877 before he hit back at Hayes, but Blaine jumped into the fray at the outset and strode forth as the champion of the " abandoned " loyal party members of the South. Within a week of the inauguration, Blaine, on two successive days on the floor of the Senate, defending the claim of William P. Kellogg, the Carpetbagger from Louisiana, to a seat in this body, plainly showed his hand when he exclaimed, " You discredit Packard and you discredit Hayes." [26]

The New York *Tribune* felt that Blaine's attack was not generally approved and that it was rash and premature, and the *Nation* watched Blaine's assault with " calm amusement," since, according to this journal, it was plain that the exhibition was a complete failure. The Chicago *Tribune* was " extremely doubtful " whether Blaine's following, " in point of numbers or respectability," would embarass Hayes' efforts " to restore peace and prosperity in the South." The *Tribune's* correspondent in Washington reported that, " outside of the carpet-bag Senators, there does not seem to be much hearty endorsement of Blaine's course." The feeling in Washington was that Blaine believed that the pacification policy was not practicable and would not be popular in the North, and that his

[25] New York *Tribune*, June 28, August 10, September 27, 1877; The Nation, XXV (July 5, August 16, 1877), 4, 95; Portland, Maine *Daily Press*, August 9, 1877.

[26] D. S. Muzzey, *James G. Blaine, A Political Idol of Other Days* (New York, 1934), pp. 130-131.

best chance to succeed Hayes in the presidency lay in the direction of keeping sectional prejudice alive. According to this explanation for Blaine's action, his idea was that Hayes would fail in his attempts to build a strong Republican party in the South, that his administration in the end would be as unpopular as Johnson's had been, and that northern Republicans would then rally with enthusiasm around a leader like Blaine who had kept steadily the old faith.[27]

If some quarters regarded Blaine's attack as being out of line, such was not the opinion of William Lloyd Garrison who praised the stand Blaine had taken. "There is a weak, timid, purblind, compromising element in the Republican party . . . whose panacea for all our national divisions is ' conciliation ' —meaning thereby a trucking to the South . . . and a stolid indifference to the fate of her colored population," Garrison told Blaine. "The elimination of this element from the party would greatly add to its strength and efficiency, as it is ever a drag in any great emergency. . . . The truly loyal at the South needs no conciliation; to the disloyal no concession should be made," declared Garrison. "If President Hayes shall be true to his inaugural professions his Administration will be a shield of defense to the oppressed against their lawless oppressors."[28]

When Hayes took the troops out of the South, Blaine was " grievously disappointed, wounded, and humiliated," and in a public letter he conveyed to Chamberlain his " profoundest sympathy " for the " heroic though unsuccessful struggle," the Carpetbagger had made for " civil liberty and constitutional government." To Packard, Blaine gave assurance that his " heart and judgment " were both with him in the contest that he was waging " against great odds for the governorship that he holds by a title as valid as that which justly and lawfully seated Rutherford B. Hayes in the presidential chair."[29]

" I can't go the new policy," Blaine wrote to Whitelaw Reid " Every instinct of my nature rebels against it, and I feel an intuition amounting to an inspiration that the North in adopt-

[27] New York *Tribune*, March 9, 1877; *Nation*, XXIV (March 15, 1877), 154; Chicago *Tribune*, March 7, 1877.

[28] Garrison to Blaine, March 8, 1877, quoted in New York *Times*, March 12, 1877.

[29] Muzzey, *Blaine*, p. 132; Blaine to Editor of Boston *Herald*, quoted in New York *Tribune*, April 12, 1877.

ing it is but laying up wrath against the day of wrath. In any event its success means the triumph of the Democratic party against which I wage eternal war." Reid wished that Blaine "did not feel bound to oppose the Southern policy of the Administration," and the editor of the New York *Tribune* went straight to the essential point when he replied, "I have no sort of faith in a local government which can only be propped up by foreign bayonets; and if negro suffrage means that as a permanency then negro suffrage is itself a failure." [30]

What had caused Blaine to change his position from that he held during the campaign and to sour on the new experiment in the South? He and his most competent biographer argue that he turned against the administration because of his strong conviction that Hayes had betrayed the party.[31] But this was an ostensible reason, a pretext to cover the real cause of Blaine's estrangement from Hayes which actually resulted from a patronage dispute. Hayes' refusal to put Representative William P. Frye of Maine in the cabinet had antagonized Blaine who according to Hayes, had claimed the appointment "as a condition of good relations with me." [32]

But Chandler produced the most spectacular and devastating attack upon Hayes' policy. No other assault equalled his in open defiance of the administration. Within a few years Chandler was to change his mind, but in 1877 he was the most fierce opponent of the new departure in the South. In the form of a public letter to the Republicans of New Hampshire Chandler let go his full blast against the administration. He pointed out, and quite correctly too, that Hayes had been elected by a bloody shirt campaign that had differed in no respect, "as far as methods and utterances were concerned . . . from the campaigns of 1868 and 1872. But, according to Chandler, the dirty work had begun when Hayes turned over federal power in the South to "rebel" Democrats, when he glorified Confederate soldiers at the expense of Union men, and when he taunted the Negro with his helplessness, and shamefully boasted

[30] Blaine to Reid, April 12, 1877; Reid to Blaine, April 13, 1877, Royal Cortissoz, *The Life of Whitelaw Reid* (New York, 1921), I, 377-378.

[31] J. G. Blaine, *Twenty Years of Congress: from Lincoln to Garfield* (Norwich, Conn., 1884-1886), II, 595-596; Muzzey, *Blaine*, p. 134.

[32] Hayes Diary, March 14, 1877, Williams, *Diary and Letters*, III, 426; George F. Hoar, *Autobiography of Seventy Years* (New York, 1903), II, 7, 12.

of his betrayal of the freedmen. Such a course, argued Chandler, gave the death blow to the Republican party in the South and nearly destroyed it in the North, and to prevent a Democratic victory in 1880, he called upon Republicans to repudiate Hayes and his policy.[33]

Letters poured in upon the New Hampshire leader praising the stand he had taken. William Lloyd Garrison thought Chandler had never done " an act more honorable to the Republican party, or more in accordance with its registered promises and pledges," and Zach Chandler called the attack " the best thing of the kind I have ever seen; a ringing, slashing and yet truthful statement that will open the eyes of some people. The drifting policy must be abandoned or the party lost in the boundless sea of irresolution and contempt." [34] A Republican from New York thanked Chandler for his " just, honorable, and courageous stand " taken in reference " to the policy of that contemptible trator [sic] Hayes." From Ohio, a Republican wrote that Hayes had " forfeited his title as a Republican, but the party should not go under, *shake him*." Another Republican from Ohio admired Chandler's " *courage* and *nerve* " and labeled Hayes' action " as the most *shameful* transaction that a President was ever guilty of. He talks about Civil Service Reform, when he sold the Governorship of two Southern States, in order to be counted in as President." [35]

But not all was praise and support for Chandler. The *Nation*, a good friend of the new southern policy, charged that what Chandler had to say was a good indication of what all machine men were thinking, and that if Chandler, and men like him, had their way, " the campaign of 1896, or even of 1916, would also be conducted ' in no respects differently from the campaigns of 1868 and 1872.' " The Springfield *Republican* wondered, " What an ass Bill Chandler is," and George William Curtis of *Harper's Weekly* looked upon Chandler's letter as a " plain threat to attempt the discredit of the Presi-

[33] *Letters of Mr. William Chandler Relative to the So-Called Southern Policy of President Hayes* (Concord, N. H., 1878).

[34] Garrison to Chandler, January 29, 21, 1878, *Ibid.*, pp. 5, 38-48; Z. Chandler to Chandler, Richardson, Chandler, p. 219.

[35] George H. Fowler, New York City to Chandler, January 5, 1878; Edward Spear, Warren, Ohio to Chandler, December 31, 1877; W. F. Herrick, Wellington, Ohio to Chandler, March 1, 1878, in Wm. E. Chandler Papers.

dent's title if he does not yield to the spoils leaders." The Washington *Post* interpreted Chandler's move to mean that " as a Republican who does not think Hayes belongs in his seat I have merely undertaken to uproot the means by which he *went into* the White House." [36]

While Chandler's letter created an uproar in Washington, one of his friends in the capital pointed out that the principal query and the most natural one in this " patronage dependent atmosphere," was what good could come from it? [37] Yet the Stalwarts did hope to take some positive action to halt the new policy in the South. Some of Grant's friends urged that he be elected again in order to reverse Hayes' strategy and win back for the Republicans both South Carolina and Louisiana. Several months after Hayes took office, about 150 Republicans met in Washington to map a course of opposition to the President and his policy. They organized a national body, elected permanent officers, and made plans for setting up branches throughout the country. [38] Unsuccessful in enlisting the aid of Blaine the movement collapsed.

Also aroused and bitter about the new policy were many southern Republicans who were more affected by the new departure than any other element in the party. From Mississippi a Republican wrote that he was " never more perplexed and discouraged in my life than at the present time, and I cannot better describe the condition of the Republican party here than to say that it is in a panic and of leading Republicans than to say that they are both dazed and alarmed by the present attitude of affairs political," Another Republican from Mississippi who had " been on the go constantly . . . in Tennessee, Alabama, Georgia and Mississippi," and who had had " an excellent opportunity of observing the effects of the policy," felt that the intentions of the President may be " all right, honest and all that; but I would prefer that his intentions should be all wrong and his *acts* all right, sensible, and patriotic, rather than the exact reverse . . . a man with good

[36] *Nation*, XXVI (January 3, 1878), 1; Chandler to George Wm. Curtis, January 1, 1878, in Wm. E. Chandler Papers; Washington *Post*, February 1, 1878.

[37] S. W. Curriden to Chandler, December 31, 1877, in Chandler Papers.

[38] *Nation*, XXVII (August 22, 1878), 109; New York *Tribune*, May 26, 1877.

intentions," this writer said, "could not manage to blunder his party out of existence in nine months." A Republican from Georgia was so angry that he asked why Hayes couldn't "quickly die? Or if he insists upon following the example of Judas Iscariot in this respect, why can't he have the good sense which he manifested & go out and hang himself." [39] The Republican state committee of Mississippi actually adopted resolutions that formally dissolved the party in that state. But the *Nation* found this action had created "little sensation in Republican circles, the best party papers declaring it the most sensible thing that could have been done." That a party which claimed a majority of 30,000 voters should so quietly disband "is an unprecedented occurrence," observed the *Nation*, "and under other circumstances would have been a most remarkable one; but in fact, in Mississippi, as in South Carolina and Georgia . . . the Republican party of late had only two excuses for existence—troops and plunder—and when these were withdrawn . . . the natural result followed. Its dissolution is therefore a sign of returning political health which even party managers have the good sense to welcome." [40]

Chandler's unsparing attack upon Hayes seemed to give new life and new hope to southern Republicans, and they responded with a warm endorsement of what the New Hampshire Stalwart had done. "We all bless you here for your grand arraignment of Hayes and his co-traders," wrote a former United States Marshal and Republican leader from Louisiana. "I trust you will drive the knife to the hilt into the Presidential huckster." From Georgia, a Negro Republican told Chandler, "We are willing to suffer if such suffering shall be of any benefit to the cause which we all have so near to our hearts. But we do not wish to be betrayed, bound hand and foot, and turned over to the tender mercies of our enemies, and this, too, by the very men whose elevation to power was brought about, in great measure, through our instrumentality." The President of New Orleans University, a Negro, in praising Chandler's letter as "manly action" in behalf of the Republi-

[39] W. Robbins, Sardis, Mississippi to Garfield, March 30, 1877; Helen Atkins, Savannah, Georgia to Garfield, April 3, 1877, in Garfield Papers; R. B. Avery, Bay St. Louis to W. E. Stevens, January 10, 1878, in Wm. E. Chandler Papers.
[40] *Nation*, XXV (July 19, 1877), 34.

can party in the South, felt that his race could neither be coaxed or driven out of the Republican party, but when Hayes announced his policy, the heads of Negroes "sunk upon their breasts and they begin to ask if their [sic] is no hope." [41]

Hayes did not appear to be surprised or offended by the attacks made upon him and his policy. The press represented him as not being alarmed by the size and vigor of the hostility toward his southern policy. He was confident that the country would approve of it, if it turned out to be successful and contributed to the peace and prosperity of the country. While he regretted that some Republicans doubted the wisdom of his course, he did not believe his party would be united against him. When Chamberlain had attacked him in a Fourth of July speech, he dismissed the incident with a refusal to quarrel with those who questioned his soundness of judgment and honesty of motives. He blunted Ben Wade's antagonism by saying Wade was an old man and disappointed in some respects, and as for Chandler's letter, Hayes told a friend, "It does not seriously disturb me. There is no change in my view or purpose." [42]

Aware that some Republican leaders wished to organize an opposition to his southern policy, before he had barely gotten it under way, Hayes expressed regret that they should feel it a duty to differ from him, but he found no fault with them. "I respect the conviction of those who honestly differ from me but am indifferent to those who propose a malignant opposition," he was reported as saying, "because I cannot see that public duty leads me in the path they would mark for my official footsteps." In press interviews Hayes made it quite clear that he had no intention of starting a controversy with those Republicans who honestly differed with him. He gave them credit for sincerity of conviction and asked them to wait patiently for results. These, he maintained, would justify the wisdom of the new policy. And as he pointed out, should his policy fail to

[41] J. R. G. Pitkin, New Orleans, to Wm. E. Chandler, January 10, 1878; S. Cass Carpenter, Columbus, Georgia to Chandler, December 31, 1877; J. S. Bean, New Orleans to Chandler, December 31, 1877, Wm. E. Chandler Papers.
[42] New York *Tribune*, May 19, April 24, 1877; New York *World*, April 24, 1877; *Ohio State Journal*, July 6, 1877; Hayes to Bryan, December 27, 1877, in Hayes Papers.

achieve the objectives he sought, he would be the first to know and no one would have to ask for a change.[43]

Privately, though, Hayes worried about the attacks upon his policy. "I deeply feel for our good old Republicans," he told William Henry Smith. "Their minds are filled with doubts, and the future is not clear to them." If anything could be done "to soften this to the really good men involved, I will be glad to do it," he promised Smith. "The thing done is simply the only possible issue. It is for the best. It will be so regarded by all wise and good people sooner or later. I shall not forget my duty to the staunch Republicans." [44] To an Ohio newspaper friend, Hayes expressed his awareness of "how sore a trial this business is to staunch antislavery veterans. . . . I expect many to condemn. I shall not worry or scold if they do. I know they mean well. It is a comfort to know also that I mean well. It will, I trust," he added, "turn out that I am right. If not, I am a sound Republican still and always." [45]

Hayes wanted to remove race antagonisms, especially the political differences resting upon the color line, so that Republicans in the South would not need the protection of the Army. In his mind the use of the military in civil affairs was repugnant to the genius of American institutions and should be dispensed with if possible. He believed that his policy would give good government to the South and that it would secure the rights, interests, and safety of the Negroes. Hayes realized that opponents would possibly thwart him, but he was confident, and he thought it was his duty to carry out his new policy. As he told Bryan, "My theory of the Southern situation is this. Let the rights of the colored people be secured and the laws enforced only by the usual peaceful methods—by the action of the civil tribunals and wait for the healing influences of time and reflection to solve and remove the remaining difficulties. This will be a slow process." [46]

Part of Hayes' optimism and confidence came from the favorable reports and support he received in many quarters. The

[43] New York *Times*, April 16, 1877 for quotation; Chicago *Inter-Ocean*, April 19, 1877.

[44] Hayes to Smith, April 19, 22, 1877, in Hayes Papers.

[45] Hayes to Wm. D. Bickham, April 22, 1877, *Ibid*.

[46] Chicago *Tribune*, March 10, April 16, 1877; Hayes to Bryan, January 10, 1879, in Hayes Papers.

information he had from Tennessee and North Carolina persuaded him to believe the Republicans would carry these two states in 1880. Reports from South Carolina indicated that the Democratic party was folding up and that Wade Hampton would be elected governor on a Republican ticket.[47] " You are steadily growing stronger in the South," wrote Bryan to Hayes and again said Bryan, " You have done more for pacification and . . . more for the destruction of sectionalism . . . than any other Republican or any other person. . . . You have done more for the South than a Democrat in your position could have done." [48] Hayes seemed to agree with some of these conclusions when he told a friend in Ohio that " on the whole, the Southern policy is doing well. The implacables in Louisiana . . . are doing all they can to offend and disapprove the ' healers of strife ' but still we do more in the right direction." [49]

Hayes believed that many of the Stalwarts opposed him, because they resented his attempts to deprive them of control of the federal patronage. How to meet and overcome this type of resistance posed a serious and delicate problem for him. One way out was to " keep cool; to treat all adversaries respectfully and kindly," but at the same time in a way to satisfy them of his sincerity and firmness.[50] Believing that most of the " best people " agreed with him, Hayes used such tactics in the tug of war over his policy.

When Congress reconvened in the fall of 1877, the Stalwarts were upset by the apparent serenity at the White House. Some had come to Washington denouncing Hayes for breaking up the Republican party, and they expected him to be conscious of his offense and to have a humble and contrite look about him. But on the contrary they found him in excellent spirits and not willing to admit that he had destroyed anything. He asked all his accusers to cite specifically where he had cut loose from the Republican party. He inquired, without resentment, if the fault were his that some Republicans in Congress distrusted him and no longer identified themselves with him. He

[47] Baltimore *Sun*, May 9, 1877, in Hayes Papers.
[48] Bryan to Hayes, August 11, 1877, December 25, 1879, " Bryan-Hayes Correspondence," *Southwestern Historical Quarterly*, XXVII (1923-1924), 245; XXVIII (1924-1925), 165.
[49] Hayes to James Monroe, Oberlin, Ohio, July 3, 1877, in Hayes Papers.
[50] Hayes Diary, October 24, 1877, Williams, *Diary and Letters*, III, 449-450.

also raised the question of whether he was not trying to carry out the 1876 platform. Surely his party could not object on this point since it had appealed to the voters on this document, which he was willing to read to congressmen who went to the White House to remonstrate with him.[51]

A few days after the sessions began, a number of the most influential Republican members of Congress held a private conference at the home of John Sherman, the Secretary of the Treasury, and newspapers reported Jacob D. Cox of Ohio as the only one present who fully endorsed the new policy. The others would support it only with reservations.[52] Garfield came away from the meeting convinced that differences of opinions " in regards to the President's policy " were so great that " the prospects of a division in our party were very strong." [53] In view of such a possibility, Garfield, Republican leader in the House, could not risk calling a party caucus. Of this decision he had this to say later. " I held the role then of trying to protect our party from splitting, and being the acknowledged leader of the House I did it by keeping our people for six months from having a caucus except to elect officers. . . . The tendency of part of our party to assail Hayes and denounce him as a traitor and a man who was going to Johnsonize the party was very strong," added Garfield, " and his defenders were comparatively few." [54]

Others substantiated Garfield's conclusion that Hayes had few supporters in Congress. Senator George F. Hoar from Massachusetts listed himself, Henry L. Dawes from the same state, and Stanley Matthews from Ohio as the only cordial friends the President had in the Senate. Even Hayes recognized this when he desired that there should be more supporters for the administration among Republicans in Congress. " Why is not the best basis for harmony the Cincinnati platform [of 1876]? " he asked in his diary. " If differences exist as to its meaning, consult the Letter of Acceptance and the state platforms after the nomination and before the election." [55] An

[51] New York *Tribune*, October 25, 1877; *Nation*, XXVI (January 3, 1878), 4.
[52] New York *Tribune*, October 22, 1877; Garfield Diary, October 19, 1877, in Garfield Papers.
[53] Garfield Diary, October 20, 1877, in Garfield Papers.
[54] Smith, *Garfield*, II, 659.
[55] Hoar, *Autobiography*, II, 7; Hayes Diary, December 18, 1877, Williams, *Diary and Letters*, III, 456.

opportunity arose for Republicans in the House to endorse the new policy when Representative Robert M. Knapp moved for a vote commending Hayes' removal of the troops from the South, but the motion was lost in a parliamentary shuffle without ever placing Republicans on record.[56]

Yet Hayes was aware that public opinion, as represented by the press and private letters, strongly supported his course in the South. " Expressions of satisfaction from all parts of the country are most gratifying," he noted. " The press and the private correspondence of [W. K.] Rogers [private secretary] and of myself are full of it." [57] When Ohio Republicans nominated Stanley Matthews for Senator, Hayes regarded the action as an endorsement of " the policy of peace and home rule—of local self government." He believed that his selection as a member of the Peabody Education Fund Board proved that the "whole country" sanctioned his pacification measures. He told Garfield that every college president and every Protestant paper in the country approved of his administration. To Bryan, Hayes reported that " In New York the better class of citizens cordially approve. . . . But many of the political leaders are more bitter than ever." For his own satisfaction Hayes privately wrote, " good people approve of what I am trying to do. The Southern question seems to be on good footing." [58]

In spite of the hammering that Hayes took from some quarters he appeared to carry the Republican party with him on the issue of the southern policy. Opposition to it, as we have seen, was pretty largely confined to former abolitionists like Phillips and Garrison, to Stalwarts like Wade, Chandler, Logan, and Blaine who joined them, to Carpetbaggers and southern Republicans who lost political status and who went unrewarded when Hayes removed the troops. While these elements were perhaps the most vociferous ones, they were a minority in the Republican party. True, the Stalwarts dominated the Republican leadership in Congress, and could and did embarasss Hayes there, but since he had eliminated himself from consideration for a second term, he had little to fear from

---

[56] *Congressional Record*, 45th Congress, I Session, p. 815.

[57] Hayes Diary, March 14, 1877, Williams, *Diary and Letters*, III, 427.

[58] *Ibid.*, March 16, October 4, 7, 1877, 427, 443, 444-445; Garfield Diary, April 19, 1878, in Garfield Papers; Hayes to Bryan, December 27, 1877, in Hayes Papers.

them concerning his future political status, and could afford to push his policy to the end of his presidency.

As we have already seen, Republicans in all parts of the country had demanded a change from military Reconstruction, and when Hayes set out to do this and ran afoul of the Carpet-baggers and Stalwarts, Republicans in all parts of the country rallied to his side and cause. " I most heartily and sincerely hope you will be sustained by the Republican party, and all good men of all parties," wrote Lucius Fairchild, American Consul to Liverpool, to Hayes. " It is true that you will have a difficult path to tread," a Reconstruction governor told Hayes, " but the policy thus far indicated if firmly pursued, as I am sure it will be, will make peace between the sections, and will receive the approval of all good men." A Pennsylvanian reported that the Southern Question was " the great and all important one " of Hayes' administration, and what the inaugural contained on this matter met " the sincere approval of Republicans generally with whom I have conversed." From Tennessee came the observation that the sentiments of the inaugural were " quite universal with our people irrespective of party." [59]

When Carpetbaggers were up in arms about the new policy, they were told that its " conciliatory purpose and intent " did honor to the President and could not " wholly fail of favorable effect upon right thinking masses." When Blaine had assailed Hayes on the Senate floor, the Philadelphia *Evening Telegraph* pointed out Blaine had "made a mistake . . . a very great mistake. . . . Mr. Blaine is just about the worst man in the Republican party to come forward as the representative of the rule-or-ruin faction of the party for the purpose of bull-dozing Mr. Hayes into continuing the evil doings of Grant . . . the efforts of the Blaine-Morton-Cameron-Conkling faction to bull-doze him [Hayes] into giving us an aggravated continuation of Grantism," continued the *Telegraph*, " deserves only the sternest reprobation from all decent people." [60]

Among his own cabinet members Hayes had stout defenders to face up to the Stalwarts, and Evarts and Sherman appeared

[59] Fairchild to Hayes, March 7, 1877; W. W. Holden to Hayes, March 8, 1877; Charles Albright, Mauch Chunk to Hayes, March 8, 1877; N. E. Alloway, Nashville to Hayes, March 8, 1877, Hayes Papers.

[60] George Mavey, Washington, D. C. to Senator George E. Spencer, Alabama. March 8, 1877, *Ibid.*, Philadelphia *Evening Telegraph*, March 7, 1877.

in public as champions of the new southern policy. Speaking before the seventy-second annual dinner of the New England Society held in New York, which Hayes attended, Evarts emphatically declared that the administration meant to go on with its course, a statement hailed by cheers that literally shook the room.[61] At Mansfield, Ohio, in a major address, Sherman defended Hayes' policy not on the abrupt grounds of necessity but upon the broader one of right. Sherman argued that it was not merely necessary to take the troops out of the South, but it was right. He confessed sharing the feeling of disappointment found among many Republicans over the result in Louisiana, but he declared that " every step taken by President Hayes was right, in strict accordance with his constitutional duty, and from the highest motives of patriotism." Some people foolishly accused Hayes of abandoning the Negro and his rights, but Sherman believed the new policy would do more to secure the practical enforcement of these rights " than the employment of an army tenfold greater than the army of the United States." [62]

The *Nation* called Sherman's speech the most courageous word uttered by any leading Republican since " Packard and Chamberlain retired from business." A Negro from Ohio was quite pleased to learn that Hayes had not abandoned the Negro, for " Nineteen out of every twenty colored men I know believe that the Republican party wishes to unload them." Thurlow Weed wrote that he had never quite understood the Louisiana issue, but after Sherman's speech, both the Louisiana and South Carolina questions could be understood and would be approved by " tens of thousands of Republicans who could not see why States that had given their Electoral votes to a Republican candidate for President had not simultaneously elected their Republican candidates for Governor." [63]

From unexpected sources came support for Hayes. Senator Oliver P. Morton, old Radical leader from Indiana and an outspoken champion of the Negro and the Carpetbagger, in a long public letter to southern Republicans, professed not to despair

[61] New York *World*, December 23, 27, 1877; see also Washington *National Republican*, April 24, 1877 and Louisville *Courier-Journal*, April 24, 1877.

[62] Mansfield (Ohio) *Herald*, August 23, 1877, in Sherman Papers.

[63] *Nation*, XXV (August 23, 1877), 4; Robert Harlan to Sherman, August 20, 1877; Thurlow Weed to Shermann, August 18, 1877, Sherman Papers.

of Hayes' fidelity to orthodox Republicanism and minimized the fears that the President intended to destroy the party. Schuyler Colfax, Grant's Vice President, took a similar stand, and went on to characterize Hayes as the representative of his ideal of a good Republican.[64] Grant also lent his support. When interviewed in St. Louis in the spring of 1877 he unequivocally endorsed Hayes' policy. " I think it is a good policy," Grant declared. " I am very anxious to see this color-line divided, so that the question becomes more one of parties and less of color or race." Grant had expected the troops to be withdrawn and he would have done the same had he remained in office, for " neither the Chamberlain nor Packard Government " could have been sustained without the show of military authority and this in America was " very repugnant to the people." Among his friends the former President invariably spoke in defense of Hayes and his program. When he was on his tour abroad, Grant told a reporter, " If I were home I would give Mr. Hayes and his policy all the support I could, because the object aimed at is a noble one, and I hope he will succeed." He had no fears that Hayes would destroy the Republican party.[65]

One of the greatest turnabouts occurred when Colonel Robert Ingersoll, who had waved the bloody shirt in a furious manner in the 1876 campaign, endorsed the new policy. Ingersoll acknowledged that he had deliberately, during the hustings, attempted to arouse northern hostility toward southern whites and to strengthen the theory that the South should be treated as a conquered province. But following Hayes' inaugural, Ingersoll delivered lectures in the leading cities of the country in which he openly repudiated nearly every doctrine that he had stressed in the late campaign and instead recommended a policy of conciliation and kindness.[66] Benjamin Butler, old Radical leader from Massachusetts, and Benjamin Harrison, a future President, added their voices to the growing support of Hayes' policy. The failure of Republican state conventions in Iowa, New York, and Maine to sanction Hayes' policy was

[64] New York *Tribune*, May 26, 1877; Schuyler Colfax to Sherman, March 9, 1877, in Sherman Papers; Louisville *Courier-Journal*, March 17, 1877.

[65] Washington *National Republican*, April 7, 1877; Chicago *Tribune*, April 7, 1877; New York *Tribune*, July 10, September 26, 1877.

[66] New York *Times*, March 15, 1877; New York *Tribune*, March 15, May 29, 1877; Nation, XXIV (April 5, 1877), 203.

offset by approval in Republican state conventions in Ohio, Massachusetts, Maryland, Wisconsin, Pennsylvania, New Jersey, and Minnesota. The New Hampshire Republican convention received Chandler's letter without favor and adopted a platform that eulogized the Hayes administration. As for himself, Chandler became the object of much personal abuse at this convention, one of the delegates calling him a " political tramp." [67]

There were mass meetings of Republicans in northern and western cities like Schenectady, Albany, Brooklyn, New York, St. Paul, and Terre Haute, where hearty endorsements of Hayes' policy were adopted. The Union League Clubs of New York and Philadelphia, and the Republican Reform Club warmly praised the new departure in the South. Even among a few Carpetbaggers like Harrison Reed, former governor of Florida, and Senator Conover of the same state, Hayes found support for his policy.[68] Surprisingly enough some of the old abolitionist element supported that part of the new policy which had produced the greatest criticism and feeling of resentment—the removal of the troops. " Let the immediate consequences be good or bad . . . there was nothing else to be done," wrote Thomas Wentworth Higginson in a public letter. " For him, in time of peace, to keep troops in any State-house in order to determine a disputed claim to the Governorship, is a stretch of power so great that no State in the Union ought to tolerate it—so great that it ought to be resisted by every peaceful means." From the West an abolitionist wrote, " My judgment clearly approves the policy of Mr. Hayes, yet my feelings rebel. It is hard . . . to desert Chamberlain, Packard, and the freedmen, yet it is inevitable . . . the bayonet rule . . . the country will no longer permit. For Hayes to attempt it would be to doom his administration to disastrous failure." [69]

Among the influential press and journals of the North there was much support for the new policy, particularly after the removal of the troops amply demonstrated that one was under way. " We fully and unequivocally . . . support President

[67] New York *Tribune*, March 14, July 3, August 2, September 6, 12, 20, 21, 29, 1877, January 10, 1878; *Nation*, XXVI (January 10, 1878), 3.

[68] New York *Times*, March 11, 13, 15, 1877; Louisville *Commercial*, August 21, 1877; New York *Tribune*, March 9, 1877.

[69] *Harper's Weekly*, XXI (May 19, 1877), 382.

Hayes in his efforts at pacification," declared the *National Republican*. " We do not believe that peace can ever come by a perpetuation of carpet-bag rule . . . and in supporting the policy of the President it [*Republican*] does not admit that it has deserted the Republican party in a single instances." The Chicago *Tribune* thought it was " folly . . . to charge upon President Hayes a desertion of the Republican party in the South, and it is false to say that the negroes are no better protected when the carpetbaggers were ousted that they were before." The New York *Tribune* felt that in recalling the troops, Hayes had put " an end to a great scandal and a great danger. . . . Bayonets will no longer hold it [the South] down. Carpet-bag devices will no longer fetter it," and the President had not turned the " colored man over to the mercies of the most malignant enemies of the race." [70]

The New York *Times* found it " satisfactory to recognize the declining importance of the Southern Question or rather of its old and irritating aspects." The *Nation* expected the end of Reconstruction would mean the end of the " Solid South," and would bring a halt to the policy of the President playing the role of a " Great Father " to southern Negroes. " The principle of the President's Southern policy is not only wise and patriotic, but it has undoubtedly the cordial support of the best sentiment in the country," stated *Harper's Weekly*. " It is one in which we most heartily concur. It is based upon the fundamental principle of equal rights. It proposes to abandon nobody and to surrender nothing." [71] In general the northern press and literary magazines like *Scribner's* and the *Atlantic* strongly approved Hayes' southern policy.

The new departure in the South also had firm friends among the business men, who were most unhappy about the economic effects that military Reconstruction had had upon the South. Hundreds of letters from anxious business men poured in on

[70] Washington *National Republican*, April 16, 1877; see also April 11, 21-23, 27, 1877; Chicago *Tribune*, April 27, 1877; see also April 3, 7, 11, 13, 14, 17, 18, 20, 23, 25, 26, 27, 1877; New York *Tribune*, April 2, 5, 24, 1877; see also April 6, 23, 27, May 1, 1877.

[71] New York *Times*, April 11, 1877; *Nation*, XXIV (March 15, April 5, 26, 1877), 154, 156, 202, 241, 244; *Harper's Weekly*, XXI (April 14, 1877), 282; see also (March 24, 31, April 7, 21, May 5, 12, 19, 26, 1877), 222, 242, 262, 302, 342, 362, 382, 402.

Hayes applauding his actions in the South, condemning the party opposition that had developed to his policy, telling him that the "better class of men" supported him and that the country needed the reconciliation of the two sections.[72] Business men told Hayes he had "started right & bravely," that "the business men of the country are with you," to "Hold the Fort," to "Stand firm," and that if "radical politicians howl it is no sign that the heart of the nation does not beat in full harmony with your efforts to bring about union-peace & harmony. You will have the moral support of all true patriots in the new departure."[73]

In New York jubilant business men of both parties staged large meetings in Wall Street and at Cooper Institute where they adopted resolutions strongly supporting the new policy. Business men gathered in other cities to express their thanks and encouragement for the historic steps Hayes was taking, and various exchanges, boards of trade, and Chambers of Commerce meeting in the South and West praised the new policy as it unfolded.[74] The leading business journal in the country, the New York *Commercial and Financial Chronicle*, concluded that the abandonment of military Reconstruction became the first step in a return to prosperity for the South and the entire nation, and that business men could "count upon the Southern question as finally put out of the way."[75] All this being the case Hayes could well agree with the observation of one of his intimates that "the people, the business interests are solid with your administration."[76]

The most paradoxical aspect of the entire controversy over the new departure in the South was the reaction of Negro Republican leaders in this section. Apprehensive, puzzled, disillusioned and even angry, they, for the most part, supported Hayes. This is all the more surprising in view of the fact that

[72] Hayes Papers, March-April, 1877.

[73] Adam Ayer, Boston to Hayes, March 9, 1877, M. D. L. Nims, Boston to Hayes, March 7, 1877; Wall Street meeting to Hayes, March 8, 1877; D. L. King, Cleveland to Hayes, March 9, 1877, in Hayes Papers.

[74] New York *Tribune*, March 9, 12, 1877; Louisville *Commercial*, March 13, October 11, 1877; New York *Times*, March 10, 11, 1877; Louisville *Courier-Journal*, March 17, 1877.

[75] *Commercial and Financial Chronicle*, XXIV (March 17, 1877), 236-237; (April 7, 1877), 309.

[76] William Henry Smith to Hayes, March 22, 1877, in Hayes Papers.

they were the ones most affected by the new policy and in view of the great pains that some of their northern friends took to point this out to them and to stir up their resentment against Hayes.

At the very beginning of this period there were certain ominous developments, so far as the Negro was concerned, that held out little hope and encouragement to him. Hayes had removed the troops, had restored " home rule " to southern whites, and had begun his experiment of conciliating the dominant group in the South. When he talked to the freedmen at Atlanta on his tour of the South, Hayes told them he thought " their rights and interests would be safer if the great mass of intelligent white men were let alone by the general governmnt." He pointed out that he had been trying this experiment for six months, " and in his opinion for no six months since the war had there been so few outrages and invasions of their rights, persons, and homes as in the last six months." [77]
While such a statement provoked " immense applause," it also produced a great uneasiness among Negroes over either the President's naiveness or his ignorance. Nor was this disquietude abated when such a staunch northern champion of the freedman as the *Nation*, following the settlements of the disputed elections in South Carolina and Louisiana, predicted that with the break-up of the last " sham " government in the South, the Negro would disappear from the national political scene. " Henceforth, the nation, as a nation will have nothing more to do with him," and as a ward of the country he could no longer be singled out for special guardianship or peculiar treatment.[78]

As Hayes unfolded his plans, some northern friends of the freedman tried to arouse him against the President. James Redpath, a former abolitionist, correspondent for the New York *Tribune* in the Civil War, and John Brown's fellow conspirator and biographer, in an open letter printed widely in southern newspapers, counselled Negroes to join the Democratic party on the best terms they could obtain, for they could expect nothing from Hayes, who now preferred their old masters. Wendell Phillips told Negroes that in view of what

[77] *Nation*, XXV (September 27, 1877), 187.
[78] *Ibid.*, XXIV (April 5, 1877), 202.

had happened, he could not blame them for leaving Republican ranks.[79]

But northern Negro friends of the administration worked hard to prevent their southern associates from leaving the Republican party. James Pointdexter, Negro leader from Ohio, said that he had favored the President's policy from the start, that it was not an abandonment of the rights of the colored men in the South, and anyone who expected them to stampede from the Republican party on account of the policy were misjudging the Negro. Other Negroes from the President's home state publicly defended his course and some sent a circular letter to their southern brethern encouraging them to aid in the implementation of the new policy, and in New Jersey, the Negro Republican State Committee approved a resolution of confidence in the notives that guided Hayes in his southern policy.[80] John Langston, then acting President of Howard University, publicly called the new policy a wise one and one that sustained the promises of the Republican party and that met the demands of the public. He placed the " fullest confidence " in Hayes and predicted that the Negro would continue to be suitably recognized and protected.[81] In view of Langston's position, a number of prominent Negroes from various states wrote to him and voiced deep concern about the purposes of the administration toward them. As no other Negro had been as pronounced, thus far, in support of Hayes' policy, they were warranted in the belief that Langston had assurances of good intentions of the President toward the colored man, of which they knew nothing. " While we have all along had abiding confidence in the President beyond the general statements contained in his inaugural," they wrote, " we have no indication whatever of the intentions of the Administration in regard to the colored people of the country, and you will agree that since the advent of this Administration many things have occurred calculated to shake, if not destroy, the confidence of the newly-enfranchised people." In reply to these queries Lang-

[79] Chicago Inter-Ocean, April 18, 1877.
[80] Ohio State Journal, July 19, September 17, 1877; W. H. West to Sherman, August 22, 1877, in Sherman Papers; Wilmington, N. C. Post, June 1, 1877; Hayes Papers, April 2, 1877.
[81] New York Tribune, April 18, 1877; Wilmington Post, May 18, 1877.

ston wrote that he had " received from his [Hayes'] own lips the most positive assurances that it was the purpose of his administration to secure by any and every legitimate means within its power and control, our protection, promotion and recognition." [82] Other Negro leaders in the South joined Langston in support of the new policy. M. W. Gibbs of Arkansas, John Thomas Rapier of Alabama, J. Willis Menard of Louisiana, Robert Smalls of South Carolina, and John R. Lynch of Mississippi pledged their support of the new policy and urged their race in the South to sustain Hayes until they had stronger reasons for not doing so.[83]

Various Negro groups in the South threw their support behind Hayes. Delegations of Negroes from Florida and Virginia, from the African Methodist Episcopal Church and from the Colored Baptist State Convention of Louisiana either called upon the President directly or sent him resolutions endorsing his new policy in the South. Negroes not dependent upon patronage, such as the President of Hampton Normal and Agricultural Institute in Virginia, were delighted with Hayes' policy and regarded it as the only solution to the " Southern Question." Perhaps many southern negroes felt as one group did in Nashville when they told Hayes he had not forsaken them. " This we do not believe," they wrote " though at times we have felt apprehensions distrustful: but . . . we heartily . . . assure you our sympathy and support." [84]

What explanation can be given for the manner in which Negro politicos commended the new policy and appealed to their race to cling to the Republican party? Did they actually look to Hayes to drive the whites out of their party and leave the patronage and control to them? Hardly could they have hoped for such a development in view of Hayes' refusal to turn over the patronage to leaders like Bruce in Mississippi and Elliott in South Carolina, and when he abandoned a Negro leader like C. C. Antoine, former Lieutenant Governor of

[82] Washington *National Republican*, June 9, 1877.

[83] Louisville *Commercial*, March 18, 1877; New York *Times*, April 4, 19, 1877; Chicago *Inter-Ocean*, April 11, 1877; New York *Tribune*, January 11, 1877; Robert Smalls to Hayes, May 9, 1877, in Hayes Papers.

[84] *Ohio State Journal*, July 30, 1877; New York *Tribune*, March 24, 1877; New Orleans *Republican*, March 16, 1877; S. C. Armstrong to Garfield, March 19, 1877, in Garfield Papers; Hayes Papers, July 25, 1877.

Louisiana, to such an extent that Antoine's wife begged the President to give her husband some kind of position since they were practically destitute, and on some days they had "not a nickel in the house." [85]

Negro leaders supported Hayes primarily because of the personal recognition they received from the President. While Hayes denied to them control of the patronage in their states, he did reward most of them with a personal appointment, with a few like Langston and Frederick Douglass receiving important posts such as Minister to Haiti and Marshal of the District of Columbia. This notorious device maintained the fiction of Republican recognition of the Negro voters and also served to muzzle the protests of their leaders. Patronage, or a lack of it, many times determined the attitude of Negro leaders toward Hayes and his policy. A Negro politico from Georgia under consideration for the post of Deputy Collector at Savannah wrote to Hayes commending " the wise policy you have inaugurated toward the Southern people believing it to be the best evolved by any statesman since the war," and having " no apprehension of evil resulting to the Colored race by the policy adopted." Failing to obtain this patronage plum, this same Negro leader expressed bitter disappointment and chagrin with Hayes and a policy that was " tantamount to the declaration that no ' Negro need apply.' " [86]

Negroes also supported Hayes' policy, because they regarded it as an experiment which would be dropped if it failed to produce the desired results. The President had promised various colored delegation that he would change his strategy quickly if it resulted in the curtailment of their rights.[87] When he failed to do this, Negroes became more openly hostile to him, but even then they were reluctant to appear to be leaving the party. They shrunk from the idea of independent action. Moreover many of them looked for a return to the policy of military interference in the South once Hayes had left office, and large numbers of them anticipated the nomination of Grant in 1880.

[85] Mrs. C. C. Antoine to Hayes, August 18, 1878, in Hayes Papers.
[86] Edwin Belcher, Augusta, Georgia to Hayes, May 18, 1877, *Ibid.*; Edwin Belcher to Sherman, October 7, 1879, June 29, 1880, in Sherman Papers.
[87] Louisville *Courier-Journal*, March 15, 1877; Washington *National Republican*, June 9, 1877; New Orleans *Republican*, March 16, 1877.

They apparently trusted the ex-President to protect them in full enjoyment of their rights despite his surrender of one reconstructed state government after another to the Democrats. Special Agents of the Treasury Department reported to Secretary John Sherman that Grant's name stirred up more enthusiasm among Negroes in the South than any other Republican save that of Lincoln.[88]

While Hayes had not flinched before the Stalwart and Carpetbagger blows, he was most sensitive about the charges that he had forsaken the Negro. Nothing hurt or troubled him so much as the accusation that he had abandoned the freedman in the South. With a patrician attitude, Hayes wanted the Negroes to look up to him as their friend and protector, and he believed that the new policy would allow the colored population to find friends among southern whites. From speaking to whites on his tour of the South, Hayes had become convinced that they were sincerely anxious to give the blacks their full civil and political rights.[89] But Hayes had also reached the conclusion that southern whites would do this only when the national government stopped interfering with their state governments, and this is what prompted his remarks at Atlanta. Hayes hoped to have the white South accept Negro suffrage, and he received pledges to this effect from leading southerners, but in removing the troops he curtailed the freedom of Negro suffrage, a result he should have anticipated.

[88] E. S. Hamlin to Sherman, September 5, 1879, in Sherman Papers.
[89] Hayes expressed this opinion in a conversation with Republican Congressman John E. Leonard of Louisiana, Louisville *Commercial*, October 3, 1877.

CHAPTER IV

COOPERATION WITH THE INDEPENDENTS

The turnover in Republican administrations over the next four years brought no change in Republican hopes and desires about winning in the South, but it did bring sharp and dramatic variations in policy. While Garfield and Arthur continued Hayes' efforts to spread Republicanism in the South, they almost completely abandoned his strategy, because they regarded it as unworkable and as a dismal failure. They used their own tactics, and they pursued them in the same spirited manner as had their predecessor.

The shocking assassination of Garfield within a few months after he had taken office brought a sudden end to his plans about the South, but not before he had had time to discuss them and to put them into partial operation. From his point of vantage as Hayes' close political associate and Republican leader in the House, Garfield had come away with an excellent understanding of how the new departure in the South had worked and how the party had reacted to it. This valuable experience along with his own in Congress with southern Democrats led him to forsake Hayes' pacificatory policy and to distrust strongly any possibility of real conciliation of the South through such an approach. " I have no doubt that the President's position had been productive of good," Garfield wrote to an intimate friend in 1879 about Hayes' policy, " for it had clearly demonstrated, more clearly, the real character of the Southern people than the old policy could have done." [1]

While Garfield had expressed the opinion following the election of 1878 that the " man who attempts to get up a political excitement in this country on the old sectional issues will find himself without a party and without support," [2] he and party chieftains did exactly this in the campaign of 1880. The Republican platform had declared that the dangers of a " Solid

[1] Garfield to Burke Hinsdale, May 20, 1879, Mary L. Hinsdale, ed., *Garfield-Hinsdale Letters* (Ann Arbor, 1949), p. 417.
[2] Buck, *Road to Reunion*, p. 111.

133

South " could only be averted by " a faithful performance of
every promise which the Nation has made to the citizen. . . .
The Solid South must be divided by the peaceful agencies of the
ballot, and all opinion there must find free expression, and
to this end the honest voter must be protected against terrorism, violence or fraud." In his letter accepting the nomination
Garfield asked that " every elector shall be permitted freely and
without intimidation to cast his lawful ballot . . . and have it
honestly counted," for " it is certain that the wounds of the
war cannot be completely healed . . . until every citizen, rich
or poor, white or black, is secure in the free and equal enjoyment of every civil and political right guaranteed by the Constitution and the laws. . . . The most serious evils which now
afflict the South," concluded Garfield, " arise from the fact that
there is not such freedom and toleration of political opinion and
action that the minority party can exercise an effective and
wholesome restraint upon the party in power." [3] The Republican Campaign Text Book for 1880 gave more than half of its
space to " bloody shirt " themes, and *Harper's Weekly*, which
had shifted from the bloody shirt to conciliation when Hayes removed the troops, now resumed its old cudgels. Garfield who
in the beginning did manifest a desire to campaign on the
financial issue soon retreated into the shelter of the war record
issue, and before election day, Republicans were declaring the
South to be the major issue of campaign.[4] And when the campaign was all over Garfield explained it to another party chieftain in this manner that, " The distrust of the Solid South and
of adverse financial legislation have been the chief factors in
the contest. I think also the country wanted to rebuke the
attempt of the Democrats to narrow the issue to the low level
of personal abuse." [5]

There was considerable speculation among Republicans over
what Garfield would do about the Southern Question when he
became President. Among officials in Washington there was a
strong belief that he would attempt to break up the one party
system in the South by strengthening the Republican organiza-

[3] Edward McPherson, *A Handbook of Politics for 1880* (Washington, 1880),
pp. 19, 192.
[4] Buck, *Road to Reunion*, p. 113.
[5] Garfield to John Sherman, November 4, 1880, in Sherman Papers.

tions there and by raising the low level of their leadership. The view also prevailed that Garfield was not interested in reviving the Whig party or converting southern Democrats to Republicanism by federal patronage. There was a general feeling in the capital that Hayes' policy was an epoch gone by, and that Garfield had no intentions of resurrecting it. The Stalwarts contended that Garfield would no longer tolerate a policy of concession to southern whites, but that he would demand a full, free, and honest count in the elections in the South.[6] Southern Republicans also felt that Garfield's election meant a return to Reconstruction days. One from Arkansas reported that it was " the General conclusion throughout the State that the incoming administration will be Strictly Radical," while a Carpetbagger from Tennessee called Garfield's victory " glorious, and . . . especially so to us ' carpetbaggers,' for it ensures to us—at least in this section—peace and tranquility not only for four years but I believe indefinitely." But when a southern Republican called on Garfield and demanded to know whether his administration would be a Stalwart one, the President lost his temper, objected to being lectured to and having his Republicanism questioned, and the visitor left sooner than he intended.[7]

Months before his inauguration, Garfield, privately but clearly, revealed his intention of abandoning the pacificatory policy toward southern Democrats. In his opinion the " final cure " for the " Solid South " lay in the education of its youth and development of its business interests. But since both of these things required time, the country was likely to have a Southern Question for many years to come. No speedy cure was possible. Patronage to the Democrats had been tried and had proved a " dreary failure," for " rebel Democrats " appointed to office by Republicans took one of the two courses-either they suffered complete ostracism by their neighbors, or they became more fierce assailants of the Republican party to keep themselves in good standing at home. In fact the South accepted all patronage at the hands of a Republican administra-

<hr>

[6] New York *Tribune*, March 19, 1881; Louisville *Commercial*, November 25, 1880.

[7] B. F. Hobbs, Arkansas to Sherman, February 7, 1881, in Sherman Papers; W. P. Chamberlain, Knoxville to Garfield, November 3, 1880; Garfield Diary, March 9, 1881, in Garfield Papers.

tion as a confession of Republican weakness and as a sign of its own superiority.[8]

Garfield's doubt of the political efficacy of giving office to southern Democrats extended to that of giving posts to southern Republicans who had the respect and confidence of their communities. " I am not sure that the appointment of Southern Republicans, however worthy, to prominent places is treated by the Solid South as any favor to that section," observed Garfield. " I do not know a better way to treat that people than to let them know that this is a modern free government, and only men who believe in it, and not in feudalism, can be invited to act in Administering it. Then give the South, as rapidly as possible, the blessings of general education and business enterprise and trust to time and these forces to work out the problem." A few days later Garfield again expressed the idea that " Time is the only cure for the Southern difficulties. In what shape it will come, if it come at all, is not clear." [9]

Garfield began to reverse Hayes' policy of conciliating southern whites in a number of ways. Carpetbaggers found him more willing than Hayes to listen to their advice and more amenable to their suggestions in strategy in the South. This was especially true in the cases of former Governor Chamberlain of South Carolina and Stephen W. Dorsey, former United States Senator from Arkansas, who had played a leading role in bringing the pivotal state of Indiana into the Republican column in 1880. Garfield regarded Dorsey as " a man of great ability and with strong and decisive views of the merits of men," and he told Chamberlain, " I shall expect and need the support of all who have special knowledge of Southern affairs and I shall have occasion hereafter, beyond doubt . . . to gain your advice and knowledge in particular matters which will arise. I urge you to give me your advice at all times, and assure you, you will not annoy me by so doing." [10]

Either because of his own painful experience or a sincere change of heart, Chamberlain actually pressed upon Garfield pretty much of what Hayes had tried to do, and the exchange

[8] Garfield to Hinsdale, December 30, 1880, in Garfield Papers.
[9] Garfield to Hinsdale, December 30, 1880, in Garfield Papers, Garfield to Hinsdale, January 11, 1881, Hinsdale, *Garfield-Hinsdale Letters*, pp. 478-479.
[10] Garfield Diary, December 14, 1880; Garfield to Chamberlain, February 3, 1881, in Garfield Papers.

of letters reveals some of Garfield's ideas about redeeming the South and some of the problems then facing any Republican President in that part of the country. Putting behind him the bitter attacks he made upon Hayes' policy, Chamberlain urged Garfield to drop all party leaders in the South tainted with Reconstruction and to embrace those who had the esteem of southern whites. Chamberlain argued that partisan zeal, services, courage, and fortitude in standing up for the party should not alone qualify a man for office in the South unless he was also honest, capable, and enjoyed a good reputation in his own community. With such a policy, a beginning could be made toward building a new Republican organization in the South capable of giving good local government, a prerequisite for party victory. Chamberlain warned though that too many Republicans were ready to aid the cause of any one who broke with the Democratic party in the South, regardless of the merits of the case, and used Mahone's movement in Virginia as a good illustration of what he meant. To countenance Mahone was to betray and dishonor the Republican party and the cause of good government. " Better by far aid the regular Democracy of Virginia," wrote Chamberlain, " who on this issue are comparatively honorable." [11]

In response to these recommendations, Garfield pointed out that he had " no faith in any sudden cure for our troubles in that direction [the South]. Nothing but wise and right methods, pursued patiently during a series of years, can give us free suffrage and its necessary complement, good local government." While he agreed that Chamberlain's " method . . . of building up a sound Republican party in the South by excluding from positions all unworthy persons is unquestionably a good one, the antagonisms and jealousies which have so abounded among our friends in the South [make] the selection of such officers . . . very difficult." Garfield wondered whether Chamberlain's analysis of the situation in the South covered the " apparent inexpungable hostility of the Southern Democrats to the Republican party of the nation? If the South treated the national administration with the respect it deserves they would greatly modify and soften the feeling of our northern people," wrote

[11] Chamberlain to Garfield, December 28, 1880, January 24, 1881, *Ibid.*

Garfield, "but they pursue the Republicans in Congress with the same spirit which led them to denounce the local Republican governments in the South." The Southern Question was receiving Garfield's earnest attention, "as you will see more fully by and by, and I may add," he told Chamberlain, "that your views . . . coincide with mine. . . . I am . . . in favor of a policy toward the South of reasonable confidence and most hearty good will, but I agree with you in regarding the action of the national administration in all Southern appointments as deserving more care and stricter principles than seemed to have marked some past administrations, and I am ready to say explicitly that I agree fully with you in your views of Mahone and his party." [12]

Negro Republicans in the South also sought a change in policy. Early in January, 1881, a group of their leaders from South Carolina, Georgia, Texas, and North Carolina headed by R. B. Elliott of South Carolina, called upon Garfield at his home in Mentor, Ohio where they asked him to give up the policy of appointing men in the South who were not in sympathy with Republican principles and who used their position to hinder the enforcement of laws passed for the protection of all citizens. These Negro leaders wanted Garfield to ignore those Republican politicians in the South who had no following and who represented no one but themselves, for such appointments only had the effect of weakening the party. These southern Negroes also pointed out that their race enjoyed citizenship in name but not in fact. Southern whites not only questioned the Negro's right to vote but denied it by force and subterfuge. Unable to redress their grievances through the courts, Negroes looked to the party that had emancipated them to raise them from their oppression.[13]

While Garfield promised the Negro leaders to give careful consideration to their problems, especially to the status of their race in the South, he pointed out that no law could confer and maintain for long, equality of citizenship not upheld by a reasonable degree of culture and intelligence. Garfield told the Negro leaders that education offered the final solution to their

[12] Garfield to Chamberlain, January 15, 1881, February 3, 1881, *Ibid.*
[13] New Orleans *Louisianian*, January 22, 1881; Wilmington, N. C. *Post*, January 23, 1881.

plight, but that this was not entirely the responsibility of the state or national government. Negro parents must help in every way, a bit of advice which, according to the New York *Age*, leading Negro newspaper of the North, meant telling the Negro to obtain "Webster's Blue Black spelling book."[14]

Garfield's advice to the Negro leaders reflected the changing attitude on the part of the North toward the freedman that we have already noted. As we have already seen, except for the Republican party interest in the Negro vote, there was not much concern among most northerners about helping Negroes. Garfield himself was somewhat pessimistic about the future of the Negro and during the election dispute of 1876 he privately told a friend, "The future of the Negro is a gloomy one unless some new method can be introduced to adjust him to his surroundings. His labor is indispensable to the prosperity of the South. His power to vote is a mortal offense to his late masters. If they control it, it will be not only a wrong to him but a dangerous increase of their power. If he votes against them, as he almost universally inclines to do, he will perpetuate the antagonism which now bears such baneful fruits."[15] Three years later, participating in a symposium on Negro suffrage, Garfield expressed some reservations about the Negro vote, "Possibly a plan of granting suffrage gradually as the negro became more intelligent would have been wiser," Garfield wrote in 1879," but the practical difficulties of such a plan would have been very great." Yet he did conclude that "on every ground of private right, of public justice, and national safety, the negro ought to have been enfranchised. For the same reasons, strengthened and confirmed by our experience, he ought not to be disfranchised."[16]

In the same symposium Blaine argued that the disfranchisement of the Negro was a political impossibility under any circumstances short of revolution, and he also stated the belief that the Negro ought to have been enfranchised. "And, if the question were again submitted to the judgment of Congress, I would vote for suffrage in the light of experience with more

[14] *Ibid.*; New York *Age*, April 13, 1889.
[15] Garfield to Hinsdale, December 4, 1876, Hinsdale, *Garfield-Hinsdale Letters*, p. 345.
[16] "Ought the Negro To Be Disfranchised? Ought He To Have Been Enfranchised?" *North American Review*, 128 (March, 1879), 246, 250.

confidence than I voted for it in the light of an experiment." [17]
When Garfield had asked Blain to read his article for the
symposium, Blaine thought it had taken all the ground from
under him by making all the strong points which he had
planned to use in his summing up. "This seemed to me altogether childish," Garfield noted in his diary. "My short article
of 18 pages has certainly not exhausted the subject. It is apparent to me that Blaine cares more about the glory of replying
to these men that about having the cause of negro enfranchise-
ment defended." [18]

In his inaugural address Garfield gave great prominence to
the supremacy of the nation and its laws; criticized southern
whites for opposing the freedom of suffrage and bluntly stated
that to prohibit Negroes from voting was "a crime, which if
persisted in, will destroy the Government itself." [19] For his
southern member of the cabinet, to head the Navy Department,
he picked, after a long search, William Henry Hunt, a native
white Republican who had allied himself with the Carpetbagger governments in Louisiana during Reconstruction and
who had been with Packard, at the time of the siege, in the
state house. Hunt retained this post until Arthur in the spring
of 1882 sent him as Minister to Russia. Southern Republicans
regarded the choice of Hunt as an earnest indication of what
Garfield meant to do in the South, and a leading party newspaper in this section called the new Secretary "a Republican
of the most approved sort. . . . It is so much better treatment
than anything southern Republicans had reason to expect that
they have been brought into good temper." [20]

Hayes had strongly urged Garfield to take a southerner into
the Cabinet regarding "it as of great importance that you
should have at least one," but Dorsey doubted the wisdom of
such a move for the reason that a southerner would be difficult
to handle and the appointment would not conciliate the South. [21]
There was even some talk about giving a post in the Cabinet
to a Negro, particularly Bruce of Mississippi, and one of Gar-

[17] Ibid., 225-231.
[18] Garfield Diary, January 23, 1879, in Garfield Papers.
[19] Richardson, Messages and Papers, VI, 4597-4598.
[20] Wilmington Post, March 13, 1881.
[21] Hayes to Garfield, December 16, 1880; Garfield Diary, December 14, 1880,
in Garfield Papers.

field's intimates predicted that this would win more support from the freedman than "a hundred negro marshals or Collectors of Internal Revenue." [22] Before he had finally chosen Hunt, Garfield had had a difficult time finding a southern Republican to head an executive department. "The southern member still eludes me," he told Blaine and John Hay in January, 1881. "one by one the southern roses fade. Nearly every name which I have considered has suffered some eclipse—total or partial. Do you know a Magnolia blossom that will stand our northern climate?" As late as a month before the inauguration he was still looking for a satisfactory southerner and reported that his search "thus far has not been fruitful in results." [23]

In spite of what Garfield had told Chamberlain about patronage in the South he set out to change Hayes' policy here. Since southern Republicans had little or no representation in Congress, Garfield laid down the rule that appointments would be made on the recommendations of the state chairmen whom he would recognize as the official head of the party in their respective states.[24] In one matter he did follow Hayes when he continued the notorious practice of giving office to a few Negro leaders so as to maintain the fiction that the Republican party rewarded the colored man. For example Robert Elliott of South Carolina became a Special Agent of the Treasury Department, Frederick Douglass the Recorder of Deeds in Washington, ex-Senator B. K. Bruce of Mississippi Register of the Treasury, and John Langston, Minister to Haiti. When a delegation of Negroes from North Carolina called on Garfield late in June, 1881 to protest against an unequal distribution of federal patronage in their state, he told them that while he sympathized with them, he followed the recommendation of the party leaders and whenever an opportunity arose he recognized the colored race.[25]

But Garfield's most pressing problem in the South was the ticklish political situation in Virginia, the handling of which

[22] George W. Carter, Washington, D. C. to Garfield, February 4, 1881, *Ibid.*
[23] Garfield to Blaine, January 24, 1881; to John Hay, January 25, 1881; to Senator George F. Edmunds of Vt., February 2, 1881, *Ibid.*
[24] New York *Age* disclosed this on September 8, 1886, when it accused Arthur of breaking his promise to follow Garfield's rule.
[25] Wilmington *Post*, June 19, 1881.

produced his sharpest break with Hayes' policy. As has already been pointed out, William Mahone had organized and assumed leadership of the Readjusters in this state who called for a scaling down of the state debt and who championed more liberal appropriations for schools and a number of social and economic measures, including better treatment for Negroes. Mahone's foes in the South and the financial interests in the northeast denounced his economic policy as a repudiation of the state debt. Actually he demanded a shifting to West Virginia, which had separated itself from Virginia, one third of the debt and a refunding of the remainder at lower interest rates. Mahone had also become personally dissatisfied with the regular Democrat organization in Virginia. During the depression of the seventies his railroad, the Norfolk and Western had fallen into the hands of a receivership. Added to this mishap was his setback at the Democratic state convention in 1877, where a combination of his opponents, defeated his gubernatorial aspirations, a situation which had aroused him to become an Independent. Supported by neither the regular party machine, nor by the upper economic and social classes, the Readjuster party swept Virginia in the state elections of 1879, winning 80 of the 140 seats in the state legislature.

Mahone's victory represented a test case for a new Republican policy in the South, for what had happened in Virginia might well be duplicated throughout the South. Other would-be Mahones had risen or were rising, and a fusion of Virginia Republicans with Mahone would test the fruits of a policy of cooperation with the Independents in the South, since Mahone, with his state ticket up for reelection in 1881, had promised to act with the administration provided the Republicans in Virginia threw in their lot with him. Powerful support of a Republican-Readjuster alliance came from white Republican leaders in the South and from northern Stalwarts like Senator Don Cameron of Pennsylvania, who expressed the opinion that Mahone could do more for the Negro and the Republican party than the federal government could do with a standing army.[26]

[26] James D. Brady to Garfield, November 4, 1880, in Garfield Papers; J. F. Lewis to Garfield, January 21, 1881, in Sherman Papers; J. F. Lewis to John Tyler, Jr., January 21, 1881; John Tyler, Jr. to Hayes, January 31, 1881, in Hayes Papers. Brady was the Collector at Petersburg; Lewis, the Republican

From the time of his election until his untimely death, Garfield was under every kind of conceivable pressure from various Republican quarters to sanction an alliance between Virginia Republicans and Mahone. Late in December, 1880, Cameron led a delegation to see Garfield and brought a statement from Mahone which gave his views on the debt question in Virginia.

Garfield regarded Mahone's declaration as " ex parte " but he wanted to hear the other side and see what Republicans said about it. As for a bankrupt state, one could only ask it to run the government economically, sustain its schools, and apply the remainder of its revenues as " the maximum of reasonable taxation to its debts. If that is Mahone's position, followed up in good faith," Garfield remarked " it is defensible. If he acts with the administration senators he shall be treated like them— but he must take the step first." [27]

But as we know from his letter to Chamberlain, Garfield, like Hayes before him, looked upon Mahone as a repudiator. Compounding this difficulty was an incident that had occurred in Virginia in the 1880 campaign. The Readjuster leaders thought that a Republican state ticket would not be put in the field in 1880, and they had a separate slate of Hancock electors in opposition to the regular Democratic list. But the Republicans entered an electoral ticket. Then many Readjusters began to fear that two Democratic electoral rosters might divide their party vote to the point where the Republicans could win, and Mahone publicly pledged his support to Hancock and predicted that " the vote of Virginia shall never be given to Garfield." [28] In an effort to aid the Mahone ticket, certain Republican leaders in Virginia and some members of the national committee conspired to have Republicans in the state vote for the Mahone slate. Two agents sent by Dorsey joined with Colonel James Brady, Collector at Petersburg in an open appeal to Republicans to vote for Hancock and to discard Garfield. Brady published a long card in the Richmond *Whig* and issued

State Chairman in Virginia; Tyler, son of a former President and a party leader in Virginia. Cameron's statement appeared in an interview with a reporter of the Philadelphia *Press*, undated clipping, unidentified newspaper, Sherman Papers, Vol. 243.

[27] Garfield Diary, December 29, 1880, in Garfield Papers.

[28] John E. Massey, *Autobiography* (New York, 1909), pp. 191-192; Thomas V. Cooper and Hector Fenton, *American Politics* (Philadelphia, 1882), I, 263.

thousands of circulars among Republicans in the state to abandon Garfield and to support Hancock.[29] Aroused by this development Garfield telegraphed to a loyal party leader in the
state that " no one has been authorized by me to abandon the
fight for the Electoral vote of Virginia," and the national committee finally issued a statement that no one had the authority
to withdraw the Republican ticket in Virginia and any one
claiming such authority " are pretenders and guilty of duplicity
and fraud." [30] Nevertheless this situation had not endeared
Mahone to Garfield.

Pressure on Garfield to come to terms with Mahone mounted
when Congress met in special session in the spring of 1881.
The opportunity for some kind of a merger grew out of the
situation in the Senate where neither the Republicans nor the
Democrats had a majority. There were thirty-seven Republicans, thirty-seven Democrats, one Independent, David Davis of
Illinois, and one Readjuster Democrat, Mahone of Virginia.
Prior to the meeting of Congress, an Associated Press report
stated that Mahone would vote with the Republicans to organize the Senate in return for which he would control the
federal patronage in Virginia.[31] The Democrats made the first
move to secure a majority in the Senate, when on March 10,
Senator George H. Pendleton from Ohio proposed a complete
list of the Senate committees with Democratic chairmen and
Democratic majorities. The next day Senator Davis, the Independent, promised to aid the Democrats organize the Senate.[32]
Ultimate control of the upper house for either party depended
upon which way Mahone voted, for if he acted with the Democrats they would have a 39-37 majority; if he sided with the
Republicans, a tie would result with Vice-President Arthur's
vote as the decisive factor.

Quite naturally the Democrats were anxious to know how
Mahone would vote. Ben Hill of Georgia attempted to force
him into the open, by charging that the Republicans could only

[29] O. H. Russell, Richmond, Virginia to T. P. Pendleton, November 1,
1880, in Sherman Papers; Brady to Republican Friends in Virginia, October 30,
1880, in Garfield Papers.
[30] Garfield to Joseph Jorgensen, October 30, 1880, in Hayes Papers; National
Committee Statement, November 1, 1880, in Garfield Papers.
[31] Louisville *Commercial*, February 28, 1881.
[32] *Congressional Record*, 47th Congress, Special Session of the Senate, p. 6.

offset Davis' decision to act with the Democrats by acquiring someone elected as a Democrat who planned disgracing the commission he holds. " I repel as an insult the charge made against any Democrat that he would be false to his colors and is intending to vote with you on the organization." In answer to Hill, Mahone declared his complete independence of the Democratic caucus and in an ensuing debate with the Georgia Democrat denied that in voting with the Republicans he would betray those who elected him.[33]

Mahone's stand in the Senate posed a difficult problem for Garfield. The Virginian's action might be the open door to larger consequences in the South, but Garfield believed the moral power of the movement had been marred by the " apparent advantage " to Mahone and to the " Republicans which his affiliation brings. The situation," confessed Garfield, " makes my policy towards the Republicans of Virginia unusually difficult." [34]

Senator Hill had mentioned a bargain between Mahone and the Republican party, and part of Mahone's price for acting with the Republicans soon became known. On March 23, Senator Henry L. Dawes of Massachusetts, leader of the Republican caucus, proposed the election of five new administrative officers of the Senate. George C. Gorham, friend and supporter of Mahone and editor of the *National Republican*, received the nomination for Secretary of the Senate, and Harrison H. Riddleberger from Virginia and one of Mahone's associates, gained the nod for Sergeant-at-Arms. Riddleberger had sponsored the measure for scaling down Virginia's debt and reducing the interest rate, the heart of the Readjuster financial program, and this made him objectionable to Democrats. Being an ex-Confederate officer and a Democratic elector in 1880 surely did not please the Republicans. As for Mahone himself, the Republican Senate leaders gave him five committee assignments, which was considerably more recognition than a freshman senator usually receives. The Democrats balked at allowing Gorham and Riddleberger to fill their administrative posts in the Senate, and the Republicans refused to go into executive session until their slate of officials took their posts. Garfield learned that the Republican leaders had resolved to hold on until Mahone "should be satisfied," realizing that this would "continue the deadlock indefinitely," but as the President told Whitelaw Reid, "When our friends have secured all the committees by the help of Mahone, they ought to stand by him until he is reasonably satisfied." [35]

As the deadlock in the Senate continued, the Republican leaders hurried to see Garfield, who appeared willing to aid an alliance with Mahone, but not at the expense of the Republican party in Virginia. The Cabinet backed up the President on this decision and expressed " a strong feeling of distrust of the Mahone Alliance and a desire to go very slow." [36] Garfield told Senator Dawes that he would do any thing he could " with honor " to secure a free vote and an honest count for voters of " all colors " in Virginia, but he would not aid in any arrangement which included in it the advancement " to a post of political honor, a man who as Editor-in-Chief of a newspaper is daily assailing me and my administration." [37]

Garfield was caught on the horns of a dilemma, for as he explained it to John Hay, " In espousing Mahone's course there may be danger of tainting our party with the flavor of repudiation which would in every way be calamitous. Not to help Mahone may lose a great opportunity to make an inroad into the Solid South." [38] The charge of repudiation against the Readjusters, a stigma which orthodox Republicanism could ill afford to bear, plagued Garfield, for he risked the loss of support from the conservative financial interests of the East if he openly embraced Mahone. After Cameron had visited him to plead the cause of the Readjuster, Garfield wrote to Whitelaw Reid and told him that " the Republican party can give no countenance to any doctrine which savors of repudiation; but a clear distinction may be made between repudiation and bank-

[35] Garfield Diary, April 4, 1881; Garfield to Reid, April 7, 1881, *Ibid.*

[36] Garfield Diary, April 29, 1881, *Ibid.*

[37] Garfield to H. L. Dawes, May 2, 1881, *Ibid.* Gorham in the *National Republican* was critical of Garfield's failure to give full recognition and support to Mahone by forcing the Democrats to accept Gorham and Riddleberger. Democrats did prevent the election of these two to their administrative positions in the Senate, and the Republican finally agreed to go into executive session without either one of Mahone's supporters receiving his post.

[38] Garfield to Hay, May 29, 1881, *Ibid.*

ruptcy." Again when newspapers reported that Garfield had approved the Readjusters' position on the debt question in Virginia, he privately denied it. Along with his worry over the odium of repudiation was his genuine fear of deserting the Republican organization in Virginia. He had no qualms about ousting Democrats " of whom there are plenty in Virgina, but I will not remove Republicans to appoint Mahone men," he told Hay. "I shall do enough for Mahone to help him against the Bourbons but not to abandon our organization." [39]

Yet for all these uncertainties, Garfield began to work out a merger with Mahone. Republican leaders in Virginia had asked the President to forego a state ticket in 1881 which would permit a combination of Republican and Readjuster forces to oppose the Democrats. Originally he had planned to wait until the Readjuster convention of 1881 had taken a stand favoring a free vote, and honest count, and the repeal of laws discriminating against the Negro, and then to ask the Republican party in Virginia to endorse that part of the Mahone program relating to the Negro and freedom of the ballot. This would permit Virginia Republicans to form an alliance for a "conscious campaign upon that basis only, carefully excluding any conclusion that would commit them to any doctrine of repudiation." But then, the President began to doubt the practicality of this scheme. Mahone did not want the Republican party in his state to hold a convention. Such a procedure, Garfield observed, would allow Mahone to " raid upon their [Republican] numbers and substantially only bear his party against" the Democrats, and this, the President feared, would demoralize and destroy the Republican party in Virginia.[40]

Despite these doubts about the practical side of a merger, Garfield had decided to work out an alliance with the Readjusters with the view in mind that the results would serve as a guide for future Republican policy in respect to the Independent movements in the South. But the death of the President in the fall of 1881 put an end to this project, and a few months later Democratic newspapers expressed the opinion that he had ignored Mahone's request for aid. The Washington

[39] Garfield to Reid, December 30, 1880; to John Hay, January 14, May 29, 1881; Garfield Diary, April 29, 1881, *Ibid.*

[40] Garfield to Hay, May 29, 1881, *Ibid.*

Post credited this information to a near friend of the late President, presumably Blaine, while the Chicago *Times* attributed it directly to this source.[41]

Both the *Post* and the *Times* represented Blaine as contending that Garfield had characterized the Readjuster plan as one of repudiation, and that under such circumstances, the late President had opposed a coalition between Republicans and Mahone, preferring a Democratic victory to such an alliance. The *National Republican*, a vigorous supporter of Mahone, called Blaine's statement a falsehood. From the time Senator Cameron and his group visited Garfield in Ohio in December, 1880, on which occasion the President called the Riddleberger Bill " an honest document," the *Republican* maintained that Garfield had always favored a merger of Republicans and Readjusters. Furthermore, this paper declared, Garfield had recommended separate conventions of Republicans and Readjusters, coalescing and harmonizing, as a means of attaining a coalition instead of a single convention called by either one of the two parties.[42] On the basis of the evidence available, one has to agree with the viewpoint of the *Republican*.

Early in February, 1881, John F. Lewis, former United States Senator from Virginia, then Republican state chairman and a United States Marshal in the state, led a delegation of Virginia Republicans to see Garfield at Mentor, Ohio. Lewis and the group with him, including Negroes as well as whites, favored an alliance with Mahone, and Garfield thought they had taken the right path if they could secure protection and justice for the colored man without endorsing repudiation in any way. When Lewis returned to Virginia, he stated in public that Garfield had approved a coalition between Mahone and Republicans in Virginia.[43]

Lewis visited Garfield again in June, 1881, and the President told him " Senator, I stand just where I did at Mentor when I stated that were I a Virginia Republican or colored man, I

[41] Chicago *Times*, December 24, 1881; Washington, D. C. *Post*, December 25, 1881.

[42] Washington *National Republican*, December 27, 1881, May 26, June 4, October 9, 1883.

[43] Garfield Diary, February 5, 1881, in Garfield Papers; Alexandria, Va. *Gazette*, February 9, 1881.

would vote with the Liberal Readjuster party." [44] The Washington correspondent of the Philadelphia *Press* reported a similar interview with another Virginia Republican who had called upon Garfield to learn his views on Mahone. The President advised this party member to give his vote to the Readjuster ticket and to discourage attempts to nominate Republican candidates.[45]

To Virginia Republicans who fought to prevent a coalition with Mahone, Garfield gave the same advice that he had given to Lewis. Twice in the spring of 1881, Congressmen Joseph Jorgensen and John F. Dezendorf led delegations of Republicans from Virginia to Washington to protest against the administration's recognition of Mahone and to ask Garfield to support only the " straightout " Republicans in the state. On the first visit, Garfield brushed aside their fears by saying that he would give the matter his full attention. On the second occasion however, he lectured the group severely and even accused Jorgensen of helping the Democrats through his refusal to aid Mahone. At this interview, Garfield advised the " straightout " Republicans to support Mahone in every possible way.[46]

In the summer of 1881, another delegation of Virginia Republican foes of Mahone conferred with the President. In the group were members of the Republican state committee including General William C. Wickham, a former state chairman and Congressmen Dezendorf and Jorgensen, with Negroes making up half the membership. As spokesman for the delegation Wickham told Garfield that regular Republicans opposed a coalition with Mahone, because it would destroy their party in the state. They wanted the administration to help them against the Readjusters, but Garfield preferred to work with Mahone rather than with the " straightout " Republicans at that time.[47]

Both Hayes and Garfield had striven for Republican success in the South. Yet to see a diminishing party vote occur in this

---

[44] Washington *National Republican*, January 2, 1882. This paper published many statements like this in 1882-1883 to prove that Arthur was simply carrying out a policy already initiated by Garfield.

[45] Philadelphia *Press*, June 8, 1881.

[46] Washington *National Republican*, April 16, May 4, 1881.

[47] *Ibid.*, June 18, 1881.

section in both 1878 and 1880 was most discouraging. Mahone's victory in Virginia, his championing of the Negro's privileges, and his falling out with the regular Democratic party presented the Republicans with the most dramatic opportunity of capturing control of a southern state since Reconstruction. Fearful of losing the support of the conservative financial interests of the Northeast, Hayes had repelled Mahone and had condemned him as a repudiator. At first, Garfield followed in the footsteps of his predecessor. But, when confronted by an offer from Mahone to act with the Republican party, plus the pressure from Republican sources within and outside of the state for a merger with the Readjusters, Garfield agreed to a partial recognition of Mahone That is, Garfield, still suspicious of Mahone's financial program, endorsed his plan to aid the Negro in Virginia and consented to an alliance between Republicans and the Readjusters only on the basis of Mahone embracing Republicanism. Garfield would not consent to the abandonment of the party organization in Virginia, nor would he turn over to Mahone the patronage in the state. Believing that Mahone needed the votes of the Republicans as much as they needed his vote-getting ability, Garfield divided the offices between both groups in the hope that this policy would result in permanent Republican gains not only in Virginia, but throughout the South. Whether Garfield's strategy would have been a political success is hard to say, for it never ran its full course. His death in the fall of 1881, and the ushering in of a new era under Arthur brought a swift end to a policy of limited cooperation with the Independents in the South.

Arthur came to the White House with the reputation of a spoilsman and a Stalwart, and the old-line Republican leaders in the South eagerly looked to him to apply these principles to his southern policy. They publicly hailed the new administration as giving the Ohio Idea in politics its death blow,[48] and they were supremely confident that the new policy would, without question, let Democrats know that they had lost the election in 1880 and that there were enough honest and com-

---

[48] The Ohio Idea in politics referred to Hayes' conciliatory policy and to the sentiment held by many northern Republican leaders that all the virtues were to be found in northern Republicans and southern Democrats and all the vices in southern Republicans and northern Democrats.

petent southern Republicans to fill the federal posts in their states. These expectations for a return to Reconstruction days were not confined to party managers in the South, for a few northern leaders entertained the same idea. For instance Grant asked Arthur to consult with one of the most unsavory characters of the party in the South, Paul Stroback, on Alabama affairs, since the former President knew that " Ala. republicanism is badly represented in Washington," and Stroback, a member of the national committee, along with Republican state chairman, George Turner, " are the most competent and reliable men in the state to obtain information from, of a political nature.' [49]

Arthur gave every indication in the beginning that his southern policy would be a throwback to Reconstruction days. He began to give important posts in the South to discredited and tainted party leaders like Stroback,[50] and he brought William E. Chandler into the cabinet, ostensibly to head the Navy Department, but really to plan and direct Republican strategy in the South. Chandler's appointment buoyed up considerably the hopes of dispirited and disconsolate southern Republicans and seemed to be, beyond the shadow of a doubt, the first major step in the return to Reconstruction tactics. It was Chandler who had fiercely assailed Hayes' conciliatory efforts and had openly demanded their repudiation. On top of this he was on the best and friendliest terms with the old-line party managers in the South, to the extent that they regarded him as their particular representative in the Cabinet and as their main refuge in the administration. They credited Chandler with having " a special interest in southern Republicanism," as being the " only man of this Administration " to whom they could explain their " situation to any purpose," and as having " been uniformly " their friend and as standing by them " under all circumstances." [51] Because Chandler corresponded so frequently

[49] U. S. Grant to Chester Arthur, October 4, 1881, Chester Arthur Papers (Division of Manuscripts, Library of Congress).

[50] Stroback was nominated for U. S. Marshal for the northern district of Alabama, but the Senate refused to confirm the appointment, Huntsville, Ala., *Gazette*, September 23, 1882, February 9, 1884.

[51] E. M. Brayton, South Carolina to Chandler, August 14, 1883; Wm. P. Canaday, North Carolina to Chandler, February 16, 1882; J. R. Chalmers, Mississippi to Chandler, July 5, 1882; J. Hale Sypher, Louisiana, to Chandler,

with southern Republicans and listened so sympathetically to
their laments, it is no wonder then that they looked upon his
appointment with an excitable interest and with the prevailing
belief that they would no longer be ignored as they had been
during the Hayes administration.

Keeping all of this in mind, southern Republican leaders
hastened to burden Chandler with plans for rejuvenating their
party. Many of them fervently, if unrealistically, believed that
the only way to do it was as Harrison Reed, former Carpetbagger governor of Florida suggested, to give him control of
the federal patronage in his state. Others, mainly native whites,
pleaded with Arthur to build a lily-white party in the South
and abandon the Negro, for as a newspaperman from Louisiana
wrote, " negro leaders are worthless, their own people will not
follow them." [52]

To the pained surprise and great consternation of these
jubilant and expectant Republican leaders in the South, Arthur
and Chandler firmly turned down both propositions. As they
saw it, the only salvation for Republicanism in the South was
through a policy of complete cooperation with the Independent
movements. In this respect they were willing, and even eager,
to go much further than Garfield. This was a radical and
unorthodox approach for two regulars and Stalwarts like Arthur
and Chandler to take, for they were asking Republicans in the
South to give up their identity and their interests and to merge
under the untried leadership of disgruntled ex-Confederates
and agrarian radicals who had quit the Democratic party. The
new policy broke sharply with Hayes' curt dismissal of the
Independents and Garfield's reluctant and limited union with
one of them. Furthermore, it left Arthur and Chandler open to
the same ugly charge that the Stalwarts had leveled against
Hayes, that of forsaking loyal party members, especially
Negroes, in the South; and it shockingly destroyed the illusions that many southern Republicans had had about Arthur's
return to Grantism in the South.

When he assumed office, Arthur's immediate problem in the

May 13, 1882, in Wm. E. Chandler Papers. These are but a few of this type
of letter from southern Republicans to Chandler.

[52] Harrison Reed to Chandler, April 16, 1882; James E. Richardson to
Chandler, August 1, 1882, *Ibid.*

South was Mahone. Early in August, while Garfield yet lived, the Virginia Republican party had formally entered into an alliance with the Readjusters. Leading Republican newspapers in the North warmly praised this move which also won the public support of Grant, who openly told the Republican chairman in Virginia, " I regard the success of the Readjusters as greatly to be desired." [53] During the state campaign Mahone learned that many Negroes, the bulk of his strength, could not pay their poll tax, and he appealed to national party chiefs for help. Senator Cameron, leading northern sponsor of the Republican-Readjuster coalition, then summering on Manhattan Island, quickly responded by raising funds in New York City. When this proved to be inadequate, internal revenue officers throughout the country were asked to contribute. Many did and the taxes were met.[54] But with Garfield steadily losing the fight for his life, and with Blaine, the Secretary of State, strenuously objecting to the Readjusters, Mahone received little assistance from Washington.

This was the situation when Arthur took over as President late in September, 1881. If the Republicans planned to come to the aid of Mahone they had precious little time left, for the bitterly-fought campaign had entered its final stages. If they hoped to put the strategy of cooperation with the Independents to its test they would have to act quickly and effectively. Arthur and Chandler realized this instantly, for they had reached the conclusion that Mahone's movement was a departure from sectional politics and therefore worthy of support and encouragement. Although strictly an organization man, Arthur committed himself wholly and irrevocably to the policy of granting full recognition and wide assistance to the Readjusters. While Garfield had attempted to divide the offices between Mahone and Republicans, Arthur worked solely with the former Confederate. Washington brusquely informed federal office holders in Virginia to work with the Readjusters

[53] New York *Times*, August 11, 1881; New York *Tribune*, August 11, 1881; Philadelphia *Press*, August 12, 1881; Washington *National Republican*, August 12, 1881; Grant to James D. Brady, October 4, 1881, quoted in Washington *National Republican*, October 17, 1881.

[54] Cooper and Fenton, *American Politics* I, 263-264; Massey, *Autobiography*, p. 203. Since Mr. Cooper was Republican State Chairman in Pennsylvania he was in a position to know about Cameron's activities to pay the poll taxes of Negroes.

or to look for another job, and those who balked were replaced by Mahone men. Such decisive and far reaching action so astonished the straightout Republican leaders in the state that they yielded to the force of circumstances and came over to the Readjuster side. Arthur gladly bartered away federal patronage in an all-out drive to snatch Mahone from defeat when he turned over to the Readjuster 200 posts in the Treasury, 1,700 in the Post-Office, seventy in the federal courts, and numerous ones in the Norfolk Navy Yard.[55]

Aid of this magnitude, while late, proved to be extremely effective, and Mahone, following his victory, gratefully acknowledged it. He told the press that the Readjusters had received only scant assistance from Garfield, but from Arthur they had had all the help the adminisration could give them. " When President Arthur assumed office it was too late to do anything," Mahone pointed out, " but the acts of the new administration, although late were effective. They indicated as plainly as could be the desires of the Administration, and wherever they were indicated they accomplished most desirable results." [56]

Arthur had gambled heavily on a Readjuster victory, because he felt that if Mahone could swing Virginia out of the Democratic column, other Independents might duplicate his feat in their states. And if they cooperated as fully and cheerfully with the administration as Mahone had been doing, then the Republicans might well be on their way to redeeming the South. For no other reason had Arthur been so generous with Mahone, and for no other reason had the administration been so willing and eager to test its new policy. Arthur had not suffered the same qualms about the Independents that had afflicted both Hayes and Garfield. With Arthur it was simply a matter of taking a chance that held out hope of recovering the South for the Republican party, and when confronted by such an enticing opportunity, he succumbed easily.

While the new policy brought apparent success in Virginia and seemed to get off to an auspicious start, it revealed a basic

[55] Washington *National Republican*, November 25, 1881; Massey, *Autobiography*, pp. 201-203; Richardson, *Chandler*, pp. 344-347.
[56] William L. Royall, *Virginia State Debt Controversy* (Richmond, 1897), pp. 46-47.

split among Republican leaders over strategy in the South.
Arthur had been warned by a close friend not to be "too
intimate with those Readjusters. Be satisfied with belonging
to a disreputable crowd in your own state, & don't go hunting
them up all over the country. You are clever undoubtedly,"
she wrote, "but there are some things you cannot do. You cannot be on the wrong side of everything in state politics, & on
the right side of everything nationally. Twice two makes four,
and not even a Readjuster can twist them into three or five." [57]
A political storm broke when Republicans realized the fullness
and closeness of Arthur's ties with Mahone. The ugly charge
of bargain reared its head again, as it had in Hayes' day, and
amusingly enough, while a number of Republican leaders in the
Senate, with much heat and indignation, denied the accusation, John Sherman defended it on the grounds that "anything
that will beat down that party [Democratic] and build up our
own is justifiable in morals and in law." [58] But the New York
Tribune raised a more serious point. Withdrawing its earlier
endorsement of the Republican-Readjuster coalition, the *Tribune*
questioned the justification of the price the party had agreed to
pay for Mahone's cooperation, and pointed out that it now appeared that instead of the Republicans purchasing Mahone, he
was buying the party and "getting it very cheap." [59] Surely
the question of whether it was a purchase or a sale made many
Republicans ponder about the wisdom of this unprecedented
step.

Nettled and harassed by these oblique blows at its policy,
the administration ran into hot water when the popular and
influential Blaine, in a press interview, branded the Republican-
Readjuster union as a grave political blunder and as "the last
degree of folly for the Republicans." [60] Favorite that he was
with the rank and file of the party and high in its councils,
Blaine's views commanded a great deal of respect and attention, and had to be rebutted, if not publicly, at least privately,
if the new policy were to have its full test. For the question
of dealing with the Independents no longer applied solely to

[57] Julia Land to Arthur, November 18, 1881, in Arthur Papers.
[58] Washington *National-Republican*, October 21, 1881; Royall, *Virginia State Debt Controversy*, pp. 53-54.
[59] New York *Tribune*, October 19, 1881.
[60] Washington *National Republican*, September 29, 1882.

Virginia. In the wake of Mahone's continued success, other disgruntled Democrats in the South hastened to attempt to duplicate his victory in their states, and an Independent movement had sprung up in nearly every southern state, and looked to Washington, as had Mahone, for political succor. Not since 1865 had the Republicans had such a wonderful opportunity to win control of the South. The belief that other Independents would take heart from Mahone's victory and from his support by Washington had prompted Arthur to embark upon his southern policy, and now that this development had come, it was necessary to deal with Blaine before he could torpedo the program and discourage the other Independents.

Chandler, who had earlier joined hands with Blaine to berate Hayes' efforts in the South, now set out to convert the " Plumed Knight " to the administration's strategy. Chandler's long and revealing letter to the Maine leader is of the greatest importance, because it discloses the thinking of the administration on the Republican problem in the South and the solution it had worked out. Chandler believed that the one chance for the recrudescence of the Republican party in the South lay in a split in Democratic ranks, and he thought he saw this opportunity in the Readjuster movement, which he felt should have been supported by the Republicans, in every possible way, in order to intensify the Democratic rift. While the first fruits of this approach had been a Readjuster victory in Virginia in 1881, other objectives remained—that of winning the House in 1882, the presidency in 1884, and in gaining permanent Republican success in the South. Chandler stressed the necessity of saving the House for the Republicans in 1882 through a policy of cooperation with southern Independents. If the Republicans lost the House in 1882, they could hardly hope to win the presidency in 1884, and, according to Chandler, they could not save the House " without fostering the Independent democratic and coalition movements in the southern states." Chandler argued that the Republicans could not carry as many northern districts in 1882 as they had in 1880, and if discontent in New York and Pennsylvania remained unhealed, they would need more than twenty southern congressmen to allow them to organize the House. " It is our imperative duty to get them if they can be obtained by honest and honorable means," wrote

Chandler. "The real question cannot be evaded by cavilling about Mahone and the readjustment of the Virginia debt . . . nor about [James Ronald] Chambers and his Fort Pillow record," for they were only incidents of a great popular revolt in the South against the regular Democratic party.[61]

Chandler pointed out that every Independent or coalition candidate in the South had flatly pledged himself in favor of a free ballot and honest count and the wiping out of a race distinction, while the regular Democrats had sworn to resist these reforms. "Shall we fail to follow our principles when they are so vital?" he asked Blaine. "Our straight republican, carpet-bag, negro governments, whether fairly or unfairly, have been destroyed and cannot be revived. Without these coalitions or support of Independents," continued Chandler, " we cannot carry southern votes enough to save the House from Bourbon democratic control, and carry the next Presidential fight. Beyond that, the safety of the colored race while exercising the suffrage depends upon the new departure." [62]

Chandler told Blaine that the administration had a popular majority in Virginia that stood for every principle it stood for. The administration looked for a majority in this state, and also felt that Tennessee could be redeemed. The point of his letter was evident said Chandler, for the country had misinterpreted Blaine's interview about the Readjusters, since he spoke of the past not of the present or future. "You want such . . . men as Mahone . . . Wm. E. Cameron, [Harrison H.] Riddleberger, [J. M.] Leach, and dozens of others to be as successful as much as I do," he told Blaine. "Do not let yourself be misunderstood; do not shirk of yourself or your prejudices; do not be narrow minded, or hesitating but place yourself unmistakably on the side of progress at the South. You do not think that we can accomplish anything there without more white votes," asked Chandler. "How are we to get them if not by the practical movements now in progress?" Blaine could decide what should be done to combat the political reform movements in New York and Pennsylvania, " but let me decide," pleaded Chandler, " who never decided wrongly for you any question, what you should do about the southern inde-

[61] Chandler to Blaine, October 2, 1882, in Chandler Papers.
[62] *Ibid.*

pendent and coalition congressional canvasses. Declare yourself immediately and emphatically in this favor and you may
save the next House of Representatives to the Republicans." [63]

Chandler's entreaty made no headway with Blaine who would
not relent in his opposition to Mahone. This forced the administration to drag the feud out into the open, which it did
when its official organ angrily accused Blaine of making a
bargain with the Democrats in Virginia against Mahone and
the administration.[64] Then other northern Republican forces
joined hands with Blaine. Whitelaw Reid openly voiced skepticism of the party's strategy to win electoral votes in the South
through a coalition with the Readjusters. The Republicans
must look for their votes in the North. " At the utmost a few
electoral votes at the South might be possibly gained," observed Reid, " but it would be at the risk of losing many more
at the North." Reid's paper assailed Arthur's policy as lacking
" moral strength " and as being " inherently and inevitably
bad." [65] Criticism also came from the reform element of the
party, when George William Curtis, editor of *Harper's Weekly*,
declared that the administration's coddling of the Independents had not improved the lot of the Negro in the South, nor
had it made Virginia a Republican state.[66]

Arthur and Chandler had hoped that the Republicans would
close ranks on the important matter of recouping their losses in
the South, and the latter told Reid that on the basis of his
argument the next Republican President could not hope to have
a Republican House. " We must have at least twenty Southern
Representatives and we cannot elect them if we formally surrender everything else, Do you not see this? " [67] Through his
newspaper, Chandler met Curtis' charge by stating that the
Negro in Virginia, under Mahone, had received more consideration than he had in any other state in the country. The
Readjusters treated the Negro like a man; they educated him
in 1,500 schools; they had secured a free ballot box and had
abolished the whipping post. As for Virginia becoming Re-

[63] *Ibid*. Cameron and Riddleberger were associates of Mahone, and Leach
was one of the leaders of the Independent movement in North Carolina.
[64] Washington *National Republican*, June 4, 1883.
[65] *Ibid*., December 17, 1883; New York *Tribune*, October 26, 1882.
[66] Washington *National Republican,* May 26, 1883.
[67] Chandler to Reid, December 17, 1883, in Chandler Papers.

publican in the same sense as " Mr. Curtis and his dough-faces
are Republicans," exclaimed the *National Republican*, " God
grant that Virginia may never become Republican." [68]

Chandler had already sketched the administration's policy in
the South in his letter to Blaine, but in order to dispel the confusion and misconceptions about it, and equally determined to
win public and party approval, the administration publicly out-
lined its plans for the South. This account pictured Arthur as
warmly and unreservedly encouraging southern Republicans to
cooperate with the Independents in their states. He believed
that wherever in the South native whites of Democratic and
Confederate antecedents were making a political departure that
involved a genuine acceptance of the constitutional amendments,
they deserved to have the support of Republicans in their
state, forged by an alliance having the blessing of the national
Republican party.[69] This was the policy that Arthur and
Chandler decided upon, and in spite of the attacks upon it,
they carried it out, with few exceptions. In general Arthur
strove to unite Republicans, Readjusters, Greenbackers, Independents, and " Liberals " under the banner of his administration for the overthrow of the southern Democracy and for the
political regeneration of the new South.

Naturally such a policy collided with orthodox Republicanism, for Arthur lavishly courted the favor of economic radicals,
like Mahone of Virginia, G. W. " Wash " Jones of Texas, J.
Hendrix McLane of South Carolina, James L. Streffield of
Alabama, Rufus K. Garland of Arkansas, and James Ronald
Chalmers of Mississippi. These men had been Democrats, but
economic distress along with bitter resentment over conservative control of their party shoved them into the Independent
ranks. There was a radical flavor to their economic policies, for
they took over the financial program of the Greenbackers and
came out for the coinage of silver dollars. They assailed the
vested interests in general and the national banks in particular.
Indirectly they championed the cause of the Negro by clamor-
ing for free elections, free opinion, free speech, and honest
count, and an enforcement of the federal laws in the South.
It was these economic radicals along with ex-Confederates like

[68] Washington *National Republican*, May 26, 1883.
[69] *Ibid.*

Chalmers and James B. Longstreet of Georgia that Arthur gathered around him as the nucleus of a new Republican party in the South.

Oddly enough, many northern Republicans who had labored to enfranchise the Negro and who had harshly condemned Hayes for forsaking the freedman swiftly fell in line with Arthur's plans to aid the Independents. Chandler, Grant, George Boutwell and others who earlier had firmly and conspicuously stood up for the rights of the colored man now just as firmly believed that the time had come when native whites, Republicans or Democrats, should lead the Republican party in the South. This was a strange aftermath to the very rough road that Hayes had had to travel when he suggested the same idea.

To appreciate fully the departure that Arthur and Chandler took and to understand adequately their strategy in the South, it is necessary to examine briefly the circumstances that gave rise to some of the Independent movements in this section and the manner in which the administration came to their aid. A successful one occurred in Mississippi under the leadership of Chalmers, a former Confederate general, whom the " bloody shirt " orators of the Republican party had always described as the villain of the " Fort Pillow Massacre." Chalmers had been elected for three successive terms to Congress on the Democratic ticket from the second district in Mississippi. In the 1880 election, Lynch, the Negro Republican leader in the state, had successfully contested Chalmer's seat, which led the latter to publish a long bitter manifesto against L. Q. C. Lamar, Democratic leader in the state, in which he savagely denounced Lamar for departing from the true Democratic faith and for throwing him overboard as a " Jonah to the Republican whale." Ringing up his defeat to Lamar's connivance with the Negroes, Chalmers left the Democratic party and announced his candidacy in 1882 on an Independent ticket that attacked the national banks, advocated the coinage of silver dollars, and called for a free ballot and a fair count.[70] While this platform challenged the economic policy of orthodox Republicanism, white Republicans in the state joined hands with Chalmers and set

[70] *Ibid.*, May 15, 1882.

out to induce the administration to make him the Mahone of Mississippi.

The state Republican convention enthusiastically put its stamp of approval upon Chalmer's candidacy, but powerful northern Republican newspapers like the New York *Tribune* and New York *Times* were openly hostile to him.[71] Arthur needed little persuasion to convince him that Chalmers was another Mahone, and he quickly threw the full weight of his administration behind the Mississippi Independent and severely took to task those party members who had fought Chalmers.[72] In Mississippi, Chalmers' candidacy brought in to the open the feud between the white and colored factions of the Republican party. For years the Negro wing, led by Lynch, James Hill, and ex-Senator Blanche K. Bruce, had guided the party in the state. The white faction run by George C. McKee, a Carpet-bagger and former Union General, deeply resented Negro domination and made a strong bid for control of the organization in 1882. Chalmers assisted the white group, and there began a lively struggle between the two Republican elements for recognition and support from Arthur. White Republicans arraigned the Negro politicos for reaching an agreement with state Democratic leaders whereby the Negro chieftains advised their followers to vote Democratic in state and local elections in exchange for support that Democratic senators gave in Washington to Negro claims for federal patronage.[73]

The Independent movement in North Carolina came in the form of opposition to prohibition legislation. The Democratic legislature had passed a bill forbidding the manufacture and sale of liquors in the state and Democratic leaders endorsed the measure and pressed North Carolinians to ratify it at a referendum in 1881. The Republican state committee fought the proposal, and with the help of an overwhelming anti-prohibition sentiment defeated it by more than 100,000 votes.[74]

The aroused and open hostility on the part of thousands of Democrats to the prohibition measure caused a great deal of

---

[71] *Ibid.*, August 29, 1882.

[72] *Ibid.*, September 4, 1882; Willie D. Halsell, "James R. Chalmers and Mahoneism in Mississippi," *Journal of Southern History* X (1944), 37-58.

[73] Willie D. Halsell, ed., "Republican Factionalism in Mississippi, 1882-1884," *Ibid.*, VII (1941), 84-101.

[74] Wilmington, N. C. *Post*, August 28, 1881.

talk in the state about "liberal" as opposed to regular Democrats, and Republicans hoped to cash in on this widespread
unrest. Democrats who had joined the Greenback party in
1880 were available, and in fact they became the nucleus of the
Independent movement shaping up in North Carolina. Men
like William Johnson of Mecklenburg, Charles Price of Rowan,
Frank Wooten of New Hanover, Thomas Clingman of Buncombe, and J. M. Leach of Davidson grabbed the reins of
leadership. They had a platform that demanded equal rights
for all men regardless of color, that advocated local self government and a national education law, and that condemned prohibition and monopolies.[75] They put up a state ticket to
oppose the Democrats that won the approval of both white and
colored Republican state conventions. From Washington came
a prompt and favorable endorsement when Arthur hailed the
Independent slate as the Republican ticket, and urged every
party member in the state to vote for it.[76]

In Texas, Congressman G. W. "Wash" Jones, a Greenbacker, revolted against the regular Democratic organization
in 1882 and hoped to repeat Mahone's performance in the Lone
Star state. Jones' platform advocated a variety of measures:
free schools, free ballot boxes, free opinion, free speech, and
a free press; enforcement of the federal laws in the South, and
promotion of national patriotism and the material interests of
Texas. Jones regarded northern enterprise as something to
emulate, not to despise, and therefore encouraged immigration
and investment in the South. The Greenbacker wanted Republicans to merge with him, and without hesitation Arthur
advised the party to take this step when he called upon Texas
Republicans to support Jones.[77]

Independents took to the field in South Carolina under the
leadership of J. Hendrix McLane who supported the financial
program of the Greenbackers. The Republican state convention endorsed McLane, and Arthur quickly followed suit. In
South Carolina Colonel [E. B. C.] Cash whom northerners had

[75] Ibid., February 12, 1882; Joseph G. de Roulhac Hamilton, History of
North Carolina (Chicago, 1919), III, 207-209.
[76] Wilmington Post, April 9, 23, June 16, 18, October 8, 1882; Washington
National Republican, September 27, 1882.
[77] Washington National Republican, June 17, 1882.

" all been made to believe . . . was guilty of murders so atrocious that they shocked a community accustomed to scenes of blood," had come forth as an Independent Greenbacker and " Forthwith the Administration adopts him, and its patronage is given in aid of his election." [78] In Alabama, the Independents led by James L. Streffield, a Greenbacker, found a friend in Arthur, who normally might have ignored them, but who in 1882 encouraged and aided them. " In Alabama the Republican party has enthusiastically endorsed the Greenback and Independent fusion State ticket," stated Chandler's *National Republican* who felt that " The cry should be ' anything to beat the Bourbons.' " [79] In Arkansas Chandler called for " a coalition of all Liberal Democrats . . . who repudiate. repudiation, [and] the Greenbackers . . . with the Republicans," in the hope this would provide a victory for the Greenback leader, Rufus K. Garland, "which would crown him as the Mahone of Arkansas." [80]

An Independent movement got under way in Georgia in the late seventies led by William H. Felton and Emory Speer and which developed into an attempt to organize a new party in the state in 1881-1881. A faction of Republicanism in Georgia, known as the " syndicate," headed by General James Longstreet, a former Confederate officer, and now a United States Marshal in the state, and various other federal office holders, were interested in supporting the Independents. Longstreet came to Washington in the summer of 1882 to confer with Arthur about the Independents, but the Republicans failed to take advantage of the movement for several reasons. There was the usual factionalism within Republican ranks in Georgia and the rival attempts to keep or to grab control of the federal patronage for the state. Then there was the customary conflict between the " lily-white " and " black-and-tan " factions

---

[78] E. M. Brayton to Chandler, August 4, 1882; William N. Taft to Chandler, November 21, 1883; J. Hendrix McLane to Chandler, January 23, March 6, 1883, in Chandler Papers; New York Tribune, October 26, 1882 for quotation.

[79] George Turner to Chandler, May 25, 1882; J. W. Burke to Chandler, June 8, 1882; in Chandler Papers; Albert B. Moore, *History of Alabama and Her People* (University, Alabama, 1934), pp. 581-582; Washington *National Republican* July 12, 15, August 5, 1882.

[80] Washington *National Republican*, July 15, 1882.

over the role and position of the Negro in the Republican party in the state. A fight developed over the attempts to oust William A. Pledger, Negro editor of the Athens *Blade*, as chairman of the Republican state committee in Georgia. While Arthur helped the " syndicate " in Georgia, the internal bickerings of the Republican party served to distract it from exploiting the Independent movement in this state.[81]

Agitation over the state debt created an Independent movement in Tennessee. Much of this debt had been incurred in support of railroad building before the Civil War; it had increased during the war as unpaid interest accumulated, and it piled up at a greater pace during Reconstruction by the issuance of bonds for aid to the railroad. Because of the failure of the railroads to pay the interest on the bonds, the burden of meeting these payments fell upon the taxpayer and led to a demand that the debt be reduced or repudiated. This demand became the major issue in the campaigns of 1880 and 1882 and split the Democrats into hostile factions. The State-Credit group, supported by the Republicans, posed as the champions of the state's obligations to pay as much of the debt as should be agreed upon by voluntary compact with the creditors. The Low Tax Democrats appeared as repudiators. In 1880 the coalition between the State Credit Democrats and Republicans had gained control of the state legislature. Despite the assistance that the administration gave to this combination in 1882, it failed to repeat its performance.[82]

Arthur did not consistently support the Independents in the South. In Louisiana and Florida, he turned his back on them and gave his blessing to the regular organization candidates, and in some parts of the South he rewarded regular Democrats and even disreputable Carpetbagger leaders. Congressman John Ellis, a Democrat from Louisiana, willingly aspired to be a Mahone in his state and to lead a movement to beat down the " Bourbon " rule there, but most Republican leaders

---

[81] *Ibid.*, August 4, September 7, 1882; James Longstreet to Chandler, September 21, 1882; Wm. N. Smythe to Chandler, June 10, 1882; J. E. Bryant to Chandler, August 7, 1882, in Chandler Papers; Judson C. Ward, " The Republican Party in Bourbon Georgia, 1872-1890," *Journal of Southern History*, IX (May, 1943), 196-209.

[82] Philip M. Hamer, ed., *Tennessee: A History, 1673-1932* (New York, 1933), II, 676-692.

were apprehensive of the proposition and promptly backed away from it. They feared, and correctly too, that an Independent movement would imperil their own political fortunes, even though one of them, a federal Marshal, predicted to the administration that three congressmen could be returned in 1882 by " due encouragement from Washington to our numerous Independents." [83] Bickering and intense factionalism darkly clouded the political picture in Louisiana, and conflicting and disturbing reports on the status of Republicanism in the state made it nearly impossible for the administration to make a sound decision. Some state Republican leaders desperately pleaded for a " political tranfusion of blood " for the party, since it was confined to " the four walls of the Customhouse " while in the rest of the state it had " long since run to weeds." Others harshly assailed " the imbecility and dry-rot of Hayeism " for infecting the party in a harmful way. Still others pessimistically concluded that the time was not altogether ripe for an Independent movement in the state, and that no one yet could be a Mahone in Louisiana. Finally a touch of realism was added when a point, long believed but seldom discussed, was made that the Republican party in Louisiana did not want success, for then it could no longer keep a small compact organization to control the federal patronage.[84]

Faced with the almost hopeless task of finding the political truth in Louisiana, Arthur cast his lot with William Pitt Kellogg, former Carpetbagger governor and United States Senator. This decision resulted from Chandler's firm belief that the principal federal office holders in the state had closed ranks in support of Kellogg, for fear that other Republican congressman would mean a redivision of the spoils, and because Negro leaders in the state like P. B. S. Pinchback and A. J. Dumont had come over to the side of the Carpetbagger. Chandler assured Kellogg of aid from Washington and promised him that he would not be annoyed by opposing factions.[85] Recognition

[83] Washington *National Republican*, January 5, 1882; J. R. G. Pitkin to Chandler, June 8, 1882, in Chandler Papers.

[84] J. R. G. Pitkin to Chandler, June 8, 1882; G. T. Ruby to Chandler, May 9, 1882; James E. Richardson to J. M. Currie, August 1, 1882, in Chandler Papers.

[85] Pitkin to D. B. Henderson, October 19, 1882; Kellogg, Pinchback, and Dumont to Chandler, October 14, 1882; James E. Richardson to Chandler, October 5, 1882; Kellogg to Chandler, October 4, 1882, *Ibid.*

of the unscrupulous Kellogg readily frightened away potential Independent Democratic support, a source of strength that Arthur had carefully and laboriously sought to cultivate elsewhere in the South. The act of taking Kellogg and rebuffing a would-be-Independent like Ellis was an inconsistent one that contradicted Arthur's approach to the Republican problem in the South.

Arthur also gave a cold shoulder to the Independents in Florida where some of the party leaders strongly urged such an alliance. Here the Independents had succeeded in electing many of their men to the state legislature, mainly from Democrtic counties. Encouraged by these results the Independents named a candidate for Congress in 1882, Daniel L. McKinnon from the first district, to oppose E. F. Skinner, a Republican, whose nomination had split the party in this part of the state. J. Willis Menard, Negro editor of the Key West News and former congressman from Louisiana, informed Chandler that all Negro and a few white leaders favored the Independent movement, and that " the men who aided you in securing this state for Hayes in 1876 are supporting Mr. McKinnon now, and I hope you will give him your support." But the administration finally made up its mind to ignore McKinnon and to string along with the Republican nominee.[86]

Arthur's open and extensive support of the Independents plainly annoyed the Democrats who acidly asked, " Why does not the Republican party unfurl its own banner in the South? " The administration answered this embarrassing query by saying that the Republican party had discovered its weakness in the South and thus had to form coalitions with the Independents in order to overthrow the southern Democrats. The Republican National Committee backed up the President on his strategy when at an informal meeting of this body in Washington in the spring of 1882, it expressed itself earnestly in favor of a union of southern Republicans with Independents who were fighting the " Bourbon Democrats." [87]

That Arthur's action was an unusual and rare thing for an

---

[86] J. Willis Menard to Chandler, September 13, October 10, November 27, 1882; N. Martin to D. B. Henderson, September 23, 1882; D. B. Henderson to Chandler, October 3, 1882, Ibid.

[87] Washington National Republican, October 24, 1883; April 17, 1882.

organization man like the President to take and that it was a radical and fundamental departure from previous Republican policy in the South was quickly and widely, if not understandably, recognized. While many a Republican in Arthur's day remained hurt and puzzled over what motivated their President to undertake so seriously such a novel course in the South, there remains little doubt today about the factors that determined the new program.

Perhaps the most important of all these factors was the political status of the South itself. The rise of Mahone combined with his two victories in 1879 and 1881 had spurred on every Independent in the South to break with the Democratic party. To Arthur this development presented the best chance that the Republicans had had for redeeming the South since the troops were removed. He had seen how his all out aid to Mahone had detached a southern state from the Democratic column, and he was very anxious to extend the Virginia experiment to other Independents in the South in the hope of producing the same result. Arthur had the same over-riding optimism for wooing economic radicals away from their Democratic ties as Hayes had had for weaning southern conservative whites away from their traditional loyalties. That is why Arthur courted them so ardently and clung to them so tenaciously as the leaders of the new Republican party in the South.

Almost equally important in determining the new policy was the special role that Chandler played and the tremendous influence that he exerted upon the President. In fact it might be argued that had it not been for Chandler, the administration might never have given a second thought to the Independents. Because of his past connection and wide contacts with southern Republicans, and his peculiar knowledge of their activities through his heavy correspondence with them, Chandler became Arthur's chief and intimate adviser of southern political affairs. He had the task of running the President's policy in the South, of conducting the congressional elections of 1882 in that section, and of rounding up southern delegates for Arthur for the 1884 national convention. As we have already seen, southern Republicans had looked upon Chandler as their champion since he had led the bitter assault upon " Hayesism " in their states. But by 1882 Chandler had experienced a drastic change of heart, the result of which could be seen in the new policy. In 1877 when he had violently assailed Hayes, Chandler had maintained that to pacify the white South was to degrade the Negro and to destroy the Republican policy of Reconstruction years which would in turn lead to intimidation, violence, and absence of legal protection. Chandler then was willing to go all the way in support of the southern Republican party, regardless of its character. But by 1882 he had reached the conclusion that no hope existed for rejuvenating the Republican party in the South through its own efforts. The old leaders of Reconstruction days wanted the party to remain small and weak, so that they could more easily control it and the patronage that accompanied control. That Chandler was well aware of this condition of affairs can be seen from a report from one of his correspondents from New Orleans who wrote, " I tell you privately . . . Louisiana republican congressmen are not wanted by Louisiana republican managers—I but tell you what every intelligent republican knows even though he dare not speak of it. The advent of new men, means a division of patronage, that some of those in place must step down and out. That is the situation in a nutshell." [88] Reports like this on the party in the South had caused Chandler to sour on some of the old party managers and had led him to conclude that Republicanism in the South had no chance to grow until it could take advantage of the Democratic rifts. Since he was in a position to put his theories into practice, Chandler prevailed upon Arthur to join hands with the Independents and to forget most of the Republican past in the South.

The need for more congressmen, especially from the South, also pushed Arthur and Chandler into a new course of action. Political reform movements of the early eighties in Ohio, Pennsylvania, and New York threatened to split the Republican party in those states and to allow the Democrats to increase their representation in Congress. This caused the administration to look to the South for extra congressmen to compensate for the anticipated losses in the North in 1882, and as Arthur and Chandler soon realized, this could only be done by electing Independents who would act with the Republicans as Mahone had done in the Senate. Finally, Arthur and Chandler prob-

---

[88] James E. Richardson to Chandler, October 5, 1882, in Chandler Papers.

ably felt that a fresh look and try in the South was what the Republican party needed. The narrow margin of Garfield's victory in 1880 and the slim hold that the Republicans had on Congress heavily underscored the almost crippling handicap that the party had in national elections in permitting the South to remain Democratic. Reconstruction tactics and the strategy of conciliating southern conservative whites had dismally failed to spread Republicanism in the South, and the new administration hoped that an entirely new approach to the problem might bring more desirable and longed-for results.

Arthur also tried to broaden his potential base of support in the South beyond that of the Independents by holding out to Democrats the hope of federal funds for internal improvements. Southern Democrats had long resented the road blocks that northern party leaders had successfully thrown up against such proposals. Anxious to exploit this Democratic cleavage, Arthur, in his first annual message to Congress, suggested the use of national aid for the removal of obstacles that impeded the navigation of the Mississippi River.[89] Then he went a step further. In March of 1882 the Mississippi River Commission, in view of the heavy floods then prevailing in the Mississippi Valley, and the numerous and extensive breaks in the levees which had already occurred and the probability that others would develop, recommended that Congress double its appropriation of $1,010,000 for " closing existing gaps in levees."[90] Arthur, in a special message to Congress a month later, not only asked for the money for this purpose, but he requested legislation for the permanent navigation of the Mississippi River and the security of the valley. Such a system of improvements, explained Arthur, might require an outlay of twenty or thirty million dollars, and yet this large an expenditure, extended over several years, could not be regarded as extravagant " in view of the immense interests involved.' ' The President reminded Congress that it had imposed and collected a tax on cotton amounting to some $70,000,000, and it was not unfair to return a portion of this income to the Mississippi Valley from whence it had come in the first place.[91]

[89] Richardson, *Messages and Papers*, VIII, 59-60.
[90] Senate Document, 47th Congress, I Session, Executive Document, 159, VI, 1-3.
[91] Richardson, *Messages and Papers*, VIII, 95-96.

As we have already seen, Hayes, on an earlier occasion had successfully exploited the cleavages between northern and southern Democrats over the issue of national aid for internal improvements. His assurances to Tom Scott, president of the Pennsylvania and Texas and Pacific Railroads, of aid from the national government for the completion of the latter line had in large part enabled the Ohioan to enter the White House under peaceful circumstances. Encouraged by this result and by the hearty reception the South had given to him on his tours, Hayes tried to divide the Democratic vote there on economic rather than on race issues in much the same way that Arthur was now attempting to do. And as in the case of Hayes, southern Democrats hailed Arthur's moves,[92] and introduced a number of measures to put the President's words into law, but they became a part of the River and Harbor Bill of 1882, which unfortunately turned out to be a piece of pork barrel legislation.[93] Convinced that the appropriations for rivers and harbors in 1882 greatly exceeded the needs of the country, Arthur vetoed the bill, which, while costing him much of the good will that he had built up in the Mississippi Valley, earned him the applause of the reformers in the North. Arthur apologized to the South for not signing the bill, since it had provided funds for work in the Mississippi River, but he was of the opinion that a pork barrel measure was unconstitutional. Congress had none of Arthur's qualms and quickly overrode the unexpected veto.[94]

Although Arthur openly and energetically aided the Independents in the South he opposed all efforts to diminish the size of the southern Republican delegations to the national conventions. Arthur wanted the nomination in 1884, and the administration worked to control a majority, if not all, of the delegations from the South. When the Republican National Committee met in 1883, Senator William P. Frye from Maine offered a new plan for sending delegates to the national con-

[92] Washington National Republican, April 27, 1882; Wilmington Post, April 30, 1882. This was especially true of Democrats in Mississippi Valley where the Vicksburg Herald hailed the President as a true friend of the valley.
[93] Congressional Record, 47th Congress, I Session, pp. 4, 1591, 1630, 1653, 1697, 1838, 1840, 2230, 2297, 2951, 3124, 3226.
[94] Richardson, Messages and Papers, VIII, 120-122; Congressional Record, 47th Congress, I Session, pp. 6800-6804, 6770.

vention in 1884 that might eventually have had the effect of stamping out Republicanism in the South. Frye's plan called for four delegates at large from each state, which involved no change, and one instead of two delegates from each congressional district which was also to have one additional delegate for each 10,000 votes or major fraction of this number of votes cast for the Republican nominee for President in 1880 in the district. This scheme would have automatically reduced the number of southern delegates for the 1884 convention from 288 to 239 and stood well to reduce it even more drastically as the years went by.[95]

Frye denied he was antagonistic to southern Republicans, but he felt that in the interest of justice the southern states, which were anti-Republican, should have a new basis of representation in choosing the party's nominees. At the same meeting Chandler argued strenuously against the proposed change, and a very lively discussion followed which wound up with the problem being referred to the national convention. Backed by the powerful support of John Sherman, Chandler moved that each congressional district select its own delegates, and when this passed it guaranteed district representation and a victory for the administration in its fight to keep its southern forces intact.[96] Interestingly enough, not all the opposition to Chandler's resolution came from the North. George McKee, national committeeman and white party leader from Mississippi, objected vigorously to it on the grounds that it was forcing the political methods of the North upon the South. A very revealing and significant interchange followed. Chandler in reply pointed out that according to his calculation McKee and a dozen other federal office holders in Mississippi would choose the state's delegates, and he felt they should be satisfied with the methods based on his proposal. McKee angrily snapped back, " So we are if you will only let us alone." [97]

The rejection of the Frye and the adoption of the Chandler plan pleased the administration immensely, and it attempted to

---

[95] New York *Tribune*, December 7, 1883; Washington *National Republican*, December 11, 1883.

[96] John Sherman to Chandler, October 25, 1881, in Chandler Papers; Washington *National Republican*, January 18, 1883.

[97] Washington *National Republican*, January 18, 1883.

use this occasion to soothe the hurt feelings of ignored southern Republicans by pointing out that instead of disparaging them, it would repay the party to give them all possible backing and encouragement "with a view to reclaiming what really belongs to us."[98] The whole thing was an anomalous situation—Arthur making a herculean effort to capture southern delegates that he had largely ignored and subordinated to the Independents.

The mixed reaction to Arthur's policy pointed up the nearly impossible task of finding a workable remedy to southern Republican ills that would please various factions within the party. Blaine and Reid had been scornful of the decision to ally the administration with economic radicals in the South, and native white Republicans from this section complained because too many Democrats received office.[99] The reform element seemed divided and confused, for while those like Curtis lashed out at the coalition with the Independents, others like Wayne McVeagh, Liberal Republican leader from Pennsylvania, openly condemned Arthur for continuing to ally himself with Carpetbaggers like Stroback and Kellogg.[100] But the sharpest attack upon Arthur's policy came from Negroes who believed, and correctly too, that the President had deserted them, especially those in the South, when he subordinated them to the ex-Confederates and Independents in their states. This was the second major abandonment of the Negro by the Republican party since it had enfranchised him. Hayes had forsaken the freedman when he removed the troops, because he hoped this would help to reconcile North and South, conciliate southern whites, and ingratiate the Republican party with them. Arthur abandoned the Negro when he chose to work with the Independents, because he felt that in order to exploit the Democratic cleavages in the South, which he concluded was the only path to Republican success there, he had to relegate the colored man to a minor role. An excellent example of this occurred in Georgia. In this state, William Pledger, a Negro editor, headed the Republican state commit-

[98] *Ibid.*, December 14, 1883.
[99] See Louisville *Commercial*, January 10, 1882; Washington *Post*, February 9, 1882; George M. Jolly to Chandler, April 25, 1883, in Chandler Papers for examples of native white complaints.
[100] New York *Tribune*, May 20, 21, 1884.

tee, but Arthur and Chandler continually ignored Pledger's recommendation which had the backing of James Deveaux, another Negro leader and Republican national committeeman from the same state. Finally the administration informed Pledger that he could have a federal post for himself if he gave up the chairmanship and recognized an Independent, Emory Speer, as head of the party. When Pledger did this, Arthur made him surveyor of customs at Atlanta.[101]

Arthur attempted to soothe the hurt feelings of Negroes by following the traditional Republican policy of rewarding several of their leaders in the South, but these few appointments failed to placate the freedman whose discontent with Republican policy in the South received a public airing.[102] Negroes demanded to know why Arthur had not consulted with their leaders on matters of party strategy and patronage in the South. Why had he instead sought the advice of men like James R. Chalmers, General Longstreet, Emory Speer, and others who were either economic radicals or former Confederates? Why was it that Negro party leaders could not even reach Arthur "unless they sneak under the coattail of . . . Chalmers, Longstreet . . . and that sort of mongrel politician." [103] As T. Thomas Fortune, Negro journalist of the North, so aptly put it, " The Republican party had eliminated the black man from its politics. This is as plain as a nose on the face. The blind alone refuse to see it. It has left the black man to fight out his own battles." Furthermore, Arthur was not concerned about the feelings of the Negro, argued Fortune. " What does Mr. Arthur care for Douglass, Bruce, Pinchback, Lynch, Quarles, Straker, Downing, or Ruffin? Has he or his lieutenants ever consulted them about the Negro vote? Some second rate men like Wm. Pitt Kellogg of Louisiana, Dezendorf of Virginia, and others of their mercenary ilk are supposed to carry the black vote in their pocket. The supposition is a lie," exclaimed Fortune, " and it is our aim to demonstrate the fact." [104]

[101] New York *Age*, September 6, 1886; New Orleans *Louisianian*, April 1, 1882; Huntsville, Ala. *Gazette*, April 1, 1882.

[102] For a full account of this Negro outburst see Vincent De Santis, " Negro Dissatisfaction with Republican Policy in the South, 1882-1884," *Journal of Negro History*, XXXVI (April, 1951), 148-159.

[103] Cleveland *Gazette*, September 1, 1883.

[104] New York *Age*, August 18, 1883.

Fortune was the harshest Negro critic of Arthur's policy in the South. Time and again he publicly castigated the President in the columns of the New York *Age*,[105] where he accused Arthur of ignoring the Negro leaders in the South, of embracing the Independents, and of holding the freedman, as a political factor, in supreme contempt. Fortune maintained that Arthur's policy satisfied " no one but Democrats and soap and water Republicans," and he urged southern Negroes to abandon the President in 1884. " We have had enough of the Garfield type of man—nerveless, vacillating, always dodging. Away with President Arthur who combines the weaknesses of his predecessors without possessing their slim stock of virtues." Fortunes's attacks went beyond the matter of castigating Arthur, for they were an arraignment of the entire Republican policy in the South since 1877.[106]

Another very severe Negro critic of Arthur was the Huntsville *Gazette* in Alabama, which, in a series of editorials from the spring of 1882 until the summer of 1883, kept pounding away at the administration for its failure to give Negroes their just share of the patronage. All that Negroes ever received from the Republican party were promises, said the *Gazette*, and empty promises at that. " Spit upon in the house of his friends, despised, and ignored at feast times, and recognized only when his services are needed—is the lot of the Negro," the *Gazette* complained. It did not advise the freedman to leave the Republican party or to act independently, but it did urge him to force party leaders to recognize him.[107]

From South Carolina came a long open letter from D. Augustus Straker, Negro leader and professor of Common Law at Allen University in Columbia, which listed the chief grievances of his race against the Republican party. Negroes felt that the Republicans had treated them unjustly for their devotion to the party from the time Hayes had recalled the troops. From that day on the Republican party had sought the best

[105] *Ibid.*, March 3, August 11, 18, 25, September 8, 1883; May 31, December 27, 1884.
[106] *Ibid.*, August 25, 1883, for quotation; August 18, 1883, December 27, 1884; Cleveland *Gazette*, September 1, 1883.
[107] Huntsville *Gazette*, March 11, April 29, June 10, July 8, 1882; February 10, March 31, April 14, 28, May 12, 26, June 9, 1883, the quote is from February 10, 1883 issue.

methods to remove the freedmen from consideration and to conciliate southern Democrats. On top of this, Negroes resented the failure of the Republican party to protect them at the ballot box, and the refusal to recognize their right to hold office equally with the whites. Colored men chafed under the policy of winking at and even fostering segregation, and they had become bitter because northern party leaders, influenced by the cry of Negro supremacy, had abandoned the idea of maintaining a republican form of government in the southern states as stipulated by the Constitution.[108]

Northern Negroes were just as unhappy as their southern brethren about Republican policies in the South. The Washington *Bee* placed the problem in a nutshell. "What do we want from the Administration? Recognition according to our voting strength, that's all," while the Cleveland *Gazette* concluded that the "promise of office by the Republican party has served too long as a delusion and snare."[109] Some northern Negro leaders sought to enlist the aid of their southern associates in an independent movement. Fortune, Peter H. Clark of Ohio, William Still of Pennsylvania, and George Downing of Rhode Island led the way in pushing this plan, and while they managed to secure the support of T. T. Harden, editor of the Savannah *Echo*, others like Bruce, Lynch, Elliott, Gibbs, and Langston spurned the independent plan.[110] Attempts were made to show that Frederick Douglass, favored such a movement, but in an open letter to the press Douglass repudiated these reports and characterized it as a step in the wrong direction.[111] However in an address before the National Convention of Negroes at Louisville in the fall of 1883, Douglass severely criticized the failure of the Republican party to protect the civil rights of the Negro, and the convention itself turned down, after much uproar, two significant resolutions; one that praised the Arthur administration, and one that affirmed the devotion of the Negro to the Republican party.[112]

[108] New York *Age*, September 1, 1883.
[109] Washington *Bee*, January 27, 1883; Cleveland *Gazette*, December 20, 1884.
[110] Little Rock, *Arkansas Mansion*, August 18, 1883. Only Fortune's and Harden's papers out of 120 Negro newspapers supported the plan.
[111] Huntsville *Gazette*, October 27, 1883.
[112] *Ibid.*; Cleveland *Gazette*, September 29, 1883; Washington *National Republican*, September 25-28, 1883.

At the same convention, Douglass took issue with Hayes over the matter of Negro support for his policy and the Negro leader moved to extricate himself from any endorsement he had given to an unpopular venture in the South. A few weeks before his inauguration Hayes had an important conversation with two prominent Negroes. " I talked yesterday (Feb. 17) with Fred Douglass and Mr. [James] Pointdexter, both colored, on the Southern question," wrote Hayes in his diary. " I told them my views. They approved. Mr. Douglass gave me many useful hints about the whole subject." [113] At the convention Douglass controverted Hayes on this, pointing out that in his interview with the President-elect he had protested against the conciliatory policy.[114] A few years later in a letter to a Negro lawyer from New York, in which he deprecated any condemnation of the Harrison administration before it got under way, Douglass wrote, " I was from first to last, outspoken, and among those known to be opposed to his [Hayes'] Southern policy, and of this no one knew better than President Hayes himself. He knew it before he came to Washington." [115]

Many Negroes held Arthur responsible for the Supreme Court's decision in 1883 which invalidated the Civil Rights Act of 1875, and the Cleveland *Gazette* predicted that this decision by a Republican court would hamper the campaign in 1884.[116] John P. Green, Negro leader from Ohio, associated the verdict with Arthur's policy of attempting to win some southern states for the party by reducing the fear of Negro supremacy, and he urged Negroes in the South to be awake. " The enemy is at hand. Our worst foes may be they of our own household." [117] The Arkansas *Mansion* called the decision a correct one, for it described the Civil Rights Act as a " law conceived in humbuggery and enacted in fraud." [118] The administration, in a tight position, recovered some lost ground when it took on civil rights as a party issue and told Negroes they would need a Republican Congress to secure those rights.[119] The New

[113] Hayes' Diary, February 18, 1877, Williams, *Diary and Letters*, III, 417.
[114] Washington, D. C. *The People's Advocate*, October 6, 1883.
[115] Frederick Douglass to T. McCants Stewart, January 7, 1889, quoted in New York *Age*, January 12, 1889.
[116] Cleveland *Gazette*, October 20, 1883.
[117] *Ibid.*
[118] *Arkansas Mansion*, November 10, 1883.
[119] Washington *National Republican*, October 18, 1883.

York *Tribune* reflected a large segment of northern opinion when it argued that the North expected the Negro to fight his own battles in the South and to stop whining about massacres and bulldozings, but the administration disagreed with this viewpoint and pointed out that the nation had to assume the responsibility for the barbarism it permitted. "If crime is legal," the administration organ concluded, " then the government is the criminal." [120] But the Athens *Banner-Watchman*, a Negro paper in Georgia, in observing the administration's flirtation with southern Independents said, " It is the initial step made by the Republican party to shake off the Negro, now that they can no longer use him. In other words the republicans see that there is no chance of ever [regaining] a foothold in the Southern States so long as their success means African political supremacy over the Caucasian, for the negro is such a treacherous ally that he cannot be depended upon." [121]

Many American political commentators have erroneously held the view that Negroes did not become dissatisfied with Republican programs and policies until the New Deal came along. Actually the Negro from the very beginning of Reconstruction was suspicious and critical of the Republican party, a development that instead of abating became wider, deeper, and public in the post-Reconstruction years. The outbreak that occurred during Arthur's administration was but one of many that happened in the two decades after the recall of the troops. Yet while the Negro remained dissatisfied he stayed in the Republican party and preferred his lot there to that of acting independently.

Such a radical change in policy in the South as the one that Arthur worked out naturally leads to the question of what did he accomplish politically? How successful was he in attaining any of the objectives he had set his heart on? That he had neither achieved any spectacular success nor broken through the Democratic ranks in the South was again evident by the failure of the Republicans to capture any states in this section in the presidential election of 1884. Yet because the policy

[120] *Ibid.*, January 4, 1884.
[121] Athens *Banner-Watchman*, April 1, 1884 quoted in Ralph Wardlaw, *Negro Suffrage in Georgia, 1867-1930, Phelps-Stokes Fellowship Studies*, no. 11, Bulletin of University of Georgia, XXXIII (September, 1932), no. 29, p. 48.

departed as sharply from Hayes' strategy as his had from Reconstruction tactics, it becomes necessary to give closer attention to the results.

The congressional elections of 1882 tested for the first time the success of Arthur's policy of all-out aid to the Independents. In terms of increasing administration strength in the House from the South, these elections seemed to vindicate Arthur's course. While the South returned only eight Republicans, one shy of the 1880 total, to the House, it elected eight Independents, an increase of four over the number in 1880, six as Readjusters from Virginia, and Chalmers of Mississippi and Tyre York of North Carolina.[122] In contrast with Hayes' policy of shunning the Independents, Arthur's strategy of embracing them had nearly doubled the size of administration strength in the House from the South and had produced results just shy of the number that Chandler had set for an administration goal.

The presidential election of 1884 provided the ultimate test for Arthur's experiment, and while the Republicans again failed to pick up any electoral votes in the South, they did take new courage from the gains they did make. Blaine polled a larger popular vote in every southern state than Garfield, save in Georgia, and South Carolina, and a larger proportional vote except in Georgia, North Carolina, and South Carolina. His aggregate in the South of 779,693 votes surpassed that of Garfield by more than 100,000 and that of Hayes by about 40,000, but his over-all proportional vote in this section of 40.10 per cent fell slightly below the 40.84 per cent of Garfield and the 40.34 per cent of Hayes.

In the congressional elections of the same year, Arthur's policy received a rude setback, when the South sent back eight Republicans but turned out of office all of the Independents, so that the administration strength from the South was halved. These results nullified all of the gains of 1882, a real blow to Republican hopes. A natural question is what happened to the Independents in 1884? Why did they vanish? The failure to elect Independents might have been the results of two factors. One was the closing of Democratic ranks when the Indepen-

---

[122] New York *Tribune Almanac* for 1878, pp. 56-57; for 1879, pp. 53-55; for 1881, pp. 37-38; for 1883, pp. 35-36.
[123] Burnham, *Presidential Ballots*, pp. 252-255.

dents threatened white and Democratic supremacy, and in the second place, 1884 was a presidential election year when both Democrats and Republicans, generally, but not always, vote a straight ticket more than they do in the off years.

But, as in the case of Hayes, the real measure of the success or failure of the new policy, lay beneath the surface returns. Like Hayes, Arthur had shifted Republican appeals in the South from Negroes to whites, but whereas Hayes had wooed conservatives, Arthur had leaned toward economic radicals. The novelty and importance of both Hayes' and Arthur's approach to the problem of rejuvenating southern Republicanism had been their reversal of appeals from blacks to whites. While this had the effect of working to the disadvantage and even to the abandonment of Negroes, both Presidents had hoped to maintain, and possibly increase, Republican strength among the freedmen while adding to the party vote among the whites. As we have seen Hayes policy had ended with the Republicans losing strength in the Black Belts and holding their own in the white counties.

In the elections of 1882 Republican losses occurred in both the Black Belts and white counties, but these setbacks were offset by victories scored by the Readjusters and Independents, whom Arthur had called his own. While the number of combined Republican-Readjuster-Independent majorities in both areas surpassed the number of Republican majorities in these counties in 1880 and 1878, they fell far below the Republican total in the Black Belts for 1876 and rose barely above the level in the white counties for 1876. Out of 217 [124] counties with 50 per cent of over Negro population, ninety-one cast Republican-Readjuster-Independent majorities as compared to seventy-six Republican counties in 1880, sixty-two in 1878, and 125 in 1876. The most distressing result of 1882 from an orthodox Republican point of view was the sharp decline in straight Republican votes in the Black Belts, for of the ninety-one that gave majorities to the coalition, only thirty-nine of them were Republican. The most alarming and serious losses of Republican counties occurred in North Carolina and Vir-

---

[124] The figure 217 instead of 294 is used, because Georgia with 63 counties and Texas with 14 counties are not included since the author has not yet been able to locate returns for these states, on a county basis, for the congressional election of 1880 and 1882.

ginia where the Independents and Readjusters made heavy inroads.

In 1880 the Republicans won seventeen of the twenty-two Black Belt counties in North Carolina and twenty-nine of the forty-three in Virginia, only to fail to win a single one in 1882 in either one of these two states, while the Independents took nineteen in North Carolina and the Readjusters won thirty-three in Virginia. The same compensation prevailed in the white counties. Out of forty-nine counties [125] with less than 5 per cent Negro population, fourteen, of which nine were Republican, cast Republican-Readjuster-Independent majorities as compared to ten Republican counties in 1880, nine in 1878, and twelve in 1876.[126] North Carolina presents a contrast of the territorial distribution of Republican strength and Negro population in the congressional elections of 1880 and 1882 and an excellent example of how Republican losses in the Black Belts were compensated for by Independent victories in 1882, victories that Arthur had labored to achieve.

In the presidential election of 1884 the Republicans continued to lose strength in the Black Belts while they managed to pick up some small gains in the white counties. Of the 293 Black Belt counties, Blaine won 125 of them as compared to 133 for Garfield and 140 for Hayes, and of the 154 white counties, Blaine took eighteen in contrast to the thirteen for both his predecessors. In the South as a whole, the Republicans garnered 219 of the 963 counties.[127]

In view of the results of the elections of 1882 and 1884, one is forced to conclude that the harvest of the new Republican venture in the South was small indeed. True the new policy had added to administration strength in Congress from the South in 1882, but only through a Republican-Readjuster-Independent coalition at the expense of orthodox Republicanism, and even these slight gains were wiped out in 1884. Thus Arthur had been no more successful than Hayes in producing a formula to break up the Democratic South.

[125] The figure 49 instead of 155 is used because Georgia with 8 counties and Texas with 98 counties are not included since the author has not yet been able to locate returns for these states, on a county basis, for the congressional elections of 1880 and 1882.

[126] *American Almanac* for 1879, pp. 350-403; for 1883, pp. 198-264.

[127] Burnham, *Presidential Ballots*, pp. 165-225, 237-243.

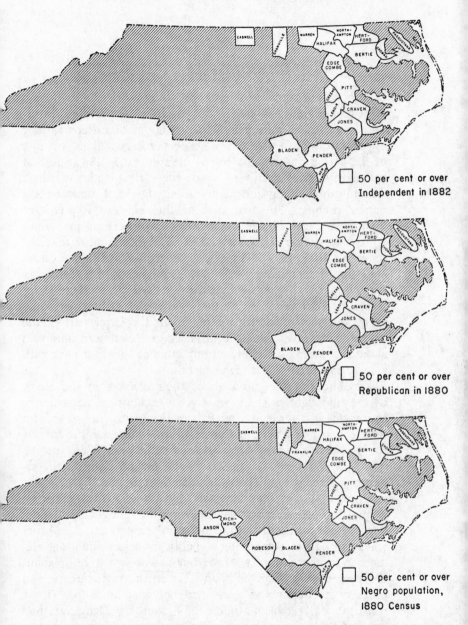

North Carolina counties with 50 per cent or over Negro population, 1880 Census, that cast Republican majorities in 1880 and Independent majorities in 1882.

Chapter V

SHADES OF RECONSTRUCTION

Although Hayes and Arthur had established the main patterns of Republican policy in the South in the post-Reconstruction years, there were yet to be serious modifications as new opportunities arose and as new leaders emerged. This was true of the period that set in after Blaine's defeat in 1884 and that ended with the Populist revolt of the early nineties in which Republican thinking and acting about the South underwent a drastic change. The first part of this era saw Republicans gloomy and pessimistic about their prospects in the South which was in sharp contrast to the exuberant optimism that had prevailed since 1877. There were developments that accentuated this despondency and which brought on the feeling in some Republican quarters that the fight for the southern states was not worth the time and money that the party had already spent and was preparing to spend. In the latter part of the period there was a strong resurgence of Republican optimism about the South and a very stormy attempt to win it back with a reversion to Reconstruction tactics.

Republicans were glum about their chances in the South in the mid-eighties for a variety of reasons. A natural discouragement had set in after two earlier major tries to redeem this section had ended in failure. Then there was the loss of the presidency for the first time since the Civil War, and because the White House had been the pivotal point in the attempt to remedy the Republican malady in the South, there was no organized party effort in this direction until the Harrison administration. Another disheartening thought for the Republicans to ponder about was the increasing success that the Democrats had had in eliminating Republicans as an important element in southern politics. Since they had no way to bring about a repeal of the Fourteenth and Fifteenth Amendments, and because the Republican party had not tried to enforce these constitutional provisions since 1877, southern Democrats had resorted to violence, intimidation, trickery, and force to suppress the Republican vote in the South and to disfranchise the Negro illegally, because they firmly believed that white supremacy was the *sine qua non* of peace and order in their states.

Added to these difficulties was the attitude of the Negroes themselves. While a few looked for the restoration of slavery following the Democratic victory in 1884, most of them failed to become upset over it. A group from Louisiana openly expressed the opinion that Cleveland's election would in all probability result in some good for the race, while P. B. S. Pinchback, the Negro leader from the same state, scornfully ridiculed the idea that the Democrats would impair the rights of the freedman and labeled the talk about re-enslavement as " absurd and disparaging to the manhood and courage of the colored men of the South." [1] The Cleveland *Gazette* still preferred a Republican administration, but felt that the Negro would receive from Cleveland all that he would have obtained from Blaine.[2] While the Washington *Bee*, also felt that the Democrats would not injure the Negro, it concluded that the time had come for the race to assume an independent role in politics. The *Bee* argued that the folly of Republicans had compelled the Negro to take this step, and it strongly urged the colored voters in the South to divide and to go where they could better their interests.[3]

These statements, along with Democratic claims of carrying large blocs of Negro voters in the South, greatly troubled Republican leaders in the eighties. Many southern Negroes smarting under the treatment they had received from Hayes and Arthur, began to look elsewhere for political allies who could offer concessions, and during Cleveland's first administration, the Democrats stoutly maintained that they were luring these disaffected Negroes from their Republican loyalties. For example, in Mississippi in counties with a relatively small white population that just about completely depended upon Negro labor, the freedman voted almost solidly for the Democrats. This resulted from the " fusion principle," a plan in which the Democratic leaders in the black counties would agree with

[1] Cleveland *Gazette*, November 29, 1884; Pinchback to some Doctor, November 25, 1884, in P. B. S. Pinchback Papers (Moorland Collection, Howard University).

[2] Cleveland *Gazette*, March 7, 1885.

[3] Washington *Bee*, November 22, 1884.

Negroes on the number of offices the latter would hold. The whites arranged that they should have nearly complete control of the more important posts, permitting the Negro to vote freely. In theory the Negro leaders chose their own candidates; actually the Democratic leaders either approved or disapproved the selections.[4]

This type of fusion gained only provisional support from the Negroes, and their desertion of the Republican party was more apparent than real. Actually this was the best bargain that the Negroes could make, for as some of them in Mississippi pointed out the Negro would vote with the Democrats or with any other political group which offered him concessions until he could again vote as a Republican.[5] A Negro editor from Tennessee echoed this viewpoint when he wrote, "Though hampered by circumstances, we are yet for the party of Lincoln, Grant, and Sherman." [6] This helps to explain why Negroes seemed to be leaving the Republican party to join the Democrats. Depressed by Republican policies since the end of Reconstruction, torn between loyalty for and resentment against the party of emancipation, and severely restricted in their privileges of voting, southern Negroes presented a picture of helplessness and confusion, and many of them temporarily forsook their Republican allies and sought to identify themselves with the Democratic party. This phenomenon lent much credence to the Democratic claims that they were making serious inroads upon the Negro strength of the Republican party in the South, and quite naturally and easily stirred up some nightmares for Republican strategists.

Another factor that heavily damaged Republican chances in the South and deepened the gloom among party leaders in the mid-eighties was the strategy that top-drawer leaders justified for this section. They repeated two earlier mistakes of the Stalwarts, and in so doing dampened considerably whatever enthusiasm Hayes and Arthur had planted among southern whites for the Republican party. For one thing they tried to

[4] Vernon Lane Wharton, *The Negro in Mississippi, 1865-1890* (Chapel Hill, 1947), pp. 202-204.

[5] *Ibid.*

[6] Edwin F. Horn of *Chattanooga Justice* to John Sherman, June 30, 1877, in Sherman Papers.

arouse resentment against Cleveland in the South, by predicting that he would initiate a program of disloyalty, and that he would encourage proscription, fraud, sectional animosity, and race prejudice. In addition to this, Republican leaders showed considerably more interest in gathering up southern delegates for the 1888 national convention than they did in a genuine rejuvenation of their party in the South. This was a notorious practice that made southern whites frankly skeptical of the sincerity of Republican motives in their states, and which encouraged the belief that the national party leaders preferred a skeletal Republican organization in the South which only became important every four years at convention time.

John Sherman and ex-Governor R. A. Alger of Michigan led the rest of the field in the mad scramble for southern delegates, with the former enjoying a strong and unique position in this fight. He was the only northern party chieftain in public office in Washington who had had much previous contact with Republican leaders in the South. He had attempted to round them up for himself for the 1880 and 1884 conventions, and he had continued to keep in touch with them through a voluminous correspondence.[7] Finally he stood only a heart beat from the presidency. When Vice President Thomas A. Hendricks died in December, 1885, Republican colleagues honored Sherman by electing him President Pro-Tem of the Senate, and Republicans in the South, as well as in the North, keenly appreciated the significance of his new position and frequently referred to him as the Vice President.

Employing his point of vantage to the fullest, Sherman left no stone unturned in his strenuous campaign for southern delegates, and for the most part, placed this consideration over that of any other concerning the party in the South. He refused to help resolve some of the great factional feuds then besetting Republicanism in the South, for fear that he would jeopardize his own position, and by this decision probably cost the Republicans at least one southern state in the 1888 election. Just before the national convention met when Mahone and John Langston, the Negro leader, battled fiercely for control of the Republican party in Virginia, Sherman refused to be drawn into the controversy and asked Langston to cooperate with the

[7] Sherman Papers in Library of Congress readily testify to this.

Readjuster, and if possible, " humor him for the good that he has done to the country and for the African race." [8] In the dispute between the Republican factions of General H. G. Malloy and N. W. Cuney, Negro national committeeman, in Texas, one of Sherman's managers pointed out to Cuney, " Senator Sherman is too good a party man to advise factional fights, for he is for the majority taking hold of party organization and the leaders of the majority having proper party recognition. That is the only way to build up a party and hold it together." [9]

At the national convention both the Sherman and Alger forces used special means to win over the delegates from the South. Mark Hanna, making his first bid as a President maker, told Sherman's manager to " notify the Chairman of the Southern delegation to report to me on his arrival and say to them that I will be prepared to purchase the surplus tickets of their Delegations for members of the Sherman Club." [10] Alger men tried to buy southern delegates away from Sherman, and they hoped to make this scheme " more successful in case of a drag of the Convention should make the expense of the Southern delegates onerous." [11] Murat Halstead of the Cincinnati *Commercial-Gazette* reported that there was " no question about the market that the Alger men had established " in their efforts to purchase delegates, and that " there never was so striking an appearance of the use of money in a national convention as there was in Chicago in behalf of Alger and Gresham." [12] Bitter over the loss of the nomination in 1888, Sherman told the press that " the friends of General Alger made a corrupt use of money in influencing the votes of Southern delegates, particularly the colored men." [13] Alger's friends angrily demanded an apology from Sherman and warned that if it were not forthcoming, they would " make public the facts about North Carolina." [14] Sherman never apologized, and the Alger men never made good on their threats, but the emphasis upon convention delegates rather

---

[8] Sherman to Langston, May 3, 1888, in Sherman Papers.
[9] Green B. Raum to Cuney, April 12, 1888, *Ibid.*
[10] Mark Hanna to Sherman, May 26, 1888, *Ibid.*
[11] C. H. Grosvenor and A. C. Thompson to Sherman, June 17, 1888, *Ibid.*
[12] Murat Halstead to Sherman, July 1, 1888, *Ibid.*
[13] New York *Sun*, June 29, 1888.
[14] Henry M. Duffield to Sherman, June 29, 1888, in Sherman Papers.

that upon strengthening the party, probably disgusted potential Republican recruits in the South.

Republican leaders also talked a great deal about the matter of the suppressed vote in the South, but they were badly split on the issue. A number of them, including Sherman and Senator George Frisbie Hoar of Massachusetts, argued that the Democratic party enjoyed an unjust advantage through its repression of Republican ballots and that the only solution to this problem lay in complete federal control of congressional elections.[15] In very sharp contrast to this position was that of Senator Philetus Sawyer of Wisconsin who suggested that the Negro divide his political affiliation in the South. " I have no faith in the Republican party in the South," blurted out Sawyer. " So What's the use of bothering about the South." He contended that it was all nonsense to talk about inaugurating a policy to win Republican votes in the South. " It cannot be done, and I don't intend to give a d – – – cent in that direction, it would be just money thrown away." [16]

Other Republican leaders joined with Sawyer in dealing a staggering blow to Republicanism in the South. Stephen B. Elkins of West Virginia, speaking in the South in the summer of 1888, bluntly pointed out that all attempts to change the situation in this part of the country by outside agitation in the interest of the Negro had wound up in failure, and he prophesied that the true solution to the Southern Question would only come when both races in the South would divide on economic and industrial questions and distribute themselves between the two major parties. Then the Negro would have the sympathy and support of his white neighbors and would receive all of his rights under the law.[17] Senator John J. Ingalls of Kansas, and Powell Clayton, Carpetbagger leader from Arkansas, went even further, when they voiced the opinion that Negro suffrage had proved to be a failure.[18] This point of view easily strengthened the belief among some Negroes that it would be better for them to abandon politics entirely and spend their time acquiring property and education, for they had

[15] Cincinnati *Enquirer*, June 17, 1887; New York *Age*, May 12, 1888.
[16] New York *Age*, May 12, 1888.
[17] *Ibid.*, June 23, 1888.
[18] *Ibid.*

reached the sad conclusion that the Republican party could not or would not protect them politically.[19] What some of the national party leaders had said seemed to confirm the observation of a native white Republican lawyer from Georgia that " To be a Republican in active politics in the South is to be a foolish martyr, and this I can never be again." [20]

Yet for all of their preoccupation with personal advancement, Republican leaders of the mid-eighties did introduce an innovation in their activities in the South when they invaded it to campaign for Republican candidates. Rarely since Reconstruction had national party leaders gone into the South to speak in behalf of the party, in spite of the frequent requests by their southern brethern for this kind of help, and seeing Sherman, William McKinley, Joseph Foraker, and others on the hustings in Virginia, Kentucky, Alabama, and Tennessee [21] amazed and delighted southern Republicans and took some of the sting out of the sharp rebuffs they had received from Washington. Two of them from Chattanooga underscored their plight as well as their appreciation when they told Sherman, " assistance of this sort we have never received as yet. Your speech in Nashville is the first speech delivered in this state by a Republican leader of a National reputation." [22]

Sherman took the lead in this endeavor as he had in the race for southern delegates, and he did say and do some significant things in the South. At Petersburg, he appealed to Virginians to lay aside their feelings of sectionalism and to join the Republican party which would give them more than the empty promises of the Democrats. In Louisville, he entreated the old Whig element to vote Republican and sought to show that Henry Clay had defended the principles of Republicanism. At Birmingham, he cheered the hearts of former Confederates when he conceded that he would "trust the patriotism of an ex-Confederate in Alabama as soon as that of an ex-Unionist

[19] R. R. Wright, Georgia to Sherman, January 16, 1886; Robert Cox, Virginia to Sherman, April 13, 1886, in Sherman Papers; Cornelius Smith, Louisiana to Chandler, May 26, 1888, in Chandler Papers.

[20] James Atkins to Sherman, March 8, 1887, in Sherman Papers.

[21] New York *Tribune*, October 30, 1885, October 3, 1886, March 25, 1887; Cincinnati *Enquirer*, March 23, 1887; Wm. Mahone to Sherman, November 8, 1885, in Sherman Papers.

[22] J. W. Brading and Francis Martin to Sherman, March 28, 1887, in Sherman Papers.

in Ohio." While he was in this city he attempted to allay the fears of Negroes that northern Republican leaders had forsaken them. When a number of them came to see him in his hotel in Birmingham and were denied admission by the manager, Sherman paid his bill and went to another hotel where he could receive his visitors.[23] At Nashville he expressed the hope of dissipating the prejudices that still existed against the Republican party in the South. He pleaded for the protection of Negro voters and referred with sorrow to some of the outrages that were still practiced. He balanced this by complimenting the South on the magnificent progress and energy with which it had met the new conditions of labor and industry and predicted a compensation, within twenty-five years, for the loss of its slaves by the results of diversified industry and the subdivision of land.

If native whites found much to applaud in Sherman's remarks, some Negroes found much to criticize. The Washington *Bee* suspected that he had proposed a division of the Negro vote in the South, which according to the *Bee*, fitted in well with the plans of Republicans to ditch the Negro and to throw upon some other party the responsibility of protecting him.[24]

In addition to asking Republican leaders to campaign in the South, native whites vainly pressed upon Washington the necessity of building a lily-white party in their states, for they were willing to "take anything rather than negro domination."[25] But Sherman, to whom the appeal was made, quickly backed away from this proposition. Then native whites wanted to set up a "High Tariff" or "Protection" party in the South, with the word Republican not to be associated with the organization in any way. Native white Republicans had happily persuaded themselves that such a plan would allow many southern Democrats to vote for Republican principles under different names. But they could not sell the project to Sherman who objected on the grounds that it would change the name of the Republican party.

[23] Cincinnati *Enquirer*, March 23, 1887.

[24] Washington *Bee*, April 2, 9, 1887.

[25] George Gilmer, Alabama to Sherman, February 18, 1886; James Atkins to Sherman, March 8, 17, 1887, Sherman Papers.

[26] D. M. Bowes, Georgia to Sherman, February 9, 20, 1888, *Ibid.*

The presidential election of 1888 both delighted and troubled Republican leaders. For while they had won control of the presidency and both houses of Congress together for the first time since 1872 [27] they still had a sectional party that had negligible appeal in the South. Since the end of Reconstruction, Republican strength in the southern states had diminished to the point where it offered practically no opposition to the Democrats, and in some parts of the South it had just about disappeared. In South Carolina it had not put up a state ticket since 1876. In other states Independent leaders like Mahone, of Virginia, dominated it. Only a handful of influential southern whites affiliated with it, and it lacked money, newspapers, and assistance from the national organization. Few Republicans ever put in an appearance in the South except at national conventions or when a Republican President had some patronage to hand out. Many Republicans would have agreed with the observation of a white party member from Tennessee when he wrote to a Pennsylvania Congressman, " in abandoning the South . . . the Republican party has thrown away its best territory for future growth and has violated sound political rules." [28]

Harrison had fared badly in the South in 1888. While his popular vote there topped that of Blaine, Garfield, and Hayes, it represented the smallest proportional vote the Republicans had gathered in the South in the post-Reconstruction years. Republican strength declined in every southern state in 1888 as compared with 1884 except in North Carolina and Virginia. The sharpest drops took place in Louisiana and Mississippi where party percentage fell sixteen and ten points respectively, and in South Carolina the Republicans polled only 17.18 per cent of the vote to skid to a new low.[29] By 1888 three presidential elections had taken place since the Republicans had set out in 1877 to redeem the South, and the results indicate that their policies seemed to be having the opposite effect.

Republican percentages of total vote cast in the South in the presidential elections from 1876-1888:

[27] Republicans had a margin of but 1 in the House after the election of 1880 and had organized the Senate only through the cooperation of William Mahone. the Readjuster from Virginia.

[28] George B. Cowlan to Wm. D. Kelley, November 9, 1888, Benjamin Harrison Papers (Division of Manuscripts, Library of Congress).

[29] Burnham, *Presidential Ballots*, pp. 252-255.

	1876	1880	1884	1888
The South	40.34	40.84	40.10	36.95
Alabama	40.01	37.09	38.52	32.67
Arkansas	39.86	38.97	40.70	38.04
Florida	50.21	45.88	46.72	39.89
Georgia	28.00	34.42	33.40	28.71
Louisiana	51.64	36.40	42.54	26.53
Mississippi	31.92	29.70	35.91	25.40
North Carolina	46.37	48.15	46.64	47.64
South Carolina	50.24	33.96	23.40	17.18
Tennessee	40.22	44.26	47.91	46.68
Texas	29.72	23.77	28.59	25.84
Virginia	40.40	39.39	48.92	49.45

In general, Hayes' and Arthur's appeals to southern whites had wound up with Republican losses in the Black Belts and with slight gains in the white counties. The same trend continued in 1888.[30]

	1876	1880	1884	1888
Counties in the South	928	943	963	991
Republican Counties	201	206	219	195
Black Belt Counties	293	293	293	293
Republican Counties	140	133	125	89
White Counties	154	154	154	154
Republican Counties	13	13	18	19

An incident occurred in Virginia in the 1888 campaign that probably cost Harrison the state and which illustrates the point that factionalism has been the bane of southern Republicanism since the close of the Civil War. While the Republican factions in Virginia had sent two delegations to the national convention they had united on a presidential electoral ticket. Harrison lost the state by only 1,539 votes, and he might have been successful had the Republicans not split the Fourth Congressional district, Mahone's home area. John M. Langston, Negro leader from the state, ran for Congress from this district in 1888, because he felt the Negro majority there should have a Negro Representative. The Republican state machine, headed by Mahone, opposed Langston, and instead backed a white,

[30] *Ibid.*, pp. 165-225, 237-243, 252-255.

Judge R. W. Arnold, for the seat. This led to a fight, in which Langston accused Mahone of not supporting him, because he was a Negro, and of believing that "no colored man would be allowed to represent the Fourth Congressional District in . . . Congress." This proved to be an effective charge in an area which had a Negro majority. Langston also called Mahone a "tyrant who must rule or ruin the republican party," and the latter replied by denouncing Langston as a "disorganizer, a bolter, and a marplot."

The Republican National Committee aided Mahone, and with the approval of this group, he prevailed upon Frederick Douglass to enter the fight against Langston. Douglass and Langston had been opponents over other issues, and the former wrote a widely circulated letter that accused Langston of some shady financial operations in connection with the Freedmen's Bank, of aspiring to head Howard University, and of political duplicity. Langston denied the charges and called them "cunning, false, and base" a masterpiece of "poor logic, irrelevant philosophy, and malicious assertions."

In spite of opposition from local Democratic leaders, Mahone, and the Republican national organization, and in spite of Douglass' letter, Langston greatly outdistanced Arnold but fell just behind his Democratic rival, George S. Venable. Langston contested and won his seat in September, 1890 and became the first and only Negro to represent Virginia in Congress.[31] But his leading the Negroes against Mahone probably prevented Harrison from taking Virginia.

If things had not been well with the Republican party in the South in 1876 they seemed to be even worse in 1888. The Southern Question that Hayes had so lightly dismissed at the end of his term still plagued the party leaders. They had failed with every strategem to build a strong party in the Dixie states. Military Reconstruction had alienated southern whites and had been a very costly price for a few years of Republican supremacy in the South following the Civil War. Since the end of Reconstruction Republican policies had appealed mainly to writes

[31] Robert E. Martin, *Negro Disfranchisement in Virginia* (Howard University, 1938), p. 106; Benjamin Quarles, *Frederick Douglass* (Washington, 1948), pp. 318-320; Allen W. Moger, *The Rebuilding of the Old Dominion* (Ann Arbor, 1940), pp. 23-24.

to win their confidence and respect, but by 1888 the Republican party had fewer white supporters in the South than it had had under Grant. The time had come for reappraisal of Republican strategy in the South, and the occasion for a fresh try to win in this section could not have been better. By this date many Republicans hoped with a county chairman in Texas " for a better time for Republicanism in the South," and surely agreed with the the Negro journalist, T. Thomas Fortune that, " The South is good missionary ground. Let the Republican party . . . contest it, and stop standing afar off and yelling, ' Stop Thief.' " [32]

Sensing that Harrison planned to do something spectacular about the South, political observers began to make their usual predictions. The most persistent was that the Republicans would revive their Reconstruction policies so as to protect party voters against fraud and intimidation. Another had Harrison planning to ignore Negroes and former Carpetbaggers and to work with those native white leaders already economically oriented toward the Northeast. Still other stories had Harrison deciding to woo high protective tariff Democrats in the South and to smash the many cliques of southern Republican bosses through a judicious handling of the patronage. [33]

Harrison had inspired some of this speculation when he asked some of his friends to submit detailed schemes on the methods of dealing with the Southern Question. [34] But most of the ideas, plans and demands came on a voluntary basis and a flood of them passed under Harrison's eye in the interval between election and inauguration. Republicans asked Harrison to avoid the mistakes of his predecessors, especially in his choice of a southern adviser on patronage matters, and in thinking that the ex-Confederate leaders controlled the southern whites. Above all he should shun " such folly " of appointing Democrats to office in the South " unless there ain't enough Republicans to go around." Republicans wanted Harrison to abandon the " self constituted " party leaders in the South and

[32] W. H. McCraven, Carthage, Texas, to Benjamin Harrison, November 17, 1888, in Harrison Papers; New York *Age*, April 21, 1886, December 17, 1887.

[33] Dallas *Morning News*, March 25, 1889; New York *Age*, November 24, December 15, 1888.

[34] See for example H. C. Parsons to Harrison, February 5, 1889, in Harrison Papers.

to give up any policy which might cause the whites to fear
Negro supremacy, for a " Negro party will always be confronted by a white party and be beaten by fair or foul means."
Finally they bombarded the President-elect with information
about election frauds and intimidation, and asked for laws and
officials to correct the ballot box outrages, to enforce the laws,
and to uphold free speech, free elections, and an honest count
in the South.[35]

But most Republicans looked upon the matter of good
appointments as the primary way to ingratiate their party with
the white South. When a white from South Carolina asked
Harrison, " why is it that heretofore we have had a bad class
of leaders—all of our Federal offices filled by men who do not
care a *rap* for the addition of good men to our ranks? " he
touched upon a sensitive but an extremely important issue.
And when he urged Harrison to " Take time—give us good
Federal officers," he drove home a point that had pricked
Republican leaders since 1865.[36] Yet while Republicans loudly
insisted that the prosperity of their party in the South depended
upon good appointments, they had various definitions of what
these meant. Some limited it to intelligent conservative whites,
others believed that only young Democrats of " protection
proclivities " filled the bill. Some wanted Harrison to choose
only the " Post-Bellum Class of men," for " the old rebel Dems.
would never change their politics, and the negroes could not
be depended upon to maintain a party by themselves." A few
wanted Harrison to make a " clean sweep " of all the southern
federal office holders and to name only those loyal to the Union
and Constitution.[37] Such varying interpretations could easily

[35] See for example R. Symmes, South Carolina to Harrison, April 9, 1889;
Francis B. Purdie, Alabama to Harrison, November 26, 1888; John E. Bryant,
New York to Harrison, March 1, 1889; Henry Booth, Alabama to Harrison,
December 4, 1888; Wm. E. Chandler to Harrison, December 22, 1889; Albert
H. Dowell, North Carolina to Harrison, February 5, 1889; W. H. Gibbs,
Mississippi to Harrison, November 17, 1888; Cecil H. Plummer, Florida to
Harrison, December 11, 1889; L. F. Miller to General J. W. C. New, Novem-
ber 27, 1888, *Ibid.* For first quotation see Miller to New, and for the second
quotation see Booth to Harrison.

[36] Wm. Perry, Wallhalla, South Carolina to Harrison, April 2, 1889, *Ibid.*

[37] Andrew Hero, Jr., Louisiana to Harrison, May 25, 1889; Harrison Reed
to Harrison, December 4, 1889; Robert A. Hill, Mississippi to Harrison,
December 18, 1889, *Ibid.*; E. J. Sanford, Tennessee to Sherman, November 19,
1888; E. North Cullom, Louisiana to Sherman, November 20, 1888; John H.

have puzzled the President, and they surely pointed up the immense difficulty of finding a formula to please everyone.

Republicans also pressed Harrison to exclude the southern Negro from party leadership and patronage.[38] The question of building a " lily-white " party had frequently confronted Republican leaders since Reconstruction, and while it had an appealing side and was vigorously pushed by southern whites, there was no assurance it would woo them away from the Democratic party. Many Republicans would have agreed with the viewpoint that Negro politicians were " the greatest rascals on earth and will do anything for money," but they would also have had to assent with William Pitt Kellogg of Louisiana, that " The President will find that without the còlored voters there is no Republican party in the South." [39]

While others had much to say about Harrison's policy in the South, he was cautious in making any statement on the subject. In his letter accepting the presidential nomination he repeated an old Republican theme when he declared that " the right of every qualified elector to cast one free ballot and to have it honestly counted must not be questioned. Every constitutional power should be used to make this right secure and punish frauds upon the ballot." Shortly after his election he pointed out privately that he could not yet make any public statement on the Southern Question, but on New Year's Eve he did say " I would like to hear a bugle call throughout the land demanding a pure ballot. A free ballot honestly expressed and fairly counted is the main safeguard of our institutions, and its suppression under any circumstances cannot be tolerated." [40]

Just a month before his inauguration, Harrison informed a friend that he would have no southern policy, because of neces-

Purnell, Alabama, to Sherman, November 24, 1888, in Sherman Papers; J. Madison Wells, Louisiana to Wm. E. Chandler, March, no date, 1889, in Wm. E. Chandler Papers. For the quotations see Reed to Harrison, Purnell to Sherman, and Sanford to Sherman.

[38] Republican Association of Harris County (Houston) Texas to Harrison, November 30, 1888; Frederick Speed, Vicksburg, Mississippi to Harrison, December 8, 1888, in Harrison Papers; Jackson, Miss. *Clarion Ledger*, November 29, 1888.

[39] James Humphries, Georgia to Harrison, January 15, 1889, in Harrison Papers; New York *Age*, June 15, 1889.

[40] New York *Age*, September 15, 1888; January 26, 1889; Francis Purdie, Alabama to Harrison, November 26, 1888, referring to Harrison's letter of November 16, in Harrison Papers.

sity his policy must be as national as a law. In his inaugural address Harrison again insisted upon the freedom of the ballot as the condition of national life and emphasized the necessity for the exercise of every power vested in Congress and the executive to secure that freedom. He tempered his insistence by suggesting to the protectionists in the South that they might make allies of the Negro through friendly instruction and co-operation. Six weeks after taking office, Harrison let it be known that he had been conscientiously studying political affairs of the South, and that he had no tendency to follow the beaten track.[41]

Harrison's major effort to win back the South for the Re-publican party centered around the Force Bill of 1890. By supporting this measure he turned his back on Hayes' idea of conciliating southern conservative whites, and he rejected the possibility of cooperating with the Independent movements which had captivated Arthur. Thus Harrison scouted the likeli-hood of winning additional Republican support in the South by accepting the elimination of the Negro as an important political force. Why he should return to a policy that had alienated the white South and which had also caused the Re-publicans to lose votes in the North deserves some explanation.

Harrison had probably become convinced of the nearly im-possible task of converting southern Democrats to Republican-ism. He had witnessed the failure of Hayes and Arthur to accomplish this aim, and he had seen a steady diminution of Republican strength in the South in the face of policies aimed at reversing such a trend. Like many other Republican leaders in the North of the eighties he had reached the conclusion that enough Republican voters lived in the South to give the party some victories, but that their vote had either been suppressed or not counted. These party strategists argued that they should work to have this vote counted instead of devising a policy to drum up Republican sentiment among southern Democrats where it did not exist or could not be cultivated.

The suppression of the voting privileges of southern Re-publicans, especially of the Negro, had become a major concern

<hr>

[41] H. C. Parson to Harrison, February 5, 1889; Samuel Melton, South Carolina to E. W. Halford, Harrison's secretary, April 17, 1889, in Harrison Papers; Richardson, *Messages and Papers of the Presidents*, IX, 5-14.

to Harrison and other party leaders. As has been pointed out already, southern Democrats had nullified the Fourteenth and Fifteenth Amendments by the use of extra legal methods. Harrison felt that he had a solemn obligation to enforce the law of the land, and he believed that with an effective federal elections law, fear and fraud could not prevent a voter from casting his ballot.[42]

By 1889 many northern Republicans contended that the Negro could not vote in the South because of his race and previous condition of servitude. This, they argued, violated the Constitution and strengthened the Democratic party in the House and in the Electoral College. Not only did a southern Democrat hold his seat illegally, but his vote was two or three times as effective in federal matters as that of a northern Republican. This was a national rather than a local evil, because congressional elections were of a national consequence. Since state action in the South had done nothing to correct the abuse, it became the nation's business to do so.[43]

To support their position Republicans focused attention on statements made by southern leaders such as the one uttered by Governor Richardson of South Carolina in a speech in the summer of 1888.

> We have now the rule of a minority of 400,000 over a majority of 600,000. No Army at Austerlitz, Waterloo, or Gettysburg could ever be wielded like that mass of 600,000 people. The only thing that stands between us and their vote is a flimsy statute—the Eight Box Law—which depends for its effectiveness upon the unity of the white people.[44]

William E. Chandler, back in the Senate and forgetful of his own abandonment of the Negro a few years earlier, carefully began to collect all sorts of evidence bearing on the problem. He received numerous letters recounting all kinds of outrages; he gathered together newspapers clippings of the southern press which made indiscreet sayings, and he analyzed returns to find

[42] Richardson, *Messages and Papers*, IX, 127-129.

[43] *Public Opinion*, VIII (1889-90), IX (1890); T. B. Reed, "Federal Control of Elections," *North American Review*, 150 (1890), 671-680; A. T. Rice, "The Next National Reforms," *Ibid.*, 148 (1889), 82-85; Hoar, *Autobiography*, II, 150-165.

[44] Robert Smalls, "Election Methods in the South," *North American Review*, 151 (1890), 594.

a suppression of the Republican vote in the South. Very much aware of the friction between the North and the South over contested seats in Congress, he readily moved an investigation of a disputed election when the opportunity arose. His real purpose was to make a speech and to give publicity to the facts that he had assembled.[45]

In its platform for 1888 the Republican party had demanded " effective legislation to secure the integrity and purity of elections," and charged that the Democratic party in Congress owed its existence to the suppression of the ballot by " a criminal nullification of the Constitution and laws of the United States." Harrison had followed this party declaration in his first annual message to Congress by calling for a more complete control of congressional elections which was a shift of sentiment on his part, since he had spoken against federal intervention in 1886 when he sat in the Senate.[46]

The fact that they controlled both the presidency and Congress at the same time gave the Republicans a long-sought opportunity to enforce the Fourteenth and Fifteenth Amendments. Harrison now stood ready to remedy the condition of suppressed Republican voters in the South. Congress sensed the mood, and when it met in December, 1889, Republican members introduced numerous bills which provided for the regulation of national elections. Out of all these came the principal measure which Henry Cabot Lodge offered in the House in March, 1890.[47]

The Force Bill, as it immediately came to be known, provided for a chief inspector for each judicial circuit of the country. It placed three supervisors, not more than two from any political party, at every registration office and polling place where the election law went into effect. They were to observe and report on registration, to watch the reception of the vote, to participate in the count, and to make their own returns. On the petition of one hundred citizens in an entire congressional district or in a city of twenty thousand inhabitants or

[45] Chandler Papers, 1888-1890; *Congressional Record*, 50 Cong., I Sess., pp. 402-406, 3138, 7819-30, 7865-81, 8980-9010.

[46] Kirk Porter, *National Party Platforms* (New York, 1924), p. 147; Richardson, *Messages and Papers*, IX, 56; *Congressional Record*, 49th Cong., I Sess., p. 1990.

[47] *Congressional Record*, 51st Cong., I Sess., pp. 96, 100, 102, 110, 250, 254, 2285, 2325, 4063. For Lodge Bill see p. 2285.

more, or on the petition of fifty citizens in any section forming
only a part of a congressional district the law went into operation. The circuit court appointed a board of canvassers of
three men and charged it with the duty of examining and
returning the votes as transmitted to it by the supervisors. If
the certificate of the board agreed with that of the state officials,
the candidate holding both would become a member of the
House. If they differed, that of the board, on a majority decision, was *prima facie* evidence of election. A contestant could
appeal the board's decision to a circuit court; and in the event
of a reversal of opinion, the candidate certified by the court
went to Congress.[48]

These were the main provisions. Additional ones dealt with
the selection of juries and with empowering the President to
use the Army and Navy to enforce the law if necessary. Democrats in the North and South immediately dubbed the measure,
the Force Bill. They attacked it on every possible ground,
except the real one that it might work. A minority report that
accompanied the bill established the pattern of all arguments
used against the bill in Congress. This maintained that the
proposal subjected the states to federal interference and control,
that it was unnecessary since state laws were adequate, and
that it was unconstitutional. Furthermore, the bill projected
the judiciary into the arena of politics, made the supervisors
instruments of party control, and cost too much.[49]

Others besides professional politicians assailed it. Washington Gladden contended that sound government could not be
based upon suffrage granted to the Negro. Godkin of the
Nation and Curtis of *Harper's Weekly*, insisted that the colored
man must be taken out of politics before his welfare could be
promoted. Those who were more partisan minded doubted the
integrity of the motives of the Republican leaders and bitterly
denounced the scheme as an effort to prolong sectional strife
for factional good. Much was also said about how northern
investments in the South could be jeopardized, and gaining
strength from northern support in this and other arguments,
southerners said they were determined to run their own affairs.[50]

[48] H. R. 11045, 51st Cong., I Sess., National Archives.
[49] *House Report*. 51st Cong., I Sess., No. 2493. part 2.
[50] Washington Gladden, "Safeguards of the Suffrage," *Century*, 37 (1889),

While numerous Republicans in the South favored the bill, approval of it among this element of the party was far from unanimous. Some southern Republicans held that the measure instead of strengthening their party would drive the better elements out and also cause it to lose the independent vote. Others added the arguments of racial animosity and the impossibility of enforcing the law in the South. "The day that bill becomes law I will cease to be a Republican," declared a white Republican from North Carolina. "That bill will draw the color line in the South as it has never been drawn before, and no white man in the Southern States can remain in the Republican party." While the Staunton *Valley Virginian*, leading Republican paper of the Old Dominion, admitted that Congress had the constitutional right to pass the elections bill, it questioned whether any good could come from its enactment and predicted that enforcement of the measure would lead to bloodshed.[51]

The chief federal supervisor of elections in North Carolina in an article in the *North American Review* objected to the federal elections bill, because he felt that it failed to provide for a national system of congressional elections and that it attempted to resurrect a dead issue in the South, the Supervisory Act of 1871. Congressman Hamilton G. Ewart, Republican from North Carolina, pointed out that in many counties in the South where few white Republicans lived, Negroes would necessarily be appointed supervisors and deputy marshals, a move that was bound to bring on bloodshed, riots, and disorder. Ewart stated that the men behind the Force Bill were asking poor Negroes to discharge a duty of supervising elections that the United States Army would be reluctant to perform, for it took unflinching nerve to act as a supervisor at a precinct surrounded by angry, hot-blooded, determined, and resolute partisans where the issue " is black against white, the powerful against the weak, the intelligent against ignorant." To the objections of northern Republicans that such a sorry plight existed in the South, Ewart replied, " But, virtuous Representatives, put yourselves in the place of these southern

621-28; E. L. Godkin, "The Republican Party and the Negro," *Forum*, 7 (1889), 246-257; *Harper's Weekly*, 1888-1889; *Public Opinion*, 6-7 (1889).
    [51] *The Nation*, LI (July 31, August 14, 1890), 82, 126-127.

people; place negro judges of elections and negro deputy marshals at the voting precincts in Michigan, in Wisconsin, in Ohio, and in Indiana, and the Republican nominees for Congress in those districts would be swept out of political existence. You very well know that you would not dare to apply this law as it will have to be applied in the South in the districts which you represent today." Ewart maintained that no Republican in his state, " black or white, is prevented from casting his vote. . . . The elections are absolutely fair. . . . There is no negro problem at the South. . . . It is a delusion to suppose that he [the Negro] is voting the Republican ticket solidly," and the colored man in the South should be treated with " wise and salutary neglect." [52] A Republican from the North who had lived in Alabama for twenty-five years, called the Force Bill one of the greatest blunders in strategy that the party had made. He thought it was " high time the Republican party was giving the Negro a rest. Let him alone." But 'according to a correspondent of the Philadelphia *Press* who had toured the South, Republicans in this section were opposed to the bill, because it did not go far enough. They wanted the national government to take complete and absolute control of federal elections.[53]

Press reaction to the Force Bill varied according to the political loyalty of the newspaper. In general Republican papers supported the measure, and in general the Democratic and Independent press opposed it. The New York *Tribune* thought it was " indeed high time for Congress to devise methods for protecting the rights of the people," and that " No other measure proposed at the present session of Congress is of greater or more far-reaching importance than this." The Chicago *Inter-Ocean* felt sure that " an effective law is needed," and the Boston *Journal* labeled the Lodge measure " a conservative bill " that promised " to accomplish the results in view with the minimum of disturbance." The Philadelphia *Press* said " It is ridiculous to speak of the measure as a force bill; there is no force about it." The Topeka *Capitol* called it " one of the most reasonable and necessary [measures] ever intro-

[52] A. W. Shaffer, " A Southern Republican on the Lodge Bill," *The North American Review*, 151 (November, 1890), 601-609; *The Nation*, LI (July 3, 1890), 5-6; *Congressional Record*, 51st Cong., I Sess., pp. 6688-6691.

[53] John H. Purnell, Opelika, Alabama to Wm. E. Chandler, July 23, 1890, in Wm. E. Chandler Papers; *Philadelphia Press*, August 1, 1890.

duced in Congress," and the Albany *Journal* argued that the bill was " in harmony with the spirit of the times." The *Ohio State Journal* predicted that " The whole nation will be the gainer by the operation," and the Brooklyn *Times* saw " nothing sectional in the bill, nothing that seems to afford a loophole of excuse to the Southern members for raising the cry of Federal interference." The St. Louis *Globe-Democrat* declared that the queston was " not one of effecting a perfect cure, but of doing as much as possible in this direction. It is idle to look for any relief through state action. . . . Congress has ample power to do all this bill proposes; and the time has unquestionably come when the assertion of this power is an imperative duty." [54]

Opposition to the Force Bill among the Democratic, and particularly the southern Democratic press, was extremely bitter. The Augusta *Chronicle* exclaimed that " no more pernicious bill could be passed by Congress," and warned that " our people will not submit to it." The Louisville *Courier-Journal* asked " Why should the North . . . seek to set the hands of the clock back and to return to the hideous experiment of putting the bottom of society on top? " The Memphis *Appeal* thundered, " With us it is a question of life or death. The Democrats of the South must subordinate all other issues to this one." The Nashville *American* quite frankly pointed out that " the white race must rule," and that the Force Bill would not change southerners from holding such a conviction. The New Orleans *Times-Democrat* put its finger on the key matter when it said that the Republicans were finding it difficult to frame a bill " that will control the South, yet not offend the North." The Philadelphia *Record* labeled the Force Bill " an act of pure despotism "; the New York *World* called it " foreign to all the institutions of our Government," and the Pittsburgh *Post* thought it was " an atrocious and criminal attempt by the Republican party . . . to dictate and rule from Washington by perversion of law and justice." [55]

Among the newspapers described as Independent, there was heavy opposition to the Force Bill. The Omaha *World Herald*

[54] *Public Opinion*, VIII (1889-1890), 164, 553; IX, (1890), 239, 262, 287, 311, 312.
[55] *Ibid.*, IX (1890), 238, 261, 262-263, 287, 310, 311.

called the measure " a disgrace to the representatives of a free people," and the Washington *Post* looked upon the bill as an " instrument bubbling over with a mischief of a most dangerous nature." The Springfield *Republican* contended that it was nothing more than " a bill to promote sectional strife," and the Providence *Journal* considered the Force Bill not only to be wrong in principle but also bad in practice.[56]

There were notable exceptions to this press reaction to the Force Bill. The New York *Times*, listed as an Independent, declared there was " no trace of partisan partiality" in the bill and that it was " an honest and courageous attempt to apply a sound principle of public policy and a high standard of political purity to a most difficult and perplexing problem." On the other hand, the Omaha *Bee*, a Republican sheet, asserted that " the masses of the Republican party" did not take any interest in the Force Bill, and that it was probable that " a majority of them do not sympathize with the proposed legislation." The *Nation* argued that the North would not submit to such treatment as was intended by the Force Bill, and the only reason for it being put forth was " to make it the text for bloody-shirt speeches. But this is as short-sighted from the politician's point of view as from the statesman's." The agitation of such propositions, contended the *Nation*, would insure the " continued solidity for the Democrats" in the South, " while instead of making the North solid for the Republicans, the readiness of Republican leaders to support such schemes renders independent voters more and more suspicious of the party. In short," concluded the Nation, " it is clearly a losing game all around." [57]

As a result of the heavy opposition to the Force Bill, some alarm developed among its supporters, and fear arose that if the attempt to pass the measure failed, much harm would result to the Republican party. Senator Hoar, chairman of the Committee on Privileges and Elections in the upper house, thought it was best to ascertain prevailing opinion and to see whether there was any chance of getting the elections bill through. If this proved to be unlikely, he believed that the

[56] *Ibid*., 309-311; VIII (1889-1890), 552.
[57] *Ibid*., IX (1890), 263; VIII (1889-90), 552; *The Nation*, XLIX (December 19, 1889), 486.

elections scheme should not be carried to the point to have a debate in either house.[58]

Accordingly, Hoar conferred with some members of the House who agreed that if the Senate were not likely to pass the Force Bill, it should be laid aside without making a serious movement for it in the lower chamber. After this arrangement, Republican Senators met in caucus on June 10 to discuss whether or not they should actively enter the fight to pass the measure. Hoar moved the appointment of a committee to study the whole question, but when objection to this arose, he was afraid that the real reason for his request might escape to the press, so he did not press his motion. In the caucus meeting no vote was taken, and no definite conclusions were reached; but the sentiment was that some legislation was necessary, although there was doubt whether the session of Congress should be prolonged for such a purpose.[59]

Despite the lack of concrete action at the Senate caucus, the bill continued to make progress in the House under the leadership of Speaker Thomas B. Reed and its sponsor, Lodge. On June 25 it became the unfinished business in this chamber with the final vote on it scheduled for July 2. Lodge opened debate on the measure by arguing that the bill simply proposed to exercise the power of the United States relative to the election of Representatives. " No local machinery is disturbed, no local officer is displaced, no man, if this law is applied to a district, will cast his vote in any manner different from that in which he now casts it. No State . . . is interfered with." Lodge held that the leading principle of the bill was " to secure complete publicity at every stage of an election," and to give full opportunity to the qualified voter. " Congress has the absolute power to deal with the election of members of this House as it pleases," declared Lodge. " If citizens . . . entitled to vote for Representatives in Congress are deprived of their rights, it is the duty of Congress to see that they are protected." To support this contention, Lodge quoted from the Constitution and from James Madison, and referred to action in the Constitutional Convention and to Supreme Court cases on this point. Lodge denied that the bill was sectional and pointed out that

[58] Hoar, *Autobiography*, II, 154.
[59] *Ibid.*; *New York Tribune*, June 15, 1890.

if all were well with elections in the South as Representatives from that section said, then there should be no objection to the bill by southern congressmen. " On the contrary, they of all people ought to desire it." [60] Congressman John J. Hemphill from South Carolina spoke for the opposition, and his arguments were mainly those which the minority report contained. " It is not elections that are troubling us," contended Hemphill, " it is the iniquity of the office holders who are sent South to oppress the people. That is the trouble with the bill." He scoffed at the accusation of corrupt elections in the South, and maintained that southern motives had been misunderstood because of sectional demagogues. Hemphill charged that there were abuses in the North, and that the Republicans had an illegal majority in the House. Bitterly did he arraign the Republicans for attempting to restore the Negro to power in the South and to renew the race struggle. But as for South Carolina, " we know that the honest and intelligent must either rule or we must leave it," and " I swear we will not leave it." Hemphill admitted that the Negro " has as many rights as I have . . . but he cannot have his rights and mine, too." [61]

A sharp struggle followed in the remaining days of debate. The arguments largely paralleled those already established by Lodge and Hemphill. The opposition was highly inflammatory and many charges such as un-Americanism, dictatorship, destruction of our government, and others filled the air as Washington's sultry days and nights shortened tempers and provoked men to desperate sayings.[62] To bolster the supporters of the bill, William E. Chandler in a public letter to Speaker Reed said, " It is not a question of party success, but one of honor and right. . . . Republicans who talk about not irritating the South with force bills are false to their proposed principles and are doing their best to discredit and defeat the party." According to Chandler, " A Republican can believe in tariff reduction or even free trade and yet properly adhere to the party. But he cannot fail to advocate the Fifteenth Amendment . . . and yet be a Republican. His only proper place is with the Negro-baiting, Republican-killing Democracy. So it is the duty

---

[60] *Congressional Record*, 51st Cong., I Sess., pp. 6538-6548.
[61] *Ibid.*, pp. 6548-6554.
[62] *Ibid.*, House Proceedings, June 26—July 2, 1890.

of all Republicans to push on in all endeavors . . . to enforce the Fifteenth Amendment. . . . Failing to do this, the party . . . dishonorably dies," [63]

Several days before the final vote, opposition arose from an unexpected source and in a disguised form. Herman Lehlbach, Republican from New Jersey, on June 30 offered an amendment which would have obliged the chief supervisor to take such action " as is requisite to secure such supervision in every Congressional district as is provided by the laws of the United States." This would have removed the stigma of a sectional measure, as it would have made its application mandatory throughout the country. Lehlbach's proposal was hotly debated and was defeated by the slight margin of six votes. [64] Lodge argued that the amendment would not have made the bill any more national than it already was. True, the operation of the bill was optional, but if everyone and every part of the country possessed the option, the measure was as national as if it were compulsory. [65]

Foes of the Force Bill made numerous efforts to emasulate it or to delay a vote on it through dilatory motions and by forcing a third reading of the entire measure, but it passed the House on July 2 by a vote of 155 to 149. Two Republicans, H. Dudley Coleman from Louisiana and Lehlbach, voted squarely against the bill, and six absented themselves without pairs. [66] Yet Republican leaders were pessimistic about the ultimate fate of the bill. Reed was convinced that it must get through now, " or our defeat is certain." Both Lodge and Senator Orville Platt of Connecticut wished that Chandler were now in Washington and not away recuperating, because they needed " people who are willing to work for results." Senator John Coit Spooner from Wisconsin rightly feared that there were not enough votes to pass the bill since there were " Republicans enough who care more for their ease than they do for their duty." Senators Nelson W. Aldrich from Rhode Island and William B. Allison from Iowa expressed grave

[63] Richardson, *Chandler*, p. 412.
[64] *Congressional Record*, 51st Cong., I Sess., pp. 6793, 6849.
[65] Henry Cabot Lodge, " The Federal Elections Bill," *North American Review*, 151 (1890), 257-266.
[66] *Congressional Record*, 51st Cong., I Sess., pp. 6940-41.

doubts as to whether the legislation would even be considered, and three other Republican Senators predicted that it would not even be debated. Three days after the Force Bill reached the Senate, Republican members met in caucus for three hours. They failed to reach an agreement over what action they should take, but the general opinion prevailed that once the bill was considered it should be pushed through.[67]

Enormous pressure was put upon the Senate to duplicate the action of the House. Senator Matthew S. Quay of Pennsylvania was bombarded with letters from his home state strongly urging passage, and the chairman of the Republican Congressional Committee issued a circular asking the Senate to take favorable action. Reed and Lodge were charged with bullying newspapers into supporting it and in prodding Negro federal office holders to appeal for its approval.[68] The Republican state chairman in Indiana pointed out that party members in his state were anxious for the passage of the elections bill and that there would be an "enormous howl" if it did not get through. "The party will take a club to every Republican senator who fails to do his duty in that connection," reported this Hoosier.[69] Hoar added his bit by determinedly moving the bill along and by having his committee favorably report it out. A portent of what was to come occurred at this time when Senator Henry Teller, Republican from Colorado, while consenting to the majority report, reserved the right to vote against the measure if he saw fit.[70] Before reporting it out, Hoar personally saw every member of the Senate and learned that not only a majority of Republicans but "a majority of the whole Senate declared emphatically for the Election Bill." [71]

The struggle in the House had been on almost entirely a partisan basis, but in the Senate the Force Bill became involved in other issues which caused a serious division among Republi-

[67] Reed to Chandler, July 6, 1890; Lodge to Chandler, July 10, 1890; O. H. Platt to Chandler, July 22, 1890, in Chandler Papers; Spooner to J. A. Johnson, July 13, 1890; to W. A. Barber, July 13, 1890, John Coit Spooner Papers (Division of Manuscripts, Library of Congress); Philadelphia *Press*, July 2, 1890; New York *Tribune*, July 11, 1890.

[68] Philadelphia *Press*, July 10, 24, 1890; New York *Tribune*, July 10, 1890; *The Nation*, LI (July 24, 1890).

[69] Louis T. Michener to E. W. Halford, July 10, 1890, in Harrison Papers.

[70] *Congressional Record*, 51st Cong., I Sess., pp. 8277-78; 2 Sess., pp. 168-169.

[71] Hoar, *Autobiography*, II, 155.

cans. The tariff and silver legislation faced the party, and the elections bill was eventually classified as a matter of secondary importance and was sidetracked by the Senate for appearing to block the passage of more significant matters. ·Yet Harrison and other party leaders had talked much about safeguarding the vote of the Negro and some like Hoar and Spooner wished to see the party meet its obligations in this respect. But it appeared that many Republicans supported the measure only for this reason, for as Spooner remarked, " The House having passed the bill . . . most of us hate terribly to run from it." [72] Two developments did occur in the Senate that seemed to remove some of the barriers blocking passage of the bill. One was the amended form of the measure as reported out which reduced the severity of penalties and which removed those sections most objectionable to the South, especially the one that allowed the President to use the armed forces to enforce the provisions of the bill. The other was the action of the Republican Senate Caucus in asking the Rules Committee to find some way to limit debate, for as Platt pointed out to Chandler, " The question whether we can pass an election law I think depends whether we can change the rules, and the persons who don't want to pass an election law don't want to change the rules." [73]

When the Force Bill reached the Senate floor, the McKinley Tariff was under debate. This piece of legislation affected practically all the business interests in the country, among which were some of the heavy contributors to the Republican campaign fund in 1888, and they anxiously awaited its enactment into law. Under Senator Arthur P. Gorman of Maryland, the Democrats began to filibuster any attempt to pass the elections bill which in turn blocked final consideration of the tariff. The two Republican Senators from Pennsylvania, Quay and Don Cameron, vitally interested in the quick and safe passage of the tariff, subordinated the plight of the Negro to it. They successfully moved to postpone action on the Force Bill until the next session and pointed out that the McKinley Tariff was an " immediate necessity; the election bill can wait." [74]

[72] J. C. Spooner to J. A. Johnson, July 13, 1890, in Spooner Papers.

[73] *Congressional Record*, 51st Cong., 2 Sess., pp. 22-26; New York *Tribune*, July 12, 1890; Platt to Chandler, July 22, 1890, in Chandler Papers.

[74] *Congressional Record*, 51st Cong., I Sess., p. 8466; Philadelphia *Press*, August 14, 1890.

Quay's maneuver immediately aroused the anger of the supporters of the elections bill who fought in vain to save it from defeat. The New York *Tribune* and Philadelphia *Press* denounced Quay's move and called upon Republican Senators to repudiate it. Spooner wrote that " The Quay resolution . . . is a cowardly surrender," and " it looks as if Aldrich and Quay has sold us out," and as for the other Republicans who opposed the elections bill, the Wisconsin Senator thought that " the almighty dollar obscures their vision." Platt accused Quay of making " a bargain with the Democrats," and a " weak and cowardly " one at that in order " to purchase the passage of the Tariff bill." [75] Hoar struggled to restore the Force Bill to the legislative calendar, while members of the Republican National Committee, including J. S. Clarkson, attempted to persuade the Pennsylvania leader from causing an open split in party ranks. House proponents of the bill were dismayed and there was considerable talk among them of holding up the tariff until the Force Bill became law.[76]

But Quay was adamant. He explained his position by saying that the Force Bill imperiled the tariff. He was not opposed to legislation regulating elections, but he was not willing to sacrifice the tariff to it.[77] Behind his move lay the charge that his " creditors—the contributors to the Harrison campaign fund— are pressing their claim." [78] They were mainly manufacturers who had advanced the cause of the party through the generous donation of funds and were now demanding their reward in the form of protection. Equally pressing upon Quay were the delaying tactics of the Democrats which they possessed under the rules of the Senate and which they had fully exploited under the direction of Gorman. Confronted by this impasse so long as the majority was determined to pass the elections bill, Quay and the other Republican protectionists had to come to terms with the Democratic minority.

[75] *The Nation*, LI (August 21, 1890), 141; Spooner to W. W. Lockwood, August 18, 1890, to Henry C. Payne, August 13, 1890, to Henry Fink, July 27, 1890, in Spooner Papers; Louis A. Coolidge, *An Old-Fashioned Senator, Orville H. Platt* (New York, 1910), pp. 232-234.

[76] *Congressional Record*, 51st Cong., I Sess., pp. 8488, 8678, 8694, 8724, 8777, 8842; Philadelphia *Press*, August 15, 22, 1890.

[77] Philadelphia *Press*, August 14, 1890.

[78] *The Nation*, LI (August 21, 1890), 141.

In his message to Congress in 1890, Harrison renewed his plea for the passage of the Force Bill. He argued that there was need for such a law in all parts of the country, for the restraints and penalties would be useful everywhere. To those who doubted its effectiveness, Harrison pointed to the character of its opposition. For those who held the measure to be unconstitutional, a new exercise of power and an invasion of the rights of the states, he referred them to Supreme Court decisions affirming the validity of such legislation and to the Enforcement Acts of 1870-1871 by which the Congress had established certain practices for the election of Representatives. Harrison vigorously scouted the sectional nature of the bill declaring that if it appeared in such a light then " crime is local and not universal." Neither would the measure revive race animosity. Instead it would provide the President with an opportunity of remedying the inadequacies of the existing laws which attempted to secure to every citizen his constitutional rights and privileges.[79]

During the summer and fall of 1890, public opinion in the country turned heavily against the Force Bill. While a large number of petitions favoring it descended upon Congress, an even greater number opposing the measure poured in. The Farmers' Alliance in National Convention at Ocala, Florida called for its defeat, and business men of southern cities in mass meetings or in trade organizations passed resolutions asking northern business men to protest against the Force Bill. In New York City more than a hundred wholesalers of every political faith joined hands to ask Congress for the defeat of the elections bill. The *Manufacturer*, organ of the Manufacturers' Club in Philadelphia, declared that " the sentiment of the Republican party, outside the circle of professional politicians, is against the adoption of the Federal Elections Bill," and in the same city, the Matthew Stanley Quay Club, a Negro organization, went on record of open hostility to the measure. Republican state convention in Wisconsin, Minnesota, Nebraska, and Michigan adopted platforms touching upon the issues of the day, but remained silent on the Force Bill, while the Tennessee Republican convention passed a resolution

[79] Richardson, *Messages and Papers*, IX, 127-129.

condemning the proposal as "a law that would unsettle the business interests," and which expressed confidence that the party would not pass it. Senator Elihu B. Washburne of Minnesota declared that "the West does not want the bill," and the St. Louis *Globe-Democrat*, an influential and moderate Republican paper, after a survey of its own, concluded that four out of five Republicans in the South opposed the Force Bill, and that the masses of the party in the West felt likewise, "The wise thing to do," said the *Globe-Democrat*, "is to frankly confess the truth . . . and the truth with regard to the Federal election bill is that it is not demanded by the sober judgment and patriotism of the country." Repercussions of the controversial elections scheme even invaded academic circles where it was reported that Harvard University failed to reelect Lodge as an overseer chiefly because of his connection with the bill.[80]

In the South opposition to the Force Bill reached its highest point since it caused a considerable amount of alarm in this section. Southern newspapers raised the specter of another Reconstruction and of Negro supremacy, and the practical effect of the measure was to have whites close ranks and solidify themselves against any type of federal intervention. Senator Zebulon Vance of North Carolina speaking at Raleigh plainly and bluntly manifested the temper of much of the South when he said that a southerner who supported the Force Bill "ought not to be allowed to live among us. Don't understand me as advocating violence," continued Vance, "but there is such a thing as driving men out by fierce intolerance and contempt; and they deserve all that can be heaped upon them." [81] The more radical and hot-headed elements in the South called for an organized boycott of all northern goods, but more sober minded southern Senators hastily condemned this proposal as a lot of foolish talk. Colquitt of Georgia, and Gorman and Vance spoke forcibly against the suggested boycott, while Butler from South Carolina advised the South to take no " con-

---

[80] *Congressional Record*, 51st Cong., 2 Sess., p. 256; *Public Opinion*, IX (1890), 428; *The Nation*, LI (July 31, August 7, 14, 21, 28, Sept. 4, 1890), 82, 102, 126, 180; St. Louis *Globe-Democrat*, August 23, 1890; Philadelphia *Press*, July 13, 1890.

[81] Shaffer, "A Southern Republican on the Lodge Bill," *North American Review*, 151 (1890), 606.

certed action in regard to the Force Bill yet awhile," for he thought that it would not pass.[82]

Yet a few felt that something had to be done, and a group of congressmen from the South published the book, *Why the Solid South*. They reviewed Reconstruction in each state and placed the responsibilities for the tragedies of their section and for the " Solid South " upon the errors made by the Republican party. Obviously the work was a piece of propaganda aimed at presenting the argument that the Force Bill was a return to the blunders of Reconstruction, and the authors hoped that Americans need not take another lesson in this.[83]

A rising opposition aligned with the delaying tactics of the Democrats and the insurgency of the silver Republicans in the Senate managed to kill the bill for good in the second session.[84] These Republican rebels showed greater concern over the free coinage of silver that they did in the dilemma of the Negro. Like Quay they willingly shelved their party's program for the South and the Negro and reached an accord with the Democratic leaders that subordinated the Force Bill to the Sherman Silver Act with its free coinage amendment. This came about in January, 1891 when the silver Republicans voted with the Democrats to remove the Force Bill from the legislative calendar and from its former position of unfinished business. The desertion of eight silver Republicans caused dismay and chagrin to the supporters of the bill, and from then on, no chance in that Congress remained to pass the measure. All but one of the eight insurgents had signed the agreement adopted by the Republican Senate Caucus in August to let the elections scheme go over until the next session upon the condition that it would then be taken up and " kept before the Senate to the exclusion of other legislative business, until it shall be disposed of by a vote." [85] Hoar could not reconcile the defection of the silver Republicans with the promise they had made in August, and he

[82] Atlanta *Constitution*, July 20, 1890; Philadelphia *Press*, July 24, 25, 29, 1890.

[83] Hilary A. Herbert and Others, *Why the Solid South or Reconstruction and Its Results* (Baltimore, 1890).

[84] Fred A. Wellborn, " The Influence of the Silver Republican Senators, 1890-1891," *Mississippi Valley Historical Review*, XIV (1927-1928), 462-480.

[85] Hoar, *Autobiography*, II, 155-156; New York *Tribune*, August 22, 1890; Philadelphia *Press*, August 23, 1890.

felt that their action meant "the death of the Republican party." [86] Spooner was greatly outraged at the treatment accorded to the election bill by mining camp Senators," and he charged that "confederates under alleged Republican leadership . . . side tracked" the measure.[87] A Republican from Ohio was of the opinion that some of his party's senators had sold themselves "for thirty pieces of Silver, or maybe they got more." [88]

Gloom and division filled Republican ranks in the Senate. "There is no touch of elbows any longer on the Republican side of the Senate," wrote Spooner, "Enough abandon us on the election bill . . . to constitute, with the Democrats, a majority of the Senate, and the trouble . . . is not with the great body of Republican Senators, but with the few who for reasons of their own desert us. We intend to have before this session ends a showing of hands on the elections bill," continued Spooner. "We would have adopted a rule long ago limiting debate, but for some weakness in our ranks, which rendered it impracticable." [89] But a showing of hands on the bill and a rule limiting debate never came even though many efforts were made to achieve them.

Republicans in the Senate abandoned their party in the South in 1890 because they had a greater interest in a high tariff and a silver measure, and because they feared that a revival of Reconstruction tactics would disrupt the community of business interests that had developed between North and South since the removal of the troops in 1877. Cameron emphasized this latter argument when he told a newspaperman in December, 1890, "I will vote against the election bill whatever form it may assume . . . Northern capital has been flowing into the South . . . and a community of commercial interests will result . . . the election law would disturb this desirable condition." [90] Others agreed with Cameron's conclusion. A Republican business man from Philadelphia opposed the Force

[86] Hoar, II, 157; *The Nation*, LII (January 8, 1891).

[87] Spooner to W. P. Roberts, January 8, 1891, to Hiram Parker, January 11, 1891, in Spooner Papers.

[88] H. Bartlett to John Sherman, January 6, 1891, in Sherman Papers.

[89] Spooner to David Williams, January 11, 1891, in Spooner Papers.

[90] *Public Opinion*, X (1890), 269.

Bill on the grounds that a more conservative course could be adopted accomplishing the same result. A Republican businessman from Brooklyn thought that if the election proposal were dropped " nobody would be disgusted, except such zealous partisans as will remain Republicans in any event." The *Manufacturer* objected to the bill on the grounds that it would stir up sectional anger and make the South more solid.[91]

There were various explanations offered for the defeat of the Force Bill. The New York *Tribune* laid the cause for its failure to get through Congress on the silver alliance of the West and South.[92] Hoar, Lodge, Spooner and other supporters of the measure blamed the opposition of northern business men, and Quay and Cameron added strength to this contention when they preferred to see the bill die rather than block the passage of the McKinley Tariff or injure northern investments in the South. Yet the special-interest-within-the-party-argument was not solely responsible for the shelving of the elections scheme. There was considerable opposition to it within party ranks, and the poll of the St. Louis *Globe-Democrat* amply demonstrated this. The Philadelphia *Inquirer*, a leading Republican paper of the East, reported the same results, when after a canvass of party opinion, it stated that most Republicans had privately hoped for the defeat of the bill.[93] James Bryce thought the elections bill was an " attempt to overcome nature by force of law," [94] and most of the public showed its bias by accepting the appelation of the " Force Bill." The St. Louis *Globe-Democrat* summed up a good bit of public sentiment by saying, " We can better afford to tolerate the evil than to attack it in the form of arbitrary Federal interference in local affairs." [95]

The defeat of the Force Bill marks the third major abandonment of the Negro by the Republicans in the post-Reconstruction years in spite of their official statements in the same years that they were the best friends that the colored man had. In

[91] Hamilton Disston to Benjamin Harrison, August 7, 1890, in Harrison Papers; *The Nation*, LI (Augst 14, 21, 1890).

[92] New York *Tribune*, January 28, 1891.

[93] Philadelphia *Inquirer*, January 27, 1891.

[94] James Bryce, " Thoughts on the Negro Problem," *North American Review*, 153 (1891), 654.

[95] *Public Opinion*, IX (1890), 470.

their platforms from 1876 through 1896 the Republicans solemnly pledged themselves to enforce the Fourteenth and Fifteenth Amendments, to secure to " every American citizen of whatever race and color complete liberty and exact equality in the exercise of all civil, political, and public rights," to protect " honest voters " against terrorism, violence and fraud, and never to relax their efforts " until the integrity of the ballot and purity of elections . . . be fully guaranteed in every state." They demanded that every citizen, white or black, be allowed to cast one free and unrestricted ballot and to have it counted and returned. They denounced what they labeled as " continuous inhuman outrages " perpetrated upon American citizens for political reasons, and the " fraud and violence practiced by the Democracy in the Southern States." [96] In Congress they moved investigations of fraud and violence in elections in the South, accused southern Democrats of holding their seats illegally and of exercising a disproportionate voting influence, and focused attention upon indiscreet statements by the southern leaders and the press such as the editorial of the *Times-Democrat* in New Orleans which exclaimed, " The aim and desire of every white citizen of Louisiana is to eliminate the Negro from politics." [97]

Actually though, the Republican party turned out to be among the poorest of friends that the southern Negro had in the post-Reconstruction years. For while the Republicans talked much about safeguarding the vote of the colored man and loudly lamented the state of political affairs in the South, they took few steps to remedy the situation or to meet their obligations to the freedman. Instead of protecting the Negro and looking after him as the ward of the nation, they deserted him and left him as the ward of the dominant race in the South. On three major occasions over these two decades, the Republicans abandoned their Negro ally. Once when Hayes recalled the troops, again when Arthur joined hands with southern Independents, and finally when Harrison and a Republican controlled Congress backed away from the Force Bill.

Such a record has left the Republican party open to the severest kind of criticism by the specialist and intelligent lay-

[96] Kirk Porter, *National Party Platforms*, pp. 95, 111, 133-136, 147, 174, 205.
[97] New Orleans, *Times-Democrat*, October 2, 1894.

men alike. Yet much of this criticism has been conducted against a background of faulty or inadequate historical information or a misunderstanding of the motives of the party. The point has been made many times that since the Republicans enfranchised the Negro they should have continued to see that he could vote, and that they could have done this by enforcing the Fourteenth and Fifteenth Amendments. But the problem is not so simple as this, and those who argue in this manner have forgotten some of the facts of history.

In the first place, because of the great diversity in election laws in the states by 1787 the Federal Convention left the suffrage requirements to the states, a prerogative that they have jealously guarded ever since and which has been reinforced from time to time with court decisions. As to Negro suffrage, it was foisted upon the South and thrust upon the freedman, because it worked to the advantage of the Republican party and acted as a bar to the reestablishment of slavery. If this were not so, why did northern and western states exclude the Negro from the suffrage while they forced the southern states to admit him? It should be remembered that in 1867, the year of the Reconstruction Acts, only Wisconsin and New York outside of the New England states allowed the Negro to vote, and even more significantly, in the same year, Kansas, Minnesota, Michigan, and Ohio voted down Negro suffrage. " There was not a shred of evidence to show that anywhere in the North, men wanted Negro voters in their midst," writes Kirk Porter in his study of the suffrage. " Done under the cloak of hypocrisy in feigned support of democratic principles, it was in truth a revengeful punitive measure directed at the South, for which the entire nation suffered." [98] Thaddeus Stevens lent credence to this latter observation when he said of Negro suffrage, " if it be a punishment to traitors they deserve it." [99]

Then there is the question of duress under which the South ratified the Fourteenth and Fifteenth Amendments which made them nationally effective. Nor should one forget that when the Supreme Court came to interpret the latter amendment, it

[98] Kirk Porter, *History of Suffrage in the United States* (Chicago, 1918), p. 134.
[99] James Albert Hamilton, *Negro Suffrage and Congressional Representation* (*New York*, 1910), p. 15.

laid down certain principles, which when taken together, made
it nearly impossible for the Republicans to enforce its provisions. The Court pointed out that the amendment did not
" confer the right of suffrage upon anyone," since that right
still came from the states; that no one could be convicted under
its provisions unless his acts constituted a discrimination on
account of race, color, or previous conditions of servitude; and
that the Amendment did not contemplate the wrongful acts
of private individuals, but only those of a state or its agents.[100]

Troublesome as all these matters were in making the practical
application of the Fourteenth and Fifteenth Amendments exceedingly difficult, had they been removed or had they not
existed, the Republicans still could have done little, if anything, to safeguard the vote of the Negro in the face of extra
legal methods employed by the South to disfranchise him. As it
has already been noted, throughout most of this period the Republicans were in no position to enforce these Amendments,
for these were not years of Republican supremacy. For their
failure to enact a Force Bill in 1890 in view of their solemn
promises to do so and in view of their control of the federal
government, the Republicans can be criticized, but even in this
case, the criticism has to be conducted against the background
of the party's motives and interests as of that date.

To say that Hayes, Arthur, and Harrison abandoned the
Negro is to tell but half the story and to allow for a severe
indictment without some deeper explanation. No one would
be foolish enough to deny that the Republicans did forsake the
Negro, but few indeed have sought to find out why. In part as
we have already seen the abandonment was beyond their control. But it was also part of the well planned strategy that
the Republicans had worked out for the South in the post-
Reconstruction years. These new plans, in the main, called for
a shift in Republican appeals in the South from Negroes to
whites, but this did not mean that the Republicans were no
longer interested in the Negro vote. On the contrary, they
wished to maintain, and even increase their Negro support, but
they also wanted to swell their ranks with white recruits.

And as we have already seen the Republican abandonment

[100] U. S. v. Reese (92 U. S., 214, 1876); James V. Bowman (190, U. S.,
127, 1903).

of the Negro was only a part of the general desertion of the freedman by northerners, of which the *Nation* and the New York *Tribune* were typical. During the eighties and nineties the northern press played up crimes in which Negroes were involved and developed the stereotype of the Negro as a criminal. Northern newspapers emphasized the Negro's hyper-sensitiveness about his civil rights, portrayed the colored man as backward, and treated the lynching of Negroes in such a manner as to create the impression that lynching was evidence of guilt. " Colored people in general," writes a recent student of the Negro in America of the last quarter of the nineteenth century, " even the ' upper class ' Negroes who were called Mr., Miss and Mrs., and even ' Hon.' and ' esquire ' were subjected to prejudice, discrimination, and segregation in the North.[101] When a stronger Civil Rights law was passed in New York in 1895, the *Times* felt that Negroes should not use it as a means to " rub shoulders with whites," and during the Republican National Convention in Philadelphia in 1900, Negro delegates were assigned to colored homes. Northern literary magazines like *Harper's, Scribner's, Century,* and to a less extent the *Atlantic,* regularly used derisive terms that are rarely used today save in local color fiction, private conversation, and among rabid Negro baiters. In these magazines " virtually every derogatory stereotype was affixed upon the Negro," who was made to appear superstitious, dull and stupid, imitative and thus not creative, ignorant, suspicious, improvident, lazy, immoral and criminal.[102]

Added to this was the invalidation of the Civil Rights Bill by the Supreme Court in 1883, an opinion which in effect indicated that the federal government could not lawfully protect the Negro against the discrimination which private individuals might choose to exercise against him. In short the court said that the system of white supremacy was beyond federal control, because the southern social order rested mainly upon human relations and not upon state-made sanctions. With this conclusion much of the northern press agreed, and the New Haven *Evening Register* stated that there was " grave doubt

[101] Logan, *Negro in American Life and Thought,* pp. 217-229 for northern press and Negro, p. 233 for quotation.
[102] *Ibid.,* pp. 233, 240-251.

if the question of social principles can be settled satisfactorily by legislation." [103] The Civil Rights decision and the attitude of most of the northern press toward it and the Negro made it easier for white southerners to convince the North that they should be permitted to solve their own race problem. Those who went into the North for money to assist the Negro emphasized that " the blacks must be for some time servants, farm laborers, and mechanics," and white reporters maintained that the Negro cared little about the loss of suffrage, accepted the idea that whites should govern, and preferred to live a segregated life.[104]

Also blocking the efforts of the Republicans to enforce the Fourteenth and Fifteenth Amendments was the ever increasing acceptance on the part of northerners in the eighties that the " Solid South " and injustice to the Negro were the inevitable results of the harsh policy of military Reconstruction, and that such remedies like the Force Bill would only serve to set back the ever developing cordiality of sentiment and the ever growing business intercourse between the two sections. " Men do not easily quarrel who are engaged in prosperous business one with another," observed *Harper's Weekly*, and the Boston *Evening Transcript*, a Republican paper, assured the South that the " beating of war-drums and making threatening faces at the South is only campaigning buncombe, and that the best and most intelligent sentiment in New England wants no more of it." [105] Whereas during Reconstruction the North was coercing the South by the mid-eighties she was appealing to the South. When William McKinley went into Virginia in 1885 to ask voters to send a protectionist to the Senate he assured them that " the Republicans of the North harbor no resentments. . . . They wish you the highest prosperity and greatest development." [106]

Edward Atkinson, a New England cotton economist who was hostile to southern textile manufactures, set the dominant theme

[103] *Ibid.*, p. 173.

[104] Buck, *Road to Reunion*, pp. 290, 296.

[105] *Harper's Weekly*, August 4, 1883, quoted from *Ibid.*, p. 187; Boston *Evening Transcript*, December 24, 1886, quoted from Logan, *Negro in American Life and Thought*, p. 180.

[106] Hesseltine, " Economic Factors in the Abandonment of Reconstruction," pp. 209-210.

in the northern reporting of the South during the eighties when he wrote in the *International Review* for March, 1881, " The old ' Solid South ' of slavery and Bourbonism is dead. A new South is rising from the ashes, eager to keep step with the North in the onward march of the Solid Nation." [107] The historian of the reconciliation of the two sections in commenting upon northern reporting of the South during the eighties writes that " the output was far greater in quantity than that of the seventies, but it was not so high in quality. Enthusiasm took the place of scholarship while boosting seemed more in vogue than analysis. Actually there was little new that could be said in description of the South that had not been said by King and Nordhoff. But every newspaper and periodical felt it necessary to send correspondents into the section on annual tours of observation, while politicians and industrialists as well as casual observers rushed into print to tell again the familiar story." [108]

Writers like J. B. Harrison, Carl Schurz, and Charles Dudley Warner, in articles in the New York *Tribune*, the *Atlantic Monthly* and in pamphlets and books in the eighties portrayed a reconciled and loyal South that was indifferent to partisan controversy and which now was devoting its resources to work, education, and the improvement of race relations. Periodicals and newspapers reiterated these themes until " every one with literary or journalistic aspirations had made a friendly raid or two into the South. Even casual tourists, unblessed by brains or insight, but prompted perhaps with the pious hope of doing their bit in the swelling chorus of reconciliation, added their observations." A new element in this reporting was the participation of business men and industrially minded politicians. A. K. McClure and W. D. [" Pig Iron "] Kelley in books about the South were almost lyrical in relating the achievement of this part of the country and in seeking to show how the growing business intercourse between the sections was speeding up the reconciliation and increasing the prosperity of both sections. Leading financiers and industrialists not only read these books but visited the South and published favorable comments on what they had seen, and even such a stalwart waver of the " bloody shirt " as Thomas Nast became converted in the

---

[107] Buck, *Road to Reunion*, p. 188.
[108] *Ibid.*

eighties and in his cartoons in *Harper's Weekly* pictured industry as the real connecting link between North and South.[109]

There is evidence of the North's interest in strengthening business ties with the South that would have been jeopardized by a revival of Reconstruction tactics. John H. Inman, of New York interested in the South since 1882, invested more than $1,000,000 in iron and coal properties in the vicinity of Birmingham and was preparing to build several large furnaces there. John S. Perry, the prominent stove manufacturer, was reported as planning to move part if not his entire works from Albany, New York to Alabama. The St. Louis *Globe-Democrat* in December, 1886, reported that the intolerance that had formerly held back northern investments in the South was disappearing as was " evidenced by the increase in the Republican vote and the decrease in the number of outrages on Republicans in certain sections of the South." The Chicago *Tribune* in the same month and year declared that " Northern capital was flowing into Tennessee at a rate that astonishes the natives," and the San Francisco *Examiner* at the same time stated that " the forces that have been silently working for the rehabilitation of the Southern States are now manifest. . . . Just now the ' late rebel states ' are attracting their full share of attention from capitalists, politicians and men of letters. . . . The days of sectional lines are past and can never be revived again." [110]

Thus the Republicans were faced with increasing northern weariness and disgust at attempts to revive the violence and chaos of a program of military Reconstruction. The party was also becoming more closely identified with the business interests of the northeast, and because of this, Republican leaders focused their attention upon the tariff and monetary policies while the Reconstruction issue steadily lost importance, a development that was in evidence in the defeat of the Force Bill in 1890.

As Harrison struggled to rejuvenate his party in the South, the Negro problem came home to roost, and the President now had an opportunity to find out what all Republican leaders had discovered, that there was no easy and simple solution to this question. Politics, tradition, and public promises compli-

[109] *Ibid.*, pp. 188-191.
[110] Logan, *Negro in American Life and Thought*, pp. 185-187.

cated the matter. In a speech on the Senate floor in the spring of 1886, Harrison stated that he was " one of those who feel that the colored race in the South since the war has been subjected to indignities, cruelties, outrages, and a repression of rights such as find no parallel in the history of civilization." [111]

Speaking before the Michigan Club at Detroit a few months before he received the Republican presidential nomination in 1888, Harrison decried the fact that the Negro Republican vote in the South had been deprived of all effective influence in the administration of the government. He demanded that " a free ballot shall not be denied to Republicans in these States where rebels have been rehabilitated with a full citizenship." He did favor the Force Bill and did urge it upon Congress, but Negroes held him as much accountable for the failure to secure the passage of this measure as they would have applauded him had it gone through.[112]

At the outset of his administration Harrison came under heavy pressure from Negroes to do something about their condition in the South, and T. Thomas Fortune called upon him to carry out the party's pledges made during the campaign of 1888. This Negro editor also asked Harrison to avoid Hayes' policy of " conciliating, bowing, and scraping, and apologizing and supplicating the white men of the South," and he demanded that Harrison consult with Negro leaders and remove every southern Democrat from office.[113]

Above everything else Negroes wanted patronage, for in their eyes this was the mark of favor and recognition from the administration. But the Negro press was divided over Harrison's intention. According to the Cleveland Gazette, the President had promised every Negro delegation that he would outdo his predecessors in giving them jobs. The New York Age related two incidents that seemed to contradict one another. A delegation of Negroes from Louisiana called upon the President to protest the policy of giving out the leading federal posts in their states to Democrats or " crawfishing Republicans," and were told by Harrison to go home and attend to their own business, and in another alleged interview with a

[111] New Orleans, *Weekly Pelican*, December 1, 1888.
[112] *Ibid.*, December 8, 1888; New York *Age*, May 16, 1891.
[113] New York *Age*, March 30, 1889.

southern delegation, Harrison proposed to appoint Negroes
to minor places in deference to the feelings of southern whites,
while in other Negro papers it was reported that Harrison had
appointed more Negroes to office than had any other President.[114]

Out of this maze of confusion and contradiction, this much
appears to be certain. Harrison continued to carry out the
traditional Republican policy of rewarding a few Negro leaders
as a means of recognizing the entire race. Names like Bruce,
Smalls, Douglass, Lynch, and their friends which had appeared
in Hayes' appointment list reappeared on Harrison's. Yet
Harrison did modify this policy somewhat, when he turned
thumbs down on some of the old Negro leaders and began to
recognize the merits of the younger men who had grown up
since the war. This was a new departure, and the Negro press
viewed it as such.[115] Harrison also attempted to give to Negroes
postmasterships in some of the large southern cities. He named
Dr. W. O. Crum for this position at Charleston, but withdrew
his name when too much Senate opposition developed. He kept
James Hill's name before the Senate for Postmaster at Vicksburg until this body refused to confirm the Mississippi Negro
leader, and he named N. Wright Cuney, Negro Republican
leader from Texas to a most important post as Collector of
the Port of Galveston.[116]

[114] Cleveland *Gazette*, October 19, 1889; New York *Age*, April 13, July 6,
1889; Kansas City, Kan., *American Citizen*, September 25, 1896.
[115] Washington *Bee*, March 15, 1890. This occurred primarily in Louisiana.
[116] *Ibid.*, July 23, August 13, 1892; New York *Age*, July 27, 1889; Charleston
News and Courier, July 6, 8, 15, October 15, 1892. The Cuney appointment
provides an interesting commentary on Harrison's dealings with the Negro.
Cuney had been under consideration for some time for this position. He was
boss of the Republican party in Texas, but he was also a Negro and was seeking
a very important patronage job in the South. The appointment dragged on.
Cuney went to Washington to find out about it. Senator William B. Allison
of Iowa took him around to see Secretary of the Treasury, William Windom,
who would have to made the recommendation to Harrison, but Windom
reportedly informed Allison that the Treasury Department had adopted a rule
not to name any Negro to office. Then Cuney called upon J. S. Clarkson,
vice-chairman of the Republican National Committee, and together they went
to the White House where they found the President with Windom signing
appointments. Clarkson gained admittance just after Harrison had signed the
appointment for the collectorship at Galveston. He held it out to Clarkson and
asked "That is right is it not and as was finally decided upon, isn't it."
Clarkson answered, "No, Mr. President, that is not the right name. In conferences some of us had with you, with some people in Texas with us, you
decided to appoint Mr. Wright Cuney to this place." Harrison got up, walked

It is also interesting to note how Negro reaction changed as Harrison continued to make Negro appointments. In the beginning Fortune accused Harrison of surpassing all " former Republican Presidents . . . in ignoring the advice and claims of colored leaders," and when the President tried to placate both white and colored Republican factions in the South, Fortune charged him with attempting to ride " the pale horse of the white league and the dark horse of colored Republicanism." But he made an abrupt change when Harrison gave office to a few Negro leaders. Then the editor of the New York *Age* ceased his attacks upon the President and exclaimed " Let the good work proceed. Turn the Southern Democratic rascals out." Evidently Harrison's policy continued to please Fortune, for when the President was renominated in 1892, the Negro leader congratulated him and pledged his enthusiastic support.[117] Along with Fortune, other Negro leaders changed their mind about Harrison. The Huntsville *Gazette*, which had raised doubts at first about Harrison's friendship for the Negro praised him when its editor, Charles Hendley, received a federal post in Alabama. Also very critical at first, the Washington *Bee* began to heap praise on Harrison and made a strong appeal to Negroes to remain in the Republican party and to despise the Democrats. The *Bee* described Harrison as " an honest man believing in honest elections " and told Negroes it would be easier for them to eat soup with a fork than to justify their consciences while voting Democratic.[118] Bruce and Lynch, the Negro leaders from Mississippi, considered Harrison to be all

around with the commission in his hand and replied, " I remember now, but the Department has for some time been advising differently and has caused me to change my mind." Then he asked Clarkson, " If you were President would you give the most important position in Texas and one of the most important in the whole South, to a Negro? " Not hesitating, Clarkson answered, " yes, and be glad of the chance." Harrison scratched out the name he had written in and wrote in Cuney's. Then he turned to Clarkson, " You are right and I am glad you called my attention to the matter in time." Maud Cuney Hare, *Norris Wright Cuney, A Tribune of the Black People* (New York, 1913), pp. 120-122; Huntsville *Gazette*, April 13, 1889; New Orleans *Weekly Pelican*, April 13, 1889.

[117] New York *Age*, March 30, May 4, June 22, 1889, July 27, 1889; Fortune to Harrison, June 10, 1892, in Harrison Papers.

[118] Huntsville *Gazette*, January 19, April 27, May 25, June 8, 1889; Washington *Bee*, August 17, November 2, 1889, May 3, June 21, November 1, 1890, July 9, 16, 1892. Quotation is from issue of July 16, 1892.

right on the question of fair dealing with Negroes and labeled the hue and cry over the administration's backwardness in recognizing the freedman as nothing more than a Democratic device and piece of propaganda, and Frederick Douglass in a speech at Thomasville, Georgia, defended some of Harrison's Democratic and white appointments in the South on the ground that the President " in distributing the patronage" has " but one object in view, and that is fitness for the place, regardless of politics or race." Even northern Negroes objected to some of the claims of their southern associates, for one from New York state, told Harrison that it was unfair to northern Negroes that patronage should go to southern Negroes who could not contribute any electoral votes.[119]

While we might think that Negroes would have blasted the Republicans for their failure to pass the Force Bill when they controlled the presidency and the Congress together, it should be noted that only Fortune's paper, among the Negro press, castigated the party of emancipation for this shortcoming.[120] Others, who had received patronage from the hands of Harrison, remained silent or blamed some other factor than the party for the defeat of this measure. Actually some southern Negroes, instead of berating the Republicans, condemned the very idea of a Force Bill. A Negro lawyer from Florida in an open letter to the press, stated that, " There is not an honest, intelligent and patriotic colored man in the South, who has the interest and welfare of his race at heart and sincerely desires its permanent prosperity in the Southern States, who can conscientiously endorse . . . the force bill." Its passage " would place the negro population in a very serious position in the South. They would have all the odds against them," and would lose all and be " irretrievably ruined in the end." This Negro argued that " no force bill, under the present circumstances, can place the race in that exalted position in the Government which it craves," and " no Congressional interference can better the political condition of affairs in these States." [121]

[119] New York *Age*, April 27, May 4, 1889; Huntsville *Gazette*, June 29, 1889; J. S. Fasset, Elmira, New York to Harrison, January 5, 1892, in Harrison Papers.
[120] New York *Age*, November 29, December 20, 27, 1890; January 3, 10, 17, 31, 1891.
[121] Charleston *News and Courier*, September 12, 1892.

By 1892 the Republican party had still failed to develop a two party South. In spite of the series of vigorous efforts and changing tactics to rebuild the Republican party in the South, it seemed to face a greater problem of rejuvenation than it had when Hayes recalled the troops. And yet when southern Republicans appeared to be at the bottom of the ladder, and when it looked as though their national leaders had begun to lose interest in their plight, a new turn in political developments raised up their hopes, infused them with new life and produced the climactic effort of the Republican party in the post-Reconstruction days to redeem the South.

Chapter VI

FUSION AGAIN

The agrarian resurgence of the 1890's revived the threats to Democratic supremacy in the South that the Independents and Readjusters had made in the seventies and eighties.[1] The conversion of agriculture from a self sufficiency to a commercial status, begun before the Civil War, but pushed on at a much greater pace after the conflict, had made the farmer a victim rather than a beneficiary of the new industrial order. While industrial power was rising to a position of economic dominance the farmer regarded himself a victim of the monopolistic prices of the trust, the freight charges of the railroads, and the interest rates of the bank. All this occurred at a period when the farmer found himself, for the first time since the Federalist era, without an effective share of control in either of the two major parties. Because of their grievances the agrarians organized the Grange and the Farmer's Alliance in the seventies and eighties and sought to relieve their situation primarily through the use of cooperatives. The failure of these devices along with the non political character of these two early organizations caused the farmers to find a means of political protest and activity, and they formed a new party, the Populist party, which proclaimed a broad program of reform and which attempted to deal with some of the important issues that the two major parties had shied away from.

The parent organization of Populism was the Alliance which in 1889 had taken separate ways into southern and northwestern branches. The constitution of the Alliance had announced it to be non-political as had the Grange before. But there was a certain ambiguity about the political character of the Alliance, for every year it put forth a series of demands that sounded like a platform and which could only be secured by political action. By 1890 the Northwest Alliance had come to the conclusion that non-partisan activities had been a failure,

[1] By far the best account of the Populist Revolt in the South is to be found in Woodward, *Origins of the New South*, pp. 235-289.

and it decided to enter politics. Kansas led the way with a People's party and other states set up independent parties under different names. Jerry Simpson, Mary Elizabeth Lease, General James B. Weaver, and Ignatius Donnelly were among the leaders of this hastily constructed movement which did obtain some success in elections in the western states.

In the South the Alliance took the position that it could control the Democratic party by working from within. Among the leaders of the southern Alliance were Benjamin R. Tillman of South Carolina, Thomas E. Watson of Georgia, Leonidas L. Polk of North Carolina, and Reuben F. Kolb of Alabama. The Alliance attacked the industrial and urban leadership of the Democratic party of the New South and had candidates pledge themselves to the Ocala platform of 1890, and in that year the Alliance elected governors in Georgia, South Carolina, Texas, and Tennessee, gained apparent control of eight state legislatures, and laid claim to forty-four Congressmen. But the supposedly Alliance state legislatures and congressmen disappointed the farmers by acting primarily as Democrats and by subordinating the Alliance platform and plans to the Democratic party. The strategy of the southern Alliance to control the Democratic party had failed, for the reverse of this had happened. Thus by 1892 Populism was a national movement, no longer confined to the West, and in which the South was now participating. The prospects of Cleveland's renomination in that year had stimulated Alliancemen in the South to become Populists in spite of Tillman's advice to remain within the Democratic party. Southern Populists now preached what southern Alliancemen had preached earlier, but support of Populism in the South was called a desertion of the white man's cause, and enormous social and economic pressures were exerted on southerners to prevent them from voting for Populism.

If the arrival of Populism in the South threatened Democratic supremacy there, it resurrected Republican hopes of cashing in on the Democratic split that took place. An optimistic national committeeman from Illinois predicted to other delegates of the National Republican League Convention meeting in Buffalo that if the party would " cultivate the tree down there [the South] . . . the fruit will drop in our hands." [2] In

---

[2] Richmond *Dispatch*, September 17, 1892.

July the Republican National Committee announced that it would make an earnest effort in 1892 to crack the Democratic South.[3] At first Democrats believed that Republican strategy would be that of furnishing money to disseminate Populist literature in the South. They seemed to be aware of some understanding between the Populists and Republicans but could not spell it out.

If national Republican leaders were hopeful about the South in 1892, national Democratic leaders were uneasy about it. In previous campaigns the South had received little attention. But the National Democratic Headquarters in New York published many interviews with southern leaders to dispel the doubt about the South remaining Democratic. As one observer put it, " The news of continued Democratic allegiance in the South at Democratic National Headquarters, in other days would have been like carrying coals to Newcastle. The news is received there now like coal at Newcastle, if the coal supply at Newcastle had given out." [4]

What troubled the Democrats and pleased the Republicans was that the Populist revolt tended to bring together southern Populists and southern Republicans in some form of concerted action. The only unifying element for these two groups was their opposition to the Democratic party in the South. Going it alone, each despaired of victory over the Democrats, but the prospects of winning through a combination of forces proved to be too tempting. Spurred on by the desire to oust the Democrats, which overrode the fact that they had little else in common, the Republicans and the Populists joined hands, which for the former meant their last all-out effort in the post-Reconstruction years to regain their ascendency in the South.

" Fusion " was the name that was generally applied to this merger of Republicans and Populists. But as the leading historian of this period of the South points out, it was nothing more than a matter of expediency on the part of both.[5] Each side realized this and acted in this manner. But while the Republicans keenly sensed the immediate practical effects of such an alliance, they also clung to their long cherished hope

---

[3] New Orleans *Times-Democrat*, July 30, 1892.
[4] Chicago *Inter-Ocean*, August 26, 1892.
[5] Woodward, *Origins of the New South*, p. 276.

that they could exploit the Democratic rift in the South to their advantage on a long term basis. They hoped that this coalition would produce more fruitful results than those with the Independents and the Readjusters.

The Republican National Committee showed its enthusiasm over the plan to cooperate with the Populists by placing Chris Magee, an influential Republican from Pennsylvania, in charge of the South for the 1892 campaign. Magee's chief task was to pull the Republican and Populist groups together in opposition to the Democrats, and he spent considerable time and money in his efforts. The Republican National Chairman, Thomas Carter of Montana, never believed too strongly in this strategy, but enough members of the committee thought the chances were good enough to make the attempt. Aware of the difficulties that any new party would have in the South and anxious to keep Alliancemen from returning to the Democratic party, the Republicans moved with great care in explaining their tactics. At first they declared that " Throughout the South we are either supporting the Alliance candidates for Congress or the Alliance is supporting our candidates." Then they spoke in more idealistic and reforming terms by pointing out that they were not trying to trade with the Independents in the South for either congressional or electoral votes. Rather they sought to combine with the Independents on the understanding that when the Independents and Republicans controlled a state legislature they would amend the election laws that disfranchised both. This appeal fitted in well with the common demand of the Republicans and Populists for " a free ballot and honest election." Finally the Republicans dropped such terms as Alliance and Independents and boldly stated that they intended " to work the third party for all there is in it in all the states [in the South] where it is at all powerful." Republicans even planned to appoint Populists as deputy marshals and supervisors of elections who would have complete charge of the election machinery so far as it lay in the hands of federal authorities.[6]

While the hope of disrupting and defeating the Democratic

[6] New Orleans *Times-Democrat*, October 27, 1892; Baltimore *American*, September 30, 1892; Mobile *Daily Register*, October 6, 1892; Florida *Times-Union*, October 6, 1892.

party in the South through fusion with the Populists caused Republican leaders to indulge in rosy visions, they faced a number of practical difficulties in making their plan work. The chief obstacle to Republican success in the South in 1892 was the fear of a Force Bill which southern Democrats injected into the campaign and which Republicans tried to keep out. The South remembered the efforts to push a Force Bill through Congress in 1890, and the Republican platform of 1892 revived their fears about such a law when it stated that the " party will never relax its efforts until the integrity of the ballot and purity of elections shall be fully guaranteed in every state. We denounce the continued inhuman outrages perpetrated upon American citizens for political reasons in certain Southern States of the Union." [7] Democratic newspapers thoroughly exploited the theme of a Force Bill and warned southern whites that this was the real issue in 1892 and that the success of the Republican-Populist coalition would mean a return to Negro rule of Reconstruction.[8] Northern Democrats also joined in when the Boston *Globe* characterized all the talk about breaking the South as " all moonshine. If Republican success did not clearly menace the South with another force bill, and the consequent revival of the race question, one or two of the Southern States might possibly be fighting ground." [9]

The administration moved to counteract the Democratic charges on the Force Bill, when Charles Foster, Secretary of the Treasury, in a press interview said, " They are trying to make a ' force bill ' issue, but they are not succeeding. The life is all out of that . . . the ' force bill ' issue is without life." [10] Republican strategists brought John R. Lynch, the

---

[7] New York *Times*, June 10, 1892.

[8] Mobile *Daily Register*, September 27, October 2, 9, 27, 30, November 6, 1892; Arkansas *Gazette*, July 1, August 20, September 1, 3, 10, 22, October 14, 29; Florida *Times-Union*, August 6, September 20, 28, November 2, 1892; Atlanta *Constitution*, July 3, 16, September 23, 26, October 17, 19, 1892; Jackson Miss. *Clarion*, July 14, October 20, 1892; Richmond *Dispatch*, July 2, 16, August 4, 25, September 17, 22, October 30, 1892; Nashville *Daily American*, August 15, 28, September 19, 1892; Louisville *Courier-Journal*, August 2, 4, September 8, 12, October 3, 21, 1892; Charleston *News and Courier*, September 13, November 8, 1892; Raleigh *News and Observer*, July 12, 13, August 7, 28, September 18, October 15, 25, November 4, 1892.

[9] Quoted in New Orleans *Times-Democrat*, July 6, 1892.

[10] *Ibid.*, August 25, 1892; Louisville *Courier-Journal*, August 24, 1892.

Negro leader from Mississippi, to speak in Chicago where he maintained that the Force Bill was just as harmless as the laws against murder and larceny.[11] As for President Harrison, he kept a tight lip about the matter and waited until September, nearly three months after his nomination, to issue his letter of acceptance.   Southern newspapers believed that the delay stemmed from the matter of the Force Bill. Harrison's hesitation on the question had the effect of bringing the Republican campaign to a standstill, and the national committee appeared to be in a quandary over what to do. A number of prominent Republicans and leading party newspapers favored keeping the issue in the background as much as possible. But Harrison, who had a hand in putting the federal elections law plank in the 1892 platform, advocated the open and vigorous support of the measure and appeared anxious to say so with candor in his letter. Yet he also reached out for the electoral vote in the South. As the New York *Times* put it, "It is a perplexing situation for an ambitious man who tries to be conscientious according to his lights."[12]

In his letter of acceptance Harrison gingerly tried to shelve the Force Bill. He neither repudiated nor supported the party platform on this issue. Instead he used the Alabama election, in which Kolb had been counted out by regular Democrats, as an example of violating the right to cast a free ballot and to have it honestly counted. "Our old Republican battle cry, 'A free ballot and a fair count' comes back to us," he said, but he took refuge in the recommendation of a "non-partisan commission" of inquiry, and he called for state and non-partisan action to revise the election laws.[13] Yet southern Democrats knew that many Republicans agreed with ex-Senator John J. Ingalls when in a speech at Topeka he confessed, "I would rather have Negro domination in the South than the domination that prevails at present." Ingalls felt that if the Republican party could not pass and execute a Force Bill, "then it is time that it should go out of business and permit some other party to do it."[14]

[11] New York *Tribune, September* 28, 1892.
[12] Quoted in Mobile *Daily Register*, August 21, 1892.
[13] New York *Times*, September 6, 1892.
[14] Mobile *Daily Register*, October 30, 1892.

Another important development that imperiled the success of the Republican-Populist venture was the attitude that southern Democrats had toward both the Populists and any coalition they might make with the Republicans. The Populists preached the same things that the Alliancemen had proclaimed, but they also had organized a political party which was regarded as a desertion of the white man's cause in the South. And by joining hands with the Republicans, the Populists brought down upon their heads the odium that had been attached to southern Republicans. A leading Democratic newspaper in Tennessee drove home this point when it declared, "Any Democrat might just as well go straight into the Republican party as into the ranks of its active ally, the People's party." [15] Subjected to heavy economic pressure and social ostracism for their sin of splitting the white vote in the South, many Populists finally deserted their party and their affiliation with the Republicans and returned to the Democratic organization. 'Republican leaders glumly admitted these defections and as one of them sadly observed, "The only trouble with the People's party is it has no people in it." [16]

Other factors that menaced Republican success in the South with their new venture was Harrison's luke warm support of the idea and the opposition that developed to it among some Republican leaders in the South. Harrison never put much stock in fusion, and only went along with it when Magee persuaded him that the Democratic leaders might spend large sums of money in the South to defeat the Populists, which otherwise would have been used to the disadvantage of the Republicans in the North and West. But Harrison was reported to be "in a furious rage" when the results of the Georgia gubernatorial election came it. Prominent Republicans who called on him following the Republican-Populist debacle in this state, told that he complained bitterly about southern Republicans duping him about political conditions in their states, and by leading him to believe that fusion would allow the Republicans to break into the winning column in the South. After the smashing Democratic victory in Georgia in 1892, it was reported that Harrison instructed the national committee

[15] Nashville *Daily American*, August 28, 1892.
[16] Raleigh *News and Observer*, October 4, 1892.

to dump the southern program overboard and to confine the money and time to the pivotal states in the North. To one caller, he reportedly said, " I have washed my hands of the south, it is a land of rebels and traitors who care nothing for the sanctity of the ballot, and I will never be in favor of making an active campaign down there until we can place bayonets at the polls. I am now more than ever in favor of ramming a force bill down their throats." [17] Republican leaders in the South also appeared to be skeptical of their party's chances for success in their states. When asked about this, P. B. S. Pinchback from Louisiana replied, " No, the south is as solid as a rock, and it is useless to talk about carrying anything there, at least under present conditions." William Pitt Kellogg from the same state regarded Republican claims about carrying the South as "utter nonsense." Former congressman H. G. Ewart of North Carolina went a step further. He assessed Republican office holders in the South for funds to carry the campaign in the doubtful states in the North.[18]

In spite of all these obstacles, fusion of some kind or another between Republicans and the Populists occurred throughout the South between 1892-1896. Republicans made their earliest bid for disgruntled Democratic votes in 1892 in Alabama. Here Reuben F. Kolb, Commissioner of Agriculture, who had unsuccessfully sought the Democratic nomintion for governor in 1890 and 1892, bolted in the latter instance, organized the Alliancemen into the " Jeffersonian Democrats," and ran against Governor Thomas G. Jones who stumped for reelection. Republicans saw in Kolb's candidacy a schism in Democrtic ranks and, instead of running their own state ticket, they agreed to support him in return for " Jeffersonian " votes for Harrison electors. The Democrats characterized Kolb and his followers as " Demopulites " and accused them of being in a " Damnable conspiracy " with the Republicans to secure the electoral votes for Harrison.[19]

The election took place in August, and Jones, who had beaten his Republican opponent in 1890 by more than 3-1,

---

[17] Atlanta *Constitution*, October 10, 1892.
[18] New Orleans *Times-Democrat*, September 6, October 30, 31, 1892.
[19] Albert B. Moore, *History of Alabama* (University, Ala., 1934) pp. 603-626: John B. Clark, *Populism in Alabama* (Auburn, Ala., 1927) pp. 134-163.

won by slightly more than 11,000 votes with the rest of his
ticket winning by larger margins. Kolb garnered the majority
of the white counties, but took only one of the Black Belt
counties. He maintained that he had carried the state by 40,000
votes, but that he lost the Black Belt areas through Democratic
frauds. The historian of the state substantiates Kolb's charges
when he describes the 1892 election as " notoriously fraudulent
and there can be little doubt that Kolb was counted out in the
Black Belt." [20]

Kolb's defeat, instead of putting an end to the fusion movement, only served to bring on a more specific coalition of the
dissatisfied elements in Alabama. The Kolbites and the Populists met in convention in Birmingham in mid-September and
chose a joint electoral and congressional ticket. The convention severely denounced Cleveland by resolution, but did not
endorse either Weaver or Harrison, so that the nominated
electors were pledged to no presidential candidate. The Republicans withdrew their electoral and congressional ticket, and
the " lily-white " leaders of the state, joined by Magee, emissary
from the national committee, attended the convention where
they expressed thorough satisfaction with the fusion ticket.
While Populists dominated the congressional slate, three Republicans and eight Kolb men, acceptable to the Republicans,
made up the electoral ticket. After the Birmingham convention, newspapers reported Republican leaders in Washington
as openly boasting that they had captured the Kolb-Populist
parties and that Harrison would win Alabama's electoral vote.[21]

The Republican National Committee had sent Magee to help
manipulate the " fusion deal " and to furnish guarantees of aid
from the national headquarters But when he arrived he discovered that Republican factionalism menaced the success of
fusion. There were two Republican groups in the state. The
one, led by Robert Mosely, state chairman, made up almost
entirely of federal office holders, " lily-white " in its outlook,
recognized by the national convention in 1892 and representing
75 to 80 per cent of Republican strength in Alabama, favored

---

[20] Moore, *History of Alabama*, p. 624.
[21] Atlanta *Constitution*, September 17, 25, 1892; New York *Tribune*, September 15, 16, 17, 23, 26, 1892; New Orleans *Times-Democrat*, September 5,
1892.

fusion as a means of bringing additional whites into the party. The other, headed by William J. Stevens, a Negro and composed almost entirely of Negroes and unsuccessful office seekers, argued there was nothing to be gained by fusion and demanded a straight out Republican ticket. Further complicating the matter was the report that Democratic leaders encouraged Stevens in his stand in their efforts to split the Republican vote in the state.[22]

Magee made three trips to Alabama to patch up the differences between Mosely and Stevens, and to have both support the Populists, but Stevens, instead of succumbing to Magee's blandishments, demanded Mosely's head as the price for reconciliation. Magee would not sacrifice Mosely, and thus the break between the two groups became wider and eventually erupted into open warfare. The Stevens group met in Birmingham late in September, filled out a congressional and electoral ticket, and decided to make the fight against the Republicans and Populists. This action undermined Magee's work, and the Republican National Committee hastily summoned Stevens to New York. Under promises of recognition in the event of Republican success in November, he was partially won over, but his followers refused to join him and Stevens elected to keep his slate in the field. Mosely retaliated by openly denouncing Stevens' move and by making a strong appeal to all Republicans in the state to vote for the fusion ticket. The Republican National Committee put strong pressure upon members in the state when the National Chairman, Carter, issued a circular which stated that the Stevens wing did not represent the Republican party in Alabama. Further pressure came from Washington when the administration denounced and even preferred charges against post-office officials in the state who fought fusion. The Populists did their bit when they asked Bruce of Mississippi and Frederick Douglass to persuade Stevens to withdraw his candidates and to support fusion.[23]

To offset Stevens' influence with the Negroes, and to remove

[22] Atlanta *Constitution*, September 16, 1892; New York *Tribune*, September 15, 16, 23, 1892; Chicago *Inter-Ocean*, September 23, 1892.
[23] Atlanta *Constitution*, September 23, October 11, 12, 13, 18, 1892; New Orleans *Times-Democrat*, September 24, 26, 30, October 10, 11, 18, 19, 1892; Mobile *Daily Register*, September 7, 17, 23, November 5, 1892.

whatever fears they had about the results of fusion, Republicans staged rallies where leading Negroes in the state disclosed the details of the bargain between Kolb and the Republicans. They urged their fellow Negroes to vote for the Kolb electors, and before they left the platform, Negro speakers exacted a promise from their audience to vote for the Kolb ticket. But Stevens firmly stuck to his guns, and kept his nominees in the field. There were a number of reports that the national Republican leaders had spent a considerable sum of money in Alabama to defeat the Democrats, and available evidence seems to back this up. Kolb admitted receiving $10,000 from Magee, and Mosely had money to pay the expenses of speakers for fusion, for as he wrote, " If you can arrange to secure a good and able speaker who favors the fusion electoral ticket . . . I will pay his actual expenses." [24]

Magee, who spent money in many different ways in Alabama in order to insure a Republican victory, actually entered into formal agreements with Republicans, promising them financial assistance, if they were to withdraw their candidacy in favor of Populists. One of these between Magee and J. T. Blakemore, who pulled out of the race in the Seventh Congressional District in favor of a Populist, fell into Democratic hands and was published. For the purpose of inducing Blakemore to give up the race, Magee agreed to furnish him an official position in Washington for four years at $100.00 a month, or to be personally responsible for providing him with the same monthly sums over the same number of years. [25]

But for all the effort and money spent, fusion failed to give the Republicans the much sought for victory in Alabama. Cleveland had a large majority of the popular vote, and Harrison ran a poor third, far behind Weaver. [26] In the congressional elections, Alabama returned all regular Democrats to Washington.

In Arkansas in 1892 there was an " understanding between Republicans and Populists. Republicans were to support the

[24] Mobile *Daily Register*, October 7, 1892; Moore, *History of Alabama*, p. 626; Robert A. Mosely to J. P. Jones, Brewton, Alabama, October 27, 1892, quoted in Mobile *Daily Register*, November 1, 1892.

[25] Arkansas *Gazette*, November 5, 1892.

[26] Cleveland 138, 135, Weaver 85, 178, Harrison 9, 184, Burnham, *Presidential Ballotts*, pp. 254-255.

Farmer's Alliance in the State ticket and secure in return Alliance support for their electoral ticket in November." [27]   In the gubernatorial election, Powell Clayton, state Republican leader, had dreamed up the plan of using the Populist candidate, Jacob P. Carnahan to decoy enough votes from William M. Fishbach, the Democratic choice, so that the Republican William G. Whipple, could win. Republicans did not want the Populists to "organize the Negroes in People's party clubs . . . but work all Democrats that you can into your party. Leave the negroes to vote the Republican ticket, for State officers of course." [28]   Thus while all three candidates remained in the field, and Republicans and Populists did not merge as they had in Alabama behind Kolb, there was a conscious effort on the part of both to work together. But once again the results were discouraging. Fishbach won the election with 90,115 votes to 33,644 for Whipple to 31,117 for Carnahan.[29]

Republicans and Populists had no greater success in their attempted fusion in the electoral and congressional vote. They divided the eight electors between them, and the Republicans agreed to support the Populist for Congress. Leaders of both parties issued circulars confirming this "deal" and asked their followers to support this combination. The Populists stated that "the supreme issue in Arkansas today is a 'free ballot and a fair count.' On this issue the Republicans are in accord with us, and we can afford to concentrate our strength with theirs." The Democrats raised the charge that the National Republican Committee paid the expenses of the Populists who opposed the Democrats for Congress. But fusion proved to be as much a failure in Arkansas as it had been in Alabama. The Democrats returned all their candidates to Congress, and Cleveland won by a wide margin over Harrison with Weaver as a poor third.[30]

While Republican leaders in Florida insisted that no "deal"

[27] Quoted in New Orleans *Times-Democrat*, September 7, 1892 in Lucia Elizabeth Daniel, "The Louisiana People's Party," *Louisiana Historical Quarterly* XXVI (1943), 1086.

[28] Arkansas *Gazette*, August 27, 28, 1892.

[29] *Ibid.*, September 18, 1892; Appleton's Annual *Cyclopedia for 1892*, pp. 19-20.

[30] Arkansas *Gazette*, October 20, 22, 30, November 2, 1892; Chicago *Inter-Ocean*, October 21, 26, 1892; Cleveland 87,834 votes; Harrison 46,983 votes; Weaver 11,824 votes, Burnham, *Presidential Ballots*, pp. 254-55.

existed between them and the Populists, the evidence shows
that both sides plainly understood each other. The Republicans
put forth no state ticket, and the state chairman, Dennis Egan,
issued a circular letter urging party members to " support the
People's party because that party in its platform stands pledged
to work for the repeal of infamous election laws in this state."
Egan pointed out that there was no " Combine, barter, trade
or personal preference in these matters. We favor them [the
Populists] simply because they are fighting the old enemy."
Republicans also failed to put any congressional or electoral
ticket in the field, but in the main supported the Populists.
Again the results were disheartening. The entire Democratic
state and national ticket triumphed over the Populist slate,
and despite the advice of Republican leaders, many Negroes
cast their ballots for the Democrats.[31]

Fusion in Georgia occurred only on the state ticket. E. A.
Buck, a native of Maine and a Republican boss and United
States Marshal in Georgia, arranged to have the Republican
convention refuse to put up a state ticket although it named
an electoral and congressional slate. Buck then apparently
reached some agreement with the Populists to divide the
electors equally between the two parties with the Republican
chieftain recognized as the common leader. But the Republican
electors thwarted him in this, when in a stormy five hour meeting at Atlanta early in October they unanimously refused to
make room for Populists, so that the full ticket remained in
the field.[32]

When the Populists named W. L. Peek, " a real dirt farmer "
for governor, Republicans asked him be their candidate too,
and he replied that while he would be happy to have their
vote, he would not compromise Populist principles. The historian of Populism in Georgia feels that the Populists would
have had greater success in 1892 had they fused with the
Republicans, but that they hung back from fear of alienating
the whites.[33] But one must also remember that Tom Watson

---

[31] Florida *Times-Union*, September 28, 29, 1892; New Orleans *Times-Democrat*, October 3, 5, 1892; William T. Cash, *The Story of Florida* (New York,
1938) II, 512. Harrison had 30,113 votes to Weaver's 4,843, Burnham, *Presidential Ballots*, p. 253.

[32] New Orleans *Times-Democrat*, October 10, 1892.

[33] Alex Matthews Arnett, *The Populist Movement in Georgia* (New York,
1922), p. 153.

was the leader of the anti-fusion Populists in the South, for as he pointed out, " I have rejected and denounced fusion between the people's party and the republicans just as I have between the people's party and the democrats," [34] and his attitude on fusion went a long way toward influencing his party's action on this question.

The Republicans eventually named Peek as their candidate for governor, and Buck sent out a circular letter to Georgia party members, especially the Negroes, pressing them to vote for the Populists. This made many Negroes angry, and one of their leaders, William A. Pledger, denounced Buck and took to the stump for Governor W. J. Northern, a Democrat, who sought re-election. When the White House learned of this, it called Pledger off, summoned him to Washington on " Official" business to make speeches for the President. Buck's action also caused a division among the state committee, and a number of the members wrote their own letters to Georgia Republicans urging them to ignore Buck's advice. Others went further by coming out for the Democratic state ticket and by organizing Republican support for it in their counties. But the same results prevailed as they had elsewhere in fusion. While Peek, with Republican support, made a creditable showing, Northern swamped him with a difference of more than 80,000 votes.[35]

The fusion that had taken place in Arkansas had aroused considerable interest among Republicans in Louisiana who had watched it very closely. But the immediate problem for the Republicans in this state in 1892 was to close the breach within their own ranks. Henry Warmoth, who had emerged out of a factional fracas of 1888-1890 as the recognized Republican leader in the state, now was seriously challenged by a faction led by A. H. Leonard. Both sides claimed to be the official Republican party in the state, and both had put up their own congressional and electoral ticket. Since such a situation men-

---

[34] Atlanta *Constitution*, October 13, 1892.

[35] *Ibid.*, July 14, 15, August 11, September 23, 27, October 1, 2, 3, 19, 1892; Nashville *Daily American*, August 28, 1892; New Orleans *Times-Democrat*, August 20, 1892; Arkansas *Gazette*, October 23, 1892; Florida *Times-Union*, September 27, 1892; Northern 140,492 votes; Peek 58,990 votes, Appleton's Annual *Cyclopedia for 1892*, p. 308.

aced the success of the national ticket, two members of the Republican National Committee, J. N. Huston from Indiana and John C. Long from Florida, came to New Orleans to unify the warring elements. Reconciliation came when Warmoth took a subordinate role, and the Leonard forces directed the campaign with a combined ticket.[36]

Once the Republicans had closed ranks, they effected the now familiar understanding with the Populists—a combined electoral and congressional ticket with each side giving half of the candidates. They further agreed not to work together after the election which underscored the idea of expediency in their compact. Both groups made a public announcement concerning the deal. The Populists denounced the old parties, monopolies and wealth and stated that fusion was necessary to secure a fair deal for both sides. Republicans simply referred to the agreement and asserted that after " due deliberation and on the advice of national leaders " they had entered into the combination to fight a common enemy and to secure a free election.[37]

The fusion agreement with the Populists revived the factional feud among Republicans in Louisiana, and every Republican who had any claim for recognition seemed to want or to do something which further complicated matters. The Leonard wing thought the understanding favored the Warmoth group and the latter faction seemed to think it favored the Leonard men. There was also a great deal of maneuvering to have the Republican nominees withdraw in those districts where the agreement called for Populists to run. On top of this not all Populists accepted fusion. The Ruston *Progressive Age*, a Populist sheet, called the agreement a " dicker " made " on the part of a few would-be leaders of the People's party " and " we do not nor will we indorse such a step." Finally the staggering defeat eliminated much of the hope that the fusionists had. The Democrats returned all their candidates to Congress, and Cleveland won the state with 77.8 per cent of the

[36] New Orleans *Times-Democrat*, August 17, September 11, 20, 25, 27, 30, October 4, 5, 1892; George M. Reynolds, *Machine Politics in New Orleans, 1897-1926* (New York, 1936), pp. 25-26; Melvin J. White, " Populism in Louisiana During the Nineties," *Mississippi Valley Historical Review*, V (1918-1919), 7-8. .

[37] New Orleans *Times-Democrat*, October 15, 21, 1892.

vote and with more than a 60,000 margin. The combined
Harrison-Weaver vote fell about 3 percentage points and ap-
proximately 4,000 votes behind that for Harrison in 1888.[38]

While fusion talk filled the air in Mississippi, it was not so
much in evidence as elsewhere in the South. When the Republicans failed to put up a state ticket, the Democrats regarded
such action as evidence of a Republican-Populist alliance.
Actually the Republicans made no nominations for Congress,
but threw their support behind the Populist candidates. This
action split the Negro leaders; Bruce and Lynch supporting
the move and Hill opposing it. Once again the Democrats sent
all their men to Congress, and Harrison suffered a tremendous
setback.[39]

Fusion failed to materialize in North Carolina, South Carolina and Virginia in 1892. In North Carolina Republican
leaders convinced the national committee that the party had a
good following in the state which might be increased were it
to make a serious fight and that to withdraw from the race
would demoralize the ranks and prove to be suicide. Republican leaders in North Carolina felt that they could use the
Populists to divide the white vote in their state, and Democrats seemed to agree with them on this. If the Republicans
and Populists had joined hands in 1892 they might well have
won, for the combined Harrison-Weaver vote in the state
amounted to more than 52 per cent of the total.[40] While Re-

[38] *Ibid.*, October 16, 18, 20, 21, 27, 28, 31, November 6, 1892; in 1892,
Cleveland 87, 922 votes, Harrison-Weaver 26, 132 votes; in 1888, Cleveland
85,012 votes and Harrison 30,701 votes, Burnham, *Presidential Ballots*, p. 255.

[39] Albert D. Kirwan, *Revolt of the Rednecks, Mississippi Politics*, 1876-1925
(Lexington, Ky., 1951), pp. 95-96; Cleveland 40,827 votes, Weaver 10,293
votes, Harrison 1,455 votes. In 1888 Harrison had polled 29,096 to Cleveland's
85,451, Burnham, *Presidential Ballots*, p. 255. The greatly reduced vote in
1892 might be accounted for, because Mississippi had adopted a new state
constitution in 1890 which had allowed for the registration of only about
77,000 voters.

[40] Raleigh *News and Observer*, August 17, 19, 31, September 1, 8, November
10, 1892; Richmond *Dispatch*, August 17, September 2, 14, 1892; F. M.
Simmons, Democratic State Chairman in North Carolina to M. J. Hawkins,
Dew County, North Carolina Democratic Chairman, October 29, 1892, in
Marmaduke J. Hawkins Papers (State Archives, Raleigh, North Carolina);
Louis E. McComas, Secretary of Republican National Committee to E. W.
Halford, October 19, 1882, Benjamin Harrison Papers; Cleveland 132,645
votes, Harrison 100,675, Weaver 45,092. In 1888 Cleveland won 147,897 and
Harrison 134,586 votes. Burnham, *Presidential Ballots*, p. 253.

publicans and Populists had their own electoral ticket in South Carolina, they both supported Benjamin Tillman in the state elections who won a smashing victory. Mahone, who still wielded the influence in Republican ranks in Virginia, favored fusion, and the administration apparently backed his plan for defeating the Democrats by having Republicans vote for the Populists. Many signs seemed to point in the direction of a Republican-Populist coalition in this state, but no fusion developed in the way it had come in Alabama, Arkansas, and Louisiana.[41]

Fusion in Tennessee produced a political sensation of the first rank. Early in the state campaign of 1892 rumors began to circulate that the Republicans and Populists were cooperating. Democrats charged that the Republicans would take their candidate for governor, George W. Winstead, out of the race and would support Governor John B. Buchanan, President of the State Alliance and the Independent candidate, in return for Independent and Populist support for Harrison in the presidential election. Both Republicans and Populists heatedly denied this, but admitted they had agreed to cooperate in some of the congressional districts. Then late in October, Democratic newspapers published the " Ivins-Hill " letters that just about destroyed fusion in Tennessee. J. J. Ivins, editor of the Knoxville *Republican*, had written to D. W. Hill, Republican National Committeeman from Tennessee, and revealed that the Republican National Committee had agreed to pay the Populist State Chairman, John H. McDowell $15,000 for supporting Buchanan for governor, for aiding Republican candidates and for giving the Republicans a " clear field " for Harrison electors. Republicans also promised to elect McDowell to the United States Senate when they and the Populists gained control of the legislature, and this coalition further agreed to repeal the election laws, which deprived the Republicans of much of their Negro strength, and thus give them " permanent control of the state." [42]

[41] W. O. Bradley, Republican National Committeeman from Kentucky to E. W. Halford, October 7, 1892, in Harrison Papers; Richmond *Dispatch*, September 18, October 26, 28, November 2, 6, 8, 1892.

[42] James A. Sharp, " The Farmers' Alliance and the People's Party in Tennessee," *East Tennessee Historical Society Publication* no. 10 (1938), pp. 104-109.

The " Ivins-Hill " correspondence immediately appeared in numerous Democratic newspapers in the South as a warning to party members that the same kind of a deal had probably occurred in their states.[43] McDowell had only lived up to that part of the bargain in bringing Buchanan into the race and had actually threatened to withdraw him when the Republican National Committee was slow in paying the agreed sum. The Democrats made few attempts to connect Buchanan with the deal or to discredit him, for their strategy was aimed at breaking up fusion. Republican and Populist leaders involved, issued denial statements, but apparently McDowell did receive the money, and apparently the " Ivins-Hill " letters fell into Democratic hands because of Republican factionalism that resulted from the decision to fuse with the Populists.[44]

The publication of the letters left the Republicans nonplussed, and they canvassed and caucussed as to how to meet the exposure. They never cried out " a democratic lie " but made the point that a traitor lived among them. But fusion also failed here. Peter Turney, chief justice of the state and Democratic nominee for governor, triumphed over the Republican Winstead with a safe margin while Buchanan trailed a very bad third. The fusion candidates for Congress lost out, and the Democrats won a majority in the state legislature.[45]

In Texas, fusion occurred between Republicans and Democrats in an effort to unseat a Democratic governor. Issues connected with the administration of Governor James S. Hogg had divided the Democrats. A division also arose in Republican ranks because of attempts to establish a " lily-white " party in the state. And in spite of a presidential election year, state questions overshadowed national ones. Hogg had won the Democratic nomination and election in 1890 on the issue of regulating the railroads, and in 1891 the state legislature took this step by enacting a Railroad Commission Act. Hogg defended this law and promised to pass a similar one for cor-

[43] Mobile *Daily Register*, October 26, 1892; Arkansas *Gazette*, October 25, 1892; Florida *Times-Union*, October 28, 1892; Atlanta *Constitution*, October 23, 1892; Nashville *Daily American*, October 23, 1892; Louisville *Courier-Journal*, October 23, 24, 25, 1892; Raleigh *News and Observer*, October 29, 1892.

[44] Sharp, *loc. cit.*; *Atlanta Constitution*, October 24, 25, 1892.

[45] Turney, 127,247 votes, Winstead 100,629 votes, Buchanan 31,515 votes, Sharp, *loc. cit.*, p. 112; *World Almanac for 1893*, p. 372.

porations. Judge George Clark, a Democrat, and his followers charged that Hogg's policies were driving capital out of the state and deterring new investments from coming in. Thus Clark opposed Hogg in the gubernatorial election and divided the Democratic vote.

But the Republicans were just as badly split. The " lily-whites " had their own candidate for governor, Andrew J. Houston, son of General Sam Houston, and they endorsed the McKinley Tariff and condemned the Force Bill. The " regulars," made up largely of federal office holders and Negroes, decided to name no candidate but came out for Clark and adopted his charge about Hogg driving capital from the state. The Populists also put up a candidate, T. L. Nugent. At this point Huston and Long, representing the Republican National Committee, and who had earlier played an important role in Louisiana factionalism, entered the picture. They sought to reconcile the " lily-white " and " Black and Tan " groups in the state by having the former withdraw Houston, thereby pledging the entire Republican support for Clark with the understanding that in congressional districts where pronounced Hogg men were running for Congress, the solid Clark vote should go to the Republican nominee. This plan had the support of President Harrison.[46]

The Republican state chairman, N. B. Moore, and N. W. Cuney, Negro chieftain issued circular letters to Texas Republicans that urged them to vote for Clark and which expressed the fear that Hogg's administration was driving northern investors away from Texas. Cuney did more than this, for he took to the stump for Clark. The St. Louis *Globe-Democrat* also threw its support behind the fusion plan by endorsing Clark with the pointed reminder that while he was a Democrat, " he is not a bourbon. . . . His candidacy represents a revolt against bourbonism." But the combined Republican-Clark forces failed to dislodge Hogg whose entire ticket swept the state.[47]

[46] Galveston *Daily News*, September 9, 13, 14, 15, October 3, 9, 1892; New Orleans *Times-Democrat*, September 15, October 1, 3, 1892; Maud Cuney Hare, *N. W. Cuney*, pp. 155-162; Florida *Times-Union*, September 20, 1892.

[47] Galveston *Daily News*, October 5, 6, 1892; Hogg, 190,486 votes, Clark 133,395 votes, Nugent 108,483 votes. All other candidates on Hogg ticket won by almost the same margin as Hogg. The " lily-white," Houston, remained in

While fusion failed to produce the magic formula that the Republicans needed to crack the Democratic South, the results in the presidential election served as a stimulus for another try. With the exception of Florida, Louisiana, Mississippi and Virginia, the combined Republican-Populist popular vote in 1892 showed a marked increase over the Republican vote in 1888 from a low of 0.18 per cent in Tennessee to a high of 15.74 per cent in Texas. But certain qualifications must be made. Take the four states where a firm agreement existed for a joint effort between Republicans and Populists to choose electors. The Republican vote in 1888 amounted to 32.67 per cent in Alabama, 38.04 per cent in Arkansas, 39.89 per cent in Florida and 26.53 per cent in Louisiana while the combined Republican-Populist vote in 1892 in these same states showed 40.54 per cent, 39.72 per cent, 13.85 per cent and 22.91 per cent respectively. Thus while the net shift in 1892 amounted to +7.87 per cent in Alabama and +1.68 per cent in Arkansas, it came out as —26.04 per cent in Florida and —3.62 per cent in Louisiana. In the remaining seven states where no fusion occurred on the electoral basis, the net shift for Republicans and Populists together amounted to +12.22 per cent in Georgia, +5.09 per cent in South Carolina, —3.44 per cent in Mississippi, +4.71 per cent in North Carolina, +0.18 per cent in Tennessee, +15.74 per cent in Texas, and —6.57 per cent in Virginia. From an orthodox Republican point of view, the most distressing result of the 1892 election was the decline in the percentage of Republican votes in every state in the South, except South Carolina, ranging from a drop of 28.73 per cent in Alabama to 3.62 in Louisiana.[48]

Fusion in the South in 1894 was highlighted by the success that it had in North Carolina, the interest it stimulated in Massachusetts, and the role it had in the revolt of the sugar planters in Louisiana. Democrats described the Republicans as making the " effort of their lives " to break into the South in 1894, but they lacked money and an enthusiasm for fusion

the field and polled 1,322 votes. No fusion occurred on an electoral basis and Cleveland carried the state with 239,963 votes, Weaver 100,778 and Harrison 74,937, Appleton's Annual *Cyclopedia for 1892*, pp. 739-741; Burnham, *Presidential Ballots*, p. 255.

[48] Burnham, *Presidential Ballots*, pp. 252-255.

that had generally prevailed in 1892. Because fusion had its
greatest success in North Carolina in 1894 the impression has
been created that the Republicans used it widely in the South
in this election. Quite the reverse is true. The 1892 arrangement of a joint effort on the state and congressional slate failed
to develop in Arkansas, Florida, Georgia, South Carolina,
Texas, and Virginia.[49]

	Republican % 1888	Republican-Populist % 1892
Alabama	32.67	40.54
Arkansas	38.04	39.72
Florida	39.89	13.85
Georgia	28.71	40.93
Louisiana	26.53	22.91
Mississippi	25.40	21.96
North Carolina	47.64	52.35
South Carolina	17.18	22.27
Tennessee	46.68	46.84
Texas	25.84	41.58
Virginia	49.45	42.88
The South	36.95	40.93

In Alabama, there was a repeat performance of the 1892
state election with the added excitement of having Republicans
in Massachusetts contribute to the fusion effort and a Republican Senator plan an investigation of the frauds. Kolb again
headed the joint Populist-Jeffersonian ticket, and again the
" lily-white " Republicans led by Mosely and ex-Governor
Lewis E. Parsons and William H. Smith supported fusion and
Kolb, while the " Black and Tans " directed by Stevens opposed
fusion and supported William C. Oates, the Democratic nominee for governor. But Kolb needed money badly to finance his
campaign, and he asked northern Republicans to aid him. He
made himself acceptable to the Republican leadership when
he came out for protection, and he went to Washington to
confer with Senator Hoar of Massachusetts whom southern
Democrats called " Old force-bill Hoar." The Senator and the

[49] Arkansas *Gazette*, July 25, October 30, 1894; Florida *Times-Union* for
1894 failed to carry any news about "fusion" in Florida in 1894; Atlanta
Constitution, August 31, 1894; Charleston *News and Courier*, September 30,
October 3, 4, 1894; Galveston *Daily News*, September 24, October 21, 1894;
William D. Sheldon, *Populism in the Old Dominion* (Princeton, 1935), pp.
108-111.

Home Market Club of Boston bestirred themselves as active allies of Kolb and began to raise money to aid the Alabama Jeffersonian. Hoar called Kolb's movement " the most promising fact that has taken place in the history of the South for many years, and if he succeeds in his movement, as we are confident he will, the solid South is broken and . . . the success of the cause of protection is assured." The Senator took the lead to obtain the money, and the Home Market Club sent out circulars to Republican chairmen throughout New England seeking to raise $50,000 for the support of Kolb.[50]

Kolb received about $5,000 although his opponents greatly exaggerated this figure. The Democrats called him a " fox . . . at last smoked out of his hole," and labeled him as the Alabama Mahone." [51] But as one Democrat campaigner reported to Senator John T. Morgan, " the exposition that Senator Hoar and sweet Reuben has conspired to scalp you and to supplant you in the United States Senate never failed to arouse our people to a deeper enthusiasm and determination that such should not be." The same writer underscored a handicap for the coalition when he concluded that " it was madmans [sic] cry that kolb uttered when he [tried] to hitch the farming population of Ala. to the high tariff coach of the East." [52]

Oates defeated Kolb with a 27,000 majority, and again the latter charged fraud as he had done in 1892. William E. Chandler, then in the Senate, introduced a resolution in that body proposing an investigation of the election as to whether it was " full, free, fair, and honest," and whether it had resulted in the choice of a legislature entitled to elect a Senator. Republican leaders in Alabama pressed Chandler to push ahead with his resolution, for as one of them told him, " We can and will show the most devilish frauds and intimidations ever heard of in a civilized country. You Republicans in the north *must* do something or we of the south will have to quit." [53]

[50] Moore, *History of Alabama*, pp. 628-641; Mobile *Daily Register*, March 27, 28, July 25, 1894; New York *Sun*, March 24, 1894.

[51] Mobile *Daily Register*, March 29, 1894.

[52] James E. Webb, lawyer, Birmingham to Senator John T. Morgan, August 10, 1894, in John T. Morgan Papers (Division of Manuscripts, Library of Congress).

[53] K. L. Daniel to Wm. E. Chandler, August 13, 1894; see also J. A. W. Smith, Birmingham to Chandler, August 11, 1894, in Wm. E. Chandler Papers.

Kolb showed great interest in Chandler's resolution, and the Jeffersonian was "prepared to show up greater frauds than in the election of 1892." Kolb proposed setting up a dual government and having his legislature elect a man "fully in line on protection. What will be the chances to get him seated?"[54] But nothing came of the resolution, and the entire Democratic ticket in Alabama went into office.

Republicans and Populists in Tennessee put out a joint congressional and state ticket with the exception that each party had its own candidate for governor. "On account of a peculiar condition in Tennessee," Republican leaders in the state had Harrison's brother urge the ex-President to come into the state campaign, but he turned down the request.[55] The Republicans named H. Clay Evans for governor. Evans had been born in Pennsylvania, had served in a Wisconsin regiment during the Civil War and had settled in Chattanooga in 1866, Here, he became an iron manufacturer, delved in real'estate which made him wealthy, and entered politics, serving as Mayor of Chattanooga on two occasions, having a term in Congress and going on to become First Assistant Postmaster General for a while under Harrison.[56] The returns gave Evans a plurality of 748, but the Democrats claimed fraud and Governor Peter Turney, up for reelection, asked the legislature to investigate.[57] The Republicans countered this move by stating that no investigation could take place until Evans had been seated since on the face of the returns he was the victor, but the Democrats refused to seat Evans until after the investigation. A justice of the peace swore him in at the state library, but the Secretary of State refused to accept this oath, and the legislative committee of seven Democrats and five Republicans investigating the charges of fraud declared Turney the winner.

Fusion paid off in North Carolina in 1894 where a combination of Republicans and Populists gained control of the legis-

[54] Kolb to Chandler, August 20, September 22, 1894, *Ibid.*

[55] L. B. Harrison to Benj. Harrison, September 22, 29, 1894; see also Newell Sanders, Republican state chairman to Benj Harrison, September 21, 1894, in Harrison Papers.

[56] Nashville *American*, August 21, 22, 23, November 5, 1894; Louisville *Courier-Journal*, November 3, 1894.

[57] Evans, 105,104 votes, Turney 104,356, Mims (Populist) 23,093, Appleton's Annual *Cyclopedia for 1894*, pp. 738-739.

lature, elected two United States Senators, and a majority of
the congressmen thereby detaching one southern state from
the Democratic control. In the fusion arrangement each party
maintained its separate organization but they put up only one
ticket, part Republican and part Populist in its makeup. They
had little in common between them save their desire for office,
and expediency was the binding force as it had been in all
other coalitions of these two groups. The Republican state
chairman had tried to prevent fusion, but the state convention
overrode his objections.[58]

While Marion Butler, the Populist, and Jeter Pritchard, the
Republican were the leaders for the fusion in North Carolina,
the "father" of it might be called Hiram L. Grant. Born in
the North, Grant had come down with the Carpetbaggers and
became Republican leader in the eastern part of the state as
well as Postmaster at Goldsboro. Realizing that the Republican-
Populist vote in 1892 was greater than the Democratic total,
Grant suggested to Butler that the two sides combine, and the
two worked out the scheme that resulted in victory.[59] The
Democrats helped this coalition along when, through fear of
Populism, they began to enforce certain technicalities of the
election and registration laws against the Populists and Republicans, and the Democratic legislature of 1893 began to
curb the activities of the State Alliance by modifying its charter.

The Republican-Populist cooperation brought the Negro into
the picture, for he made up a large part of the Republican party
in North Carolina. In the eastern part of the state some Negroes appeared on the county tickets, although the Populists
refused to endorse publicly Negro officeholders. While most
Negroes continued to vote Republican they disliked fusion, and
a number of them openly denounced the agreement and called
it a "Populist-fused, negro hating ticket."[60] Negroes de-

[58] Helen G. Edmonds, *The Negro and Fusion Politics in North Carolina,
1894-1901* (Chapel Hill, 1951), pp. 34-38; Raleigh *News and Observer*, August
26, 29, 31, 1894; William A. Mabry, *The Negro in North Carolina Politics
Since Reconstruction* (Durham, 1940), p. 35; Simeon Alexander Delap, "The
Populist Party in North Carolina," *Trinity College Historical Society Papers,
Series, XIV No. 2* (1922) pp. 55-64.

[59] Josephus Daniels, *Editor in Politics* (Chapel Hill, 1941), pp. 123-125.

[60] Edmonds, *op. cit.*; for examples of Negro opposition to fusion see Wilmington, N. C. *Weekly Star*, October 5, 19, 1894; Raleigh *News and Observer*,
August 22, September 28, October 3, 4, 17, 30, 1894.

veloped a hostility to fusion for several reasons. A number of Republican leaders in the western part of the state had been trying since 1888 to eliminate the Negro from the party and to build a " lily-white " organization. Those Republicans who had been foremost in this movement became the strongest advocates of fusion in the state, and the Negro resented supporting any one who had sought to get rid of him. Negroes also distrusted the Populists and saw little difference between them and the Democrats, for as a Negro pointed out in a public letter, " We can't vote a fusion ticket. It will never do. We might as well eat the devil as to drink his broth." [61]

The turn of events in Louisiana in 1894 excited the hopes of Republican leaders from New Orleans to Washington and produced a fusion of forces along economic lines, an objective the Republicans had long sought to attain in the South. The Wilson-Gorman Tariff of 1894, a Democratic measure, had made a change from a specific to an ad valorem duty on sugar which aided the Sugar Trust and hurt the producers. The new tariff also refused to extend the bounty provision of the McKinley law. As a result, a very large portion of the sugar planters in Louisiana bolted their party and went over to the Republican camp. The decision to take this action came from a series of meetings which saw the planters at first declare for protection, then denounce the Democratic party and advocate a Republican alliance, and finally accept this alliance, adopt strong Republican resolutions and organize a new party. They called themselves National Republicans, allowed no Negroes, and set up a separate campaign committee distinct from the regular Republican organization in the state.[62]

When the bolt occurred many explained it by calling the planters northerners, but one of them, who refused to rebel, in an open letter pointed out that " with very few exceptions, the entire mass of sugar planters . . . are Southern born and bred . . . most of whom and their fathers, too, fought gallantly for the South in the War and afterwards in overthrowing the Carpetbag Republican rule, and have loyally and stanchly supported the Democratic party until this recent extraordinary

[61] Raleigh *News and Observer*, September 25, 1894.
[62] See New Orleans *Times-Democrat*, September 18, 1894 for details of meetings.

desertion of it." [63] About three hundred of the planters had met to take this action and nearly all of them were men of wealth and large influence and with power to control a considerable following. They realized the importance of breaking with the Democratic party, but they felt that the Negro question was no longer an issue because, as they argued, whites would govern the South.[64]

National Democratic leaders had looked for dissatisfaction on the part of the sugar planter, but they had not anticipated schism. They adopted the attitude of letting things take their own way for a while and trusting to time and reflection to bring the sugar planter back to the party. At first the Democratic National Committee made light of the whole matter and manifested an air of indifference. But Louisiana Democrats, up for reelection in the sugar districts, called upon such leaders as Secretary of the Treasury John G. Carlisle and Senator Faulkner of West Virginia, Chairman of the Democratic Congressional Campaign Committee, who in turn issued statements reaffirming their " friendliness " for the sugar industry but also favoring a revenue duty on sugar.[65]

As election time grew near the anxiety on the part of the Democratic leaders, concerning the bolt, increased rather than diminished, and how to close the breach puzzled them. Recovering from their first shock, Democratic newspapers and politicos began to denounce the sugar planters, to ostracize them, and to raise the bugaboo of Negro rule. While the planters themselves were rich and powerful enough to ignore the social ostracism, their followers had neither the social prestige nor the wealth to withstand this form of pressure and began to drop away.[66] Added pressure came in the form of a decision of Cleveland to remove all federal office holders in Louisiana who had received their positions through the influence of any one connected with the revolt unless the official could furnish proof that he was " working for the success of the regular national Democracy." Governor Murphy J. Foster

[63] Charleston *News and Courier*, September 18, 1894.

[64] Birmingham *Age Herald*, September 7, 1894.

[65] New Orleans *Times-Democrat*, September 22, 1894.

[66] Eugene Young, " The Sugar Planters' Revolt," *The Independent* XLVI (October, 1894), 1370-71.

not only threatened, but actually removed a number of state officeholders who had identified themselves with the revolt. The state committee proposed that the Democrats and National Republicans unite in the question of white primacy, but the sugar planter rejected this as an " insidious attempt to raise the race issue . . . The plain issue is free trade or protection and this we will not allow to be sidetracked by any pretended fear of negro domination or any prevalent issue." [67]

National Republican leaders at first did not regard the bolt as " one toward Republicanism." They only looked upon it as one of the " favorable signs of an awakening of the Southern people to a new life, free from the racial issue that have distracted them ever since the War." [68] The Republican managers of the 1894 campaign decided it would not be a good policy to interfere openly at first. They hoped for a greater rupture and they planned to give the bolters encouragement in every way needed to infuse new life into the Republican party in Louisiana, but as Tom Platt observed, " Let's see if those people down in Louisiana mean anything before we indorse them." As for Joseph H. Manley, Republican leader from Maine, he thought the conversion was " too sundden [sic]." Other members of the national committee agreed with Platt by pointing out that " Before we whoop up that Louisiana business we want to see what they will do for themselves." [69]

But Warmoth, former Carpetbagger governor of Louisiana and now associated with the Magnolia Sugar and Railroad Company, reported, " We are getting along with our new move. Our people are very skittish but out of the thousands that have come over we hope to keep hundreds in line." Warmoth predicted that " we will elect 3 members [to Congress] unless we are counted out in the city [New Orleans] so badly that we can't catch up." [70] The planters had named for Congress one Democratic and two Republican leaders from the first three congressional districts in the state, and the Republican party

[67] New Orleans *Times-Democrat*, October 2, 5, 12, 18, 1894; Chicago *Inter-Ocean*, October 12, 1894.

[68] Young, *loc. cit.*

[69] New Orleans *Times-Democrat*, October 4, 1894.

[70] H. C. Warmoth to Wm. E. Chandler, September 13, November 9, 1894, in Wm. E. Chandler Papers.

had indorsed all three as its nominees.[71] A leading Republican paper of the North called this action " a movement of importance to the Republican party of the Union," and Republican leaders now busied themselves in their efforts to aid the revolt.[72] Protection was their ace card, and McKinley was linked closely to it by virtue of the tariff that bore his name. Off he went to New Orleans, speaking in Lexington and Chattanooga on his way. A committee of business men headed by Warmoth and Robert Bleakley, the President of the Commercial Club, greeted him, and a crowd of more than eight thousand, mostly whites, heard him at the Auditorium Club where he connected the McKinley tariff with protection to the sugar planters, but did not promise that the Republicans would restore the bounty on sugar.[73]

But the election proved that the Republicans had become too optimistic and the Democrats had grown too concerned about the bolt of the sugar planters. The Democrats triumphed in each one of the sugar districts, and with the exception of the third, they had about the same margin of victory they had enjoyed in 1892.[74]

While fusion was failing to give Republicans control of the South they were preparing for one more try. The great success they had had with it in North Carolina in 1894 and the split in Democratic ranks over Bryan's nomination persuaded them to make another attempt in 1896. Leading Democratic newspapers in the South labeled the convention that named Bryan as " subversive of everything in the history and tradition of the Party," and the platform as " not only Populistic," but " full of socialism." [75] The Louisville *Courier-Journal* in an editorial titled " Is This Your Party " called upon every Democrat to examine the platform to determine whether or not it was a Democratic document, and whether it " is any kin to him." The anti-Bryan Democrats organized themselves into the National or " Gold " Democratic Party and named John M. Palmer of Illinois for President and Simon Bolivar Buckner for Vice

[71] New Orleans *Times-Democrat*, September 18, 23, 25, 29, 30, 1894.

[72] Chicago *Inter-Ocean*, October 14, 1894.

[73] New York *Tribune*, October 21, 1894; New Orleans *Times-Democrat*, October 20, 21, 1894.

[74] *World Almanac for 1893*, p. 344, for 1895, p. 402.

[75] Woodward, *Origins of the New South*, p. 287.

President, whom a leading Democratic newspaper of the South regarded as "honorable men and honest men," and as representing the principles for which the Democratic party had ever contended." [76]

With the exception of Arkansas, the Palmer-Buckner ticket appeared in every southern state, and this presented the Republicans with far more reaching possibilities in the South than they had either in 1892 or in 1894. Fusion with the Populists was based on expediency, but fusion with the Gold Democrats could be put on a firmer footing, such as economic issues that could bring about a realignment of parties in the South. On the other hand, many Democrats looked upon the Palmer-Buckner ticket as no more than a decoy to aid McKinley, and W. N. Haldeman of the Louisville *Courier-Journal* and director of the southern headquarters of the Gold Democrats made no attempt to conceal his plans to draw votes away from the Democrats to give McKinley the victory and to "settle the fate of Bryan and Sewall." [77]

But as always, troubles arose to plague Republican efforts in 1896. One difficulty was the difference of opinion among the top Republican strategists over what course to take in the South. Hanna had placed Quay in charge of the eastern and southern end of the campaign, and he became so impressed with the opportunities in the South, especially in Alabama, Florida, and Tennessee, that he in turn convinced the national committee to spend money in these states. But when Hanna had studied the proposal he ordered a halt to Quay's plans and cancelled the idea of spending any more money in Alabama and Tennessee but authorized some for Florida.[78]

Another handicap for the Republicans to overcome was the fact that McKinley had voted for the Force Bill of 1890 and had remained silent on the subject in his letter of acceptance. He had asked the voters to heed Washington's admonition, "There should be no North, no South, no East, no West, but a common country," but the Richmond *Dispatch* reminded southern Democrats that "McKinley had honeyed words for

[76] Louisville *Courier-Journal*, July 11, 1896; Charleston *News and Courier*, October 10, 1896.

[77] Woodward, *Origins of the New South*, p. 287.

[78] New York *Times*, October 2, 1896.

the South. He is bidding for southern votes, and had precedent for resorting to his mellifluous utterances . . . Judging McKinley by his record and out of his own mouth, so far as the past is concerned, his desire to humiliate the South and bind it to the Republican chariot by force bill chains is as much bred in the bone as is his affection for his protection offspring." [79] The revival of the fear of a Force Bill in the South and the linking of McKinley to it worried Republican strategists. The New York *Times* came to the rescue with the solution of informing the South that it had no reason to apprehend any new efforts to regulate elections by federal authority. "But," said the *Times*, "with Congress in control of a strong Republican party majority there might be a renewed effort in that direction if there shoud be a feeling of exasperation at the practice of flagrant frauds in support of such as Bryan represents." [80]

Finally, there was the handicap of fusion itself to bedevil Republican strategists in the North as well as in the southern states where it was expected to take place. Hanna had "arrangements there" which he hoped would give the Republicans at least Virginia and North Carolina." [81] These arrangements turned out to be attempts at fusion primarily with the Gold Democrats assisted by handsome contributions from Hanna. But the stumbling block came from either lack of fusion among the fusionists themselves or from fusion in the wrong direction. The Republicans and Populists who had been attracted to one another in 1892 and 1894 over the matter of expediency repelled one another in 1896 over the currency issue. While the Republicans and Gold Democrats had an affinity for each other, because they both supported the gold standard, the latter were reluctant to join in any formal alliance and preferred to use their ticket as a decoy to take votes away from Bryan or to urge suport for McKinley through speeches and letters. And to hope that all three groups would fuse together was nothing more than an idle dream. Actually fusion occurred more frequently between Republicans and Populists than between Re-

[79] Louisville *Courier-Journal*, August 27, 1896; Richmond *Dispatch*, September 1, 1896.

[80] New York *Times*, October 31, 1896.

[81] Powell Clayton to William E. Chandler, August 26, 1896, in Wm. E. Chandler Papers.

publicans and Gold Democrats, but it happened more often in state elections than it did in the congressional or presidential elections, a development that failed to please national Republican leaders since they sought electoral votes and more congressmen in Washington.

In Arkansas, Florida, Mississippi, and South Carolina the Republicans failed to fuse with the Populists or Gold Democrats in either the state or national elections.[82] In Alabama, the Republicans fused with the Populists on the state ticket and cooperated with the Gold Democrats in some of the congressional districts and with the Populists in others but put out their own electoral ticket.[83] In Georgia, the Republicans " unofficially " supported the Populist state ticket, but rejected the offer by Gold Democrats for a combined electoral ticket on the basis that most of the latter would vote for McKinley anyway.[84] Texas Republicans not only had a " lily-white " and a " regular " organization, but they had several factions within the regular group. In order to secure assistance from the national committee, the Republican leaders in Texas tried to create the impression that theirs was a doubtful state, and they urged fusion as the means to put it in the Republican column. National Republican headquarters did turn loose some money and informed Cuney, the Negro leader, that " Texas is beginning to attract attention and Hanna and others are coming to believe that something tangible may come out of the fusion with the Populists and sound money Democrats." Straightening out the differences between the Republican factions proved to be a more arduous task than working out a fusion agreement, even though that arch " fixer " Huston spent considerable time in Texas. Just when harmony had been restored and fusion appeared to be in sight, Willie " Gooseneck Bill " McDonald, Negro Republican leader in the state, took to the stump for the Democrats and upset all that had been done.[85]

[82] Arkansas *Gazette*, October 11, 1896; Appleton's Annual *Cyclopedia for 1896*, pp. 290, 493, 705-706.

[83] Moore, *History of Alabama*, p. 642; New York *Times*, September 28, 1896; New Orleans *Times-Democrat*, October 12, 1896; Birmingham *State Herald*, October 2, 1896; Nashville *American*, September 29, 1896.

[84] Atlanta *Constitution*, September 2, October 2, 3, 4, 13, 16, 21, 22, 24, 1896; New York *Times*, October 8, 23, 1896; New York *Tribune*, October 8, 1896; Nashville *American*, October 2, 1896.

[85] Roscoe C. Martin, *The People's Party in Texas* (University of Texas Bul-

Hanna also became interested in carrying Tennessee and apparently promised to send money into the state. National Republican leaders regarded the monetary split making a great wedge in Democratic ranks in the state and they looked upon it as a better battleground than some of the other doubtful states in the South. Powell Clayton, who headed the Speakers' Bureau of the national committee, asked a number of leading Republicans in the state to take to the stump and promised to pay their expenses while they were on the hustings. But the Republicans fused with no one except for some cooperation they gave to both the Gold Democrats and Populists in some of the congressional fights.[86]

In Louisiana, the Republicans did join with the Populists on the state ticket and wanted to fuse with the Gold Democrats on the electoral slate but were turned down. Hanna's greatest difficulty here was, as in the case of Texas, reconciling the "Regular" and National Republicans [the Sugar Planters]. The regulars had insisted upon recognizing Negroes and placing them on the electoral ticket, and Hanna backed them up on this. But the Nationals refused to have anything to do with the Negro. Under Hanna's proddings the factions smoothed over their differences, but the agreement came too late to prevent state officials from placing two Republican tickets on the ballots. The difficulties of uniting the two Republican groups seriously weakened the chances for any Republican-Gold Democratic combination in the state, and the Populists preferred the Democrats to the "goldbugism" they found in the Republican party.[87]

Hanna also proved to be generous in Virginia in his effort

letin No. 3308, 1933), pp. 233, 243; Maud Cuney Hare, *Cuney*, p. 210; Rupert Norval Richardson, *Texas the Lone Star State* (New York, 1943), p. 362; Galveston *Daily News*, September 9, 10, 11, 30, October 1, 2, 4, 10, 11, 12, 20, 21, 23, 26, 1896.

[86] Nashville *American*, August 13, September 20, 25, October 2, 8, November 1, 1896; Atlanta *Constitution*, October 2, 1896.

[87] W. L. Brian, Secretary of State, Louisiana to Marion Butler, September 25, 1896, in Marion Butler Papers (Southern Historical Collection, University of North Carolina); Reynolds, *Machine Politics in New Orleans*, p. 31; Hicks, *Populist Revolt*, p. 340; Lucia E. Daniels, "The Louisiana People's Party," *Louisiana Historical Quarterly* XXVI (1943), 1099-1104; New Orleans *Times-Democrat*, July 19, 27, 29, 31, August 5, 13, 18, 29, October 1, 2, 3, 6, 7, 14, 16, 23, 26, 1896.

to break into the winning column in the South. In this state,
the Gold Democrats cooperated very closely with state and
national Republican leaders, and the New York *Times* observed, "The Republicans and sound money-men have an
abundance of money." [88] Among the Gold Democrats in Virginia were leaders of the Democratic party such as, Basil B.
Gordon, Democratic state chairman in 1889 and 1891, Governor Charles T. O'Ferral and other party leaders in the state
who came out openly for McKinley.[89] National Republican
leaders were very hopeful about Virginia and the Secretary of
the Republican National Committee advised McKinley, "We
have got the matter in Virginia in good running shape. Mr.
[N. B.] Scott [Rep. National Committeeman from West Va.]
is in daily communication with the Committee there, and I
think from present appearances we have an excellent chance of
carrying the State. In fact from reports the prospects are better
there than in some of the States out west." [90]

Republicans became so enthusiastic about Virginia that Hanna
spent $160,000 in the state and they pressured ex-President
Harrison to campaign there. Harrison showed little real zeal
for the task and pointed out from his own experiences with the
state, " I cannot believe that Virginia is one of the states we
can expect to capture, and . . . I do not think I can speak in
Richmond . . . You do not seem to appreciate that it is very
unusual for an ex-President to enter generally into a political
campaign." [91] But in spite of these protests, Harrison did come
to Richmond to stump for the Republicans.

A leading figure in the attempt to win Virginia for the Republicans was M. E. Ingalls, President of the Chesapeake and
Ohio Railroad. He stumped for McKinley, carried free over
his lines anti-Bryan men to various parts of the state to attend
Republican rallies, and served as the connecting link between
the Republican National Committee and the Gold Democrats
in Virginia. Ingalls held conferences with Republican leaders

---

[88] New York *Times*, October 25, 1896.

[89] Moger, *The Rebuilding of the Old Dominion*, pp. 109-114.

[90] Wm. M. Osborne to William McKinley, August 11, 1896, in William
McKinley Papers (Division of Manuscripts. Library of Congress).

[91] Moger, *op. cit.*, pp. 108-109; W. T. Durbin, Republican national committeeman from Indiana to Harrison. September 10, 1896, Harrison to Durbin,
September 16, 1896, in Harrison Papers.

and the sound money men and persuaded Hanna to aid the coalition with money.[92]

North Carolina presented at the same time a hopeful, a frustrating, and a confusing picture. That the Republican National Committee was optimistic about the situation in North Carolina can be seen in the report it gave McKinley. "We have had a long session today with the North Carolina people and have come to the conclusion to make the fight in North Carolina," wrote the secretary. "From all the statements and information we can get I have not any doubt in my mind but that we can carry the state."[93] Out of the welter of confusion to all parties in North Carolina this much appears to be clear. The Republicans and Populists fused on most of the state ticket, except for governor and lieutenant governor, on the county tickets, and in some of the congressional races. The Republicans and Populists did attempt to combine on the electoral ticket, but the latter demanded Republican support of free silver as a basis of fusion, and the Republicans turned them down. As for the Gold Democratic leaders in the state, they asked their followers to vote for McKinley, and the Populists and Democrats finally joined hands in the electoral ticket.[94] Then the fun began. Populist leaders became worried by the fact that the fusion agreement with the Republicans had some inconsistency in it. Populists assumed the role of helping to elect a legislature that could return a gold standard man to the United States Senate. The Populists were also angry by the failure of the Republicans to take down their candidate for governor, Daniel L. Russell. On top of all this came the turmoil resulting from Republican-Populist cooperation on the national ticket. As the leader of the anti-fusionist forces in the South pointed out to the champion of fusion in the same section, "A fusionist you have always been, and you bargain with the Republicans in one campaign and with the Democrats

[92] Moger, op. cit.; Richmond Dispatch, September 11, 13, 1896.
[93] Wm. M. Osborne to McKinley, September 1, 1896, in McKinley Papers.
[94] Hamilton, History of North Carolina, III, 256-262; Charleston News and Courier, November 2, 1896; Mobile Daily Register, September 11, 1896; Raleigh News and Observer, September 11, October 4, 1896; New York Times, September 11, 1896; Hal W. Ayer, Populist State Chairman in North Carolina in circular letter to North Carolina Populists, no date, 1896, in Marion Butler Papers.

in the next. In this campaign you have bargained with both Republicans and Democrats. God only knows which bargain you intend to keep." [95] Even the Populist candidate for governor was confused by the various agreements in North Carolina, for as he wrote, " I confess that I myself am " befogged " at present, hardly know where to go, what to say when I speak, or ' where I am at.' " [96] Fusion with the Republicans also worried Butler who looked upon this cooperation as bringing on the " demoralization and disruption, if not the death, of the People's Party. It is clear," he predicted, " that this is the last year that there will be cooperation in North Carolina." [97]

With or without fusion, the Republicans still sought in vain for the formula that would give them success in the South. While they had improved their position in every state in the South in 1896 except in Arkansas, Louisiana and South Carolina, they had yet to bring one into the Republican column, and in every southern state save Georgia and Texas, McKinley had polled a smaller proportional vote than Harrison had gathered in 1888. [98] While the Gold Democrats had helped to swell the Republican vote in the South, the combination of Populists and Silver Democrats offset this defection and frustrated Republican hopes in such states like North Carolina, Tennessee, and Virginia where a good possibility for a Republican victory had existed.

By 1896 the Republicans had striven for two decades to break into the Democratic South, and they had used a variety of plans and tactics to recoup their lost political fortune in this section. But success still eluded them. Plagued by factionalism among their southern brethren, by fear of another Reconstruction among southern whites, by bickering among their own top strategists over what to do about the South, Republicans actually found their party to be worse off in the South in 1896 than it had been in 1876, when they set out to redeem it. Compared with what strength they had in 1876, which they determined to multiply, and with what they had in 1880, when they measured

---

[95] Tom Watson to Marion Butler, October 28, 1896, in Marion Butler Papers.

[96] William A. Guthrie to Marion Butler, September 26, 1896, *Ibid.*

[97] Marion Butler to J. A. Simms, Concord, North Carolina, February 17, 1896, *Ibid.*

[98] *World Almanac*, 1897, pp. 425-471; Burnham, *Presidential Ballots*, pp. 252-255.

the first effects of their new policy, the Republican vote in the South as a whole, and in all of the southern states save Georgia, Tennessee, Texas, and Virginia had substantially declined by 1896. While McKinley became the first Republican President since Grant to win a majority of the popular vote in the nation, the Republicans gathered less than a third of the popular vote in the South and in the case of Mississippi only 7.27 per cent.[99]

Republican percentages of the popular vote in the South in the presidential elections of 1876, 1880, and 1896.

	1876	1880	1896
South	40.34	40.84	29.45
Alabama	40.01	37.09	28.13
Arkansas	39.86	38.97	25.13
Florida	50.21	45.88	24.21
Georgia	28.00	34.42	36.85
Louisiana	51.64	36.40	21.80
Mississippi	31.92	29.70	7.27
North Carolina	46.37	48.15	46.87
South Carolina	50.24	33.96	13.47
Tennessee	40.22	44.26	46.21
Texas	29.72	23.77	30.75
Virginia	40.40	39.39	45.83

The Republicans were still without much support in the South. Twenty years of planning, scheming, maneuvering, and fusing still left them without electoral votes in this section. They still remained a sectional party without any great appeal for southern whites. Yet they had not permitted the South to become Democratic by default. They had not written it off as hopeless. They had fought for it. They had tried to Republicanize it, and while the fruits of their efforts seem small, they girded themselves for a fresh attack in the twentieth century.

[99] *Ibid.*

INDEX

Abolitionists: endorse removal of troops, 125

Adams, Henry: on election of 1872, 38–39

African Methodist Episcopal Church: supports Hayes' southern policy, 130

Alabama: Democrats return to power in, 23; fusion in between Republicans and Populists, 234–237, 247–249, 257; Republican factionalism in, 235–236; fusion in between Republicans and Gold Democrats, 257

Albany, N. Y.: Republican support for Hayes' southern policy, 125

Albany *Argus*: on opposition of businessmen to Reconstruction, 48

Albany *Journal*: favors Federal Elections Bill, 202

Alcorn, James L.: considered by Hayes for cabinet, 74

Aldrich, Nelson W.: on Federal Elections Bill, 206–207

Alger, R. A.: and southern Republican delegates, 185–187

Allison, William B.: on Federal Elections Bill, 206–207

Arkansas: Democrats return to power in, 23; fusion in between Republicans and Populists, 237–238

Arkansas *Mansion*: and Supreme Court's decision on Civil Rights Act, 176

Arnett, Alex Matthews: on fusion in Georgia, 239

Arthur, Chester: and southern Independents, 13, 152, 160–169; receives advice on southern policy, 152; southern policy of, 156–158, 159, 167; and Mahone, 153–154; splits Republican party with southern policy, 155–159, 172; favors internal improvements in South, 169–170; and southern Republican delegates, 170–172; and the Negro, 172–177; political effects of southern policy, 177–180

Athens *Banner-Watchman*: on Republican abandonment of Negro, 177

Atkinson, Edward: on new South, 219–220

Augusta *Chronicle*: opposes Federal Elections Bill, 202

Bateman, Warner: on Republican defeat in Ohio and Hayes' southern policy, 110

Black Belts: and Hayes' southern policy, 100–102; and Arthur's southern policy, 179–180

Blaine, James G.: discusses Southern Question, 61; opposes confirmation of Key, 106; attacks Hayes' southern policy, 111–113; endorses Negro suffrage, 139–140; opposes Republican-Readjuster alliance, 148, 155

Blakemore, J. T., 237

Bloody shirt: used by Republican party, 10, 34; wavers of admit failure of Reconstruction, 24; not representative of northern opinion, 35

Boston *Evening Transcript*: on business men and new southern policy, 48; assures South, 219

Boston *Globe*: on Solid South, 231

Boston Home Market Club: supports fusion in Alabama, 248

Boston *Journal*: favors Federal Elections Bill, 201

"Bottom rails": connection between them and Granger movement, 49

Bowles, Samuel: criticizes Reconstruction, 38; on disputed elections, 82

Boynton, Henry Van Ness: on Wade Hampton aiding Republicans. 79

Bristow, Benjamin: criticizes Reconstruction, 27

Brookes-Baxter War: and Republican factionalism in South, 31

Brooklyn, N. Y.: Republican support for Hayes' southern policy, 125

Brooklyn *Times*: favors Federal Elections Bill, 202

Brown, John C., 75

Bruce, Blanche K.: opposes Independent Negro movement, 175; supports Harrison's southern policy,

263

Logan, John A.: attacks Hayes' southern policy, 104, 106
Logan, Rayford W.: on the North and the Negro, 51, 218
Long, John C.: and Republican factionalism in Louisiana, 241; in Texas, 245
Longfellow, Henry W.: supports Hayes on South, 72
Longstreet, General James: and Independents in Georgia, 163
Louisiana: Democrats return to power in, 23; disputed elections in, 52–53, 80–82; Republicans attack Hayes' southern policy, 92, 116; Negroes support Hayes' policy, 130; Negroes on Cleveland's election, 183; Negroes protest Republican policy in South, 222; Republican factionalism in, 240–241, 258; Republicans and Populists fuse in, 241–242, 258; Republicans and sugar planters cooperate in, 251–255
Louisiana Returning Board: rewarded by Hayes, 91
Louisville: National Convention of Negroes meet in (1883), 175
Louisville *Commercial*: on Hayes' southern policy, 93
Louisville *Courier-Journal*: on Hayes and internal improvements in South, 88; opposes Federal Elections Bill, 202
Lowell, James Russell: on election of 1872, 38–39; supports Hayes on South, 72
Lynch, John R.: on effect of Key's appointment, 78; supports Hayes' southern policy, 130; opposes independent Negro movement, 175; supports Harrison's policy, 225; defends Federal Elections Bill, 232; supports Republican-Populist fusion in Mississippi, 242

McClure, A. K.: relates achievements of South, 220
McCormick, Richard, Secretary of Republican National Committee: urges new policy, 59
McDonald, Willie " Gooseneck Bill ": and Republican factionalism in Texas, 257

McDowell, John H.: and fusion in Tennessee, 243–244
McKee, George; opposes use of northern political methods in South, 171
McKinley, William: campaigns in South, 188; assures South, 219; and sugar planters' revolt in Louisiana, 254; avoids sectional issue in 1896, 255; assisted by Gold Democrats in Virginia, 259–260
McKinley Tariff: and Federal Elections Bill, 208
McKinnon, Daniel L.: leads Independents in Florida, 166
McLane, J. Hendrix: leads Independents in South Carolina, 162–163
McVeagh, Wayne: condemns Arthur's policy, 172
Magee, Chris: heads 1892 Republican campaign in South, 230; and fusion in Alabama, 235–237
Mahone, William: aids the Republicans, 22; and Readjusters, 94–95; and Garfield, 142–150; and Arthur, 153–154; seeks control of Republican party in Virginia, 185, 191–192; favors in Virginia, 243
Maine: Republican convention tables endorsement of Hayes' policy, 111
Malloy, General H. G.: and Republican factionalism in Texas, 186
Manley, Joseph H.: and sugar planters' revolt in Louisiana, 253
Manufacturer: opposes Federal Elections Bill, 210, 214
Marion, Ohio *Independent*: on Hayes's southern policy
Maryland: Republican state convention endorses Hayes' southern policy, 125
Massachusetts: Republican state convention approves Hayes' southern policy, 125
Matthew Stanley Quay Club: opposes Federal Elections Bill, 210
Matthews, Stanley: recommends southern Democrat for cabinet, 75; advises Carpetbagger claimants in disputed elections, 81–82; advises Hayes on disputed elections, 82
Maynard, Horace: on the South, 27
Medill, Joseph: criticizes Reconstruction, 27